THE RANCH 2.0

by

Chris Peck

Gotham Books

30 N Gould St.
Ste. 20820, Sheridan, WY 82801
https://gothambooksinc.com/

Phone: 1 (307) 464-7800

© 2024 *Chris Peck*. All rights reserved.

No part of this book may be reproduced, stored in a retrieval system, or transmitted by any means without the written permission of the author.

Published by Gotham Books (January 9, 2024)

ISBN: 979-8-88775-643-1 (H)
ISBN: 979-8-88775-641-7 (P)
ISBN: 979-8-88775-642-4 (E)

Because of the dynamic nature of the Internet, any web addresses or links contained in this book may have changed since publication and may no longer be valid.

The views expressed in this work are solely those of the author and do not necessarily reflect the views of the publisher, and the publisher hereby disclaims any responsibility for them.

About This Book

You are about to read a literary work unlike any other on the market. (planet)

1. Take a deep breath…. hold it… OK let it go

2. Close your eyes look up into your eyelids an try to cleanse yourself of all you have been taught about what books are supposed to be like. This book is not like those books. Any of them. You will need to be flexible in your approach and get up to speed at your own pace. Based on many personal surveys of my known readers I feel you will grow to love this story. If you read the whole thing WOW thank you. If you smile or laugh…hey all the better. Humor is like chocolate chips in your writing, it sweetens the story and makes you wanting more. Humor can make you feel better about what you are reading so enjoy.

3. Please do not try to speed read "The Ranch" You could hurt your self, and I can't guarantee that the story I wrote and the story you read super fast are going to be the same story.

4. This book is based on the life of an actual sailor who served in the US. Navy during the height of the Viet Nam War from 1967 to 1971. His story is totally unique and the subject "Jessy" is an equally unique but very real person who lived this story. The adventures in these pages all really happened. The names and descriptions of some of the characters have been modified to protect the writer (me).

Rant: I have included Notes and Rants in this writing. The notes are mostly historical items that aren't part of the story but provide background for the story. They are right on the page and not in tiny letters at the bottom. You are welcome. I have also gone off on some rants about subjects that effected me personally. These rants may even include my personal beliefs on religion and or politics but don't reflect the beliefs of a particular party or religion. I refer to God in terms we can all understand so instead of God I may use a pro noun like "Lenny" or "Carl" or "Karen" when defining the deity who may have been on duty at some particular time. Sorry if that last remark gave someone a migraine. That was not my intension. Keep in mind if you plan to hunt me down and set me on fire in my own driveway, I am armed. I have a one shot black powder 54 caliber Hawkins rifle that I built from a kit. It's real pretty and shoots really big holes in stuff. Note: I only need one shot.

CONTENT

CHAPTER 1	1
CHAPTER 2	27
Blue Navy Blue	27
CHAPTER 3	55
J.E.T.S... Jets Jets Jets	55
CHAPTER 4	69
California Dreaming	69
CHAPTER 5	90
The Job	90
CHAPTER 6	100
Crime And Punishment	100
CHAPTER 7	109
The "A" Team	109
CHAPTER 8	122
Jessy's Transformation	122
CHAPTER 9	132
Favorite Destinations	132
CHAPTER 10	144
"And now, THE NEWS"	144
CHAPTER 11	146
The Letter	146
CHAPTER 12	159
Special Services	159

CHAPTER 13	168
The Golf Course	168
CHAPTER 14	179
Training Day	179
CHAPTER 15	187
The Case	187
CHAPTER 16	191
The Visitor	191
CHAPTER 17	204
The Horse Ranch	204
CHAPTER 18	220
The Night Shift	220
CHAPTER 19	225
This is the end my friend	225
CHAPTER 20	234
Much Closer to The End My Friend	234
CHAPTER 21	241
The End of Days	241
Acknowledgments	259
Gene Shepherd	260

FOREWORD

Welcome to the world of free form writing. The book you are about to read is the first attempt by a newcomer to the literary trade. By profession I was a telephone man and don't yet consider myself a master wordsmith but I do consider myself trainable. This book is about "Jessy McCartney" and his very different military experience during the Viet Nam War. We were friends and served at the same time during America's misadventure in southeast Asia. There has been a deep seated need in my heart to tell this story for a very long time and after some soul searching, confidence building, and a sizable but well regulated quantity of alcohol and some very well cared for flowers from an also well regulated plant that grows wild all over the earth, I figured "what the hell I'm going to be dead sooner than later and Jessy's story is an amazing one and it simply must be told."

Jessy grew up without a father at a time and place when and where almost everyone else had at least one. He could remember being asked by the kids in grade school what happened to his father. Jessy was normally getting back on his feet when this question was asked after being knocked to the ground because he was small and skinny and didn't have a father. His mother would wait until he was twenty-one to tell him the story of the hansom, forgetful (because once he found out he was going to be a dad... he forgot to come back), Irish, heavy equipment operator who left her to raise Jessy. Jessy was forced to make up a story. That story revolved around a war hero who was killed in the heat of battle when a German soldier shot him with an RPG. (rocket propelled grenade) Jessy was born in December of 1948. The Germans had stopped shooting anyone with anything in May 1945. When he was seven he hadn't learned much about the second World War. If his school mates were a little smarter they would have done the math and realized that his mother would have had to been pregnant for at least three and a half years. Jessy's sad little story didn't have a leg to stand on but it worked and kept the whole getting knocked to the pavement thing to a minimum.

Being the son of a war hero was sort of cool and Jessy even started to convince himself that his story was true. In Jessy's young yet marginally twisted mind he could see his dad standing on top of a burning Sherman tank, smoking the stub of a nasty cigar, blazing away with a Thompson submachine gun, in each hand. He shrugs off the bullets that are tearing away at his uniform and his body when suddenly he is transformed into a crimson cloud of smoke and flying body parts by a shoulder mounted rocket fired by a German soldier wearing a Nazi helmet. "That's what you get for splitting and leaving mom to raise me alone, bitch," Jessy thought. The story got better the more times Jessy told it and before long his fantasy father had killed enough Germans to fill up a Volkswagen factory before they blew him to red white and blue smithereens. He sold himself this story to such an extent that he felt he had something to live up to. Jessy wasn't exactly born to be in the service but somehow convinced himself that someday he would become the best damn soldier since John Wayne. (John Wayne was a famous actor in the day but he wasn't a soldier but he was an important front man for the US military).

Note: For young men and women considering the military option... get up to speed on how wars work. We are all brought up to believe that wars are fought for freedom and glory...Most wars are fought for money and power or a malignant need in the spider webs of some madman's mind to control as much of the planet as possible, and all too often in the name of God or Bruce or Nancy.

I've been employed in and around the Veterans Medical Center here In Albuquerque, New Mexico since 1978. During that time I've met and gotten to know veterans from all of our wars going back to World War II until this current batch who served in Iraq and Afghanistan. Every one of these Veterans is different but they are also very much the same. Those of us who joined up or were drafted, all have the basic military experience in common. It doesn't matter if you wound up storming the beach at Normandy or driving the Admiral to the golf course in a very clean Jeep, there is a commonality involved with anyone who has been indoctrinated into military life.

This isn't a war novel, so if you are expecting descriptions of huge fiery explosions with bloody assholes and elbows flying in all directions from cover to cover you need help, you also need to find yourself a different author. There is one chapter that involves a terrible deadly aircraft accident and another where torture, rape and murder are important elements, and of course, some typical nearly deadly Navy horse ranch adventures, but this book is mostly a study of the fact of war and how Jessy personally dealt with the one that was thrown directly in his path. I've included a number of rants directed at the rich and powerful who put monetary gain ahead of the lives of the young men and woman who are sacrificed every day in the name of wealth and misplaced glory.

I must now warn you that I have dropped a few carefully targeted "F" bombs here and there to remind you, the reader, that people in the service curse from time to time (all the time). Jessy and I are both from New Jersey where the word fuck was invented and this amazing word can be used five or six times in a sentence without being repetitious or redundant. People in the military swear like sailors and when they return home they have to readjust to the world they came from. If you come from New York or Boston for instance that adjustment is minimal but a farm boy from Kansas could raise a few eyebrows when he slips and asks his mother "Mama could you please pass the fucking okra." Just guessing but his next sentence could very well be "Daddy could you please put down that fucking axe handle?"

This book is a mostly nonfictional, account of a few very important years of Jessy's life, and I feel that we were brutally honest as we tried to describe the good the bad, the humorous and the stunningly sad. The legal and the not so much. This is Jessy's story, I am just his lowly scribe. I don't make Jessy out to be a role model in this story but I've tried to rationalize all the crazy shit he did and the madness that surrounded those who were trying to serve their country during that seemingly insane time in our nations history. In the process Jessy didn't hurt anyone. (well there was a guy in judo class but that was mostly unintentional) Jessy did like to think he helped turn a few heads around. I hope you can forgive Jessy for some things you will read about here. If you can't...you might want to take a deep breath and try relaxing, just a little bit.

The men and women who have served overseas in the line of fire while "defending our country" deserve our undying thanks and respect. They also deserve an education, a job, free health care and a VA loan when they get back home from their tour of duty. Not two years after they get back, I mean the day they get back. They earned these things and many of them have paid a very high price. For those who don't make it back, their families deserve a more than a star in the window and a folded flag in a triangular case for their book shelf. How about a check for a few hundred thousand dollars to help pay off a mortgage and college educations for the kids who are still alive. High school kids who join the service are thinking many things when they sign the paperwork at the recruiters office. Today some are hoping to get an education, some are planning how to spend the sign-up bonus, some are trying to find a way to make a difference, and some just want to cash in on all the "tail" they think they will get when they put on the uniform. None of these young wide eyed kids sees themselves in a wheel chair or a plastic bag with their arms and legs strewn all around someone else's neighborhood, ten thousand miles from the town they grew up in. This book is for those young men and women who are considering a lifetime, or at least what may seem like a lifetime in the military. My greatest wish is that this book will make you laugh, perhaps shed a tear, and what is more important, I hope that this story makes you THINK.

The United States armed forces has nearly as many job descriptions as it has people wearing odd looking hats. There are practical reasons for the shape of those hats of course but you wouldn't see someone on Wall Street for instance wearing a "Jump Cap," a "Dixie Cup," or a "Cunt cap." Sorry about that last one. I didn't make up the name. It's called a garrison cap in mixed company.

The US military employs cooks and mail delivery personnel, there are drivers of trucks and drivers of flight line maintenance equipment. There are those who paint ships, those who navigate ships. There are people who drag deadly weapons to the flight deck and attach them to the wings of some of the scariest airplanes in the world, and then, of course, the pilots of those sexy aircraft who fly those armed weapons over to somebody's house or place of employment and push a button that, after a few seconds, removes that building from the landscape forever, along with the people who were living or working there. This list of military jobs is almost endless. Each and every military branch is a well run self contained unit. Everything that is done in civilian life is duplicated within the confines of the military structure, whether it is writing paychecks, repairing plumbing, feeding the troops, providing communications services, distributing prescription medications, or perhaps feeding and caring for a herd of large four legged creatures on a "Navy horse ranch." This is a story about the experiences revolving around the very odd and "Twilight Zone" like jobs that Jessy performed in his nearly four year career as a member of the most expensive and dangerous navy that a giant shit load of tax payers money can buy. Mostly however, this story is about how Jessy wound up doing his jobs and the carnival of changes that took charge of his life along the way.

CHAPTER 1

In the beginning there was chalk

Let us begin this story in the prehistoric year of 1966. That's a long, long, very long time ago to those of you who "twitter." This means I am older than sunlight, and I don't generally regard the opinion of people who were born after the end of the Viet Nam war. This is just a guideline not a hard as nails rule. There are plenty of damn smart kids out there with their hearts and minds in the right place who deserve respect and I pray they get a chance to lead our brave new world in the right direction……someday sooner than later please.

One particularly overcast New Jersey afternoon Jessy was seated at his desk in high school science class. The desk was big and made from solid wood with a thick black fireproof coating that had two gas outlets protruding from the surface, one for each student. The fireproof feature came in handy when some kids would try to use the burners to light cigarettes the instant the teacher left the room. The science room had eight of these lab desk work stations. There was the aroma of formaldehyde from the biology class that shared the same class room and the students were surrounded by the ghostly spirits of the countless frogs and piglets that had given their lives for science.

This was Jessy's senior year in the above middle class town of Cedar Grove, New Jersey, and Jessy was about halfway through the process of determining his destiny. At the time he probably should have been listening to his science teacher, who was doing his very best to explain how a television worked. Fortunately Jessy knew he would be totally stumped by this question when he asked it. Jessy had gone over the whole science book early on in the school year and if something wasn't in the lesson plan, Mr. "looks up girls dresses all day" wouldn't have a clue and would ramble on hopelessly for the rest of the period. It was a little game Jessy played with his unknowing instructor and his classmates loved him for it, especially the beautiful young girl who sat next to Jessy in the front row with the short skirt and the most wonderful tanned legs in the whole school. Her name was Rhea, and she had recently moved to New Jersey from Southern California.

Rhea knew that when Jessy asked Mr. "Really, I'm sick and need help," one of his patented trick questions, their teacher would get so involved in trying to fake his way thru the answer that he would forget to drop a pencil in front of her desk so he could take way, way, way, too long picking it up while he stared up her skirt and the panties that lived there. Rhea and Jessy had a connection that was only destined to last a short while longer. Soon, her father would again be transferred. This time to some foreign desolate godforsaken city in a state far away. Rhea was grateful whenever Jessy was able to deflect their twisted science teacher's passions away from her vagina and back toward the pursuit of science. Jessy however used this spare time to ponder his plans for the future.

Jessy's dream back in high school was to one day get a job designing cars in Detroit. This was way back in the day when all the baddest, coolest, most powerful, affordable cars in the world were being produced by American union workers in "Motown," and Jessy loved cars. Muscle cars were tearing up the streets and highways of our country and we had the music to go with it. "Jan and Dean" and of course the "Beach Boys" were turning out songs for us to drive to ("Steppenwolf" would soon take that honor) and gasoline was going for 30 cents a gallon. Red hot, 400hp cars were a culture back then and "compact was a thing your date carried in her purse, it certainly wasn't something you would pick her up in." Life was great for a white teenager back then. If you were a black teen in 1967, well...probably not so much. Black kids were still having a good time on Friday night but had a much harder time getting home from the party.

Jessy wanted to be the person who designed the next Corvette, Pontiac GTO or Thunderbird with a trainload of pissed off horses under the hood. He had been reading "Hot Rod magazine" ever since he was a twelve year old juvenile delinquent. Jessy didn't have much disposable income at the age of twelve so he was forced to use the old five finger discount method of payment for his magazines and cigarettes. They really shouldn't have kept those items so close to the front door. This is a personal observation.

Due to his dream to be an automobile designer Jessy had signed up for mechanical drawing, drafting, and designing courses all through high school. He had the same teacher (there was only one) for all four years. The highlight of the design class was a year long homework project in his senior year where he was challenged to design a car from the future. The idea was to come up with a car that could possibly be produced within the next few years. Jessy got a grasp of the teachers idea immediately but that didn't stop some of the class from creating cars with wings, ray guns and radar antennas. This was, by far, the hardest he had ever worked on a project in his entire school career. Jessy had built a eight sided house with pocket doors out of balsa wood in his junior year. The model was beautiful with little pine trees and a circular driveway but his teacher had a childhood fear of octagons and gave Jessy a "C".

Jessy spent two long months coming up with a viable concept car and at least that long perfecting the model. The year was 1966 and the car that Jessy had created would later turn out to be a perfect cross between the 1969 Pontiac GTO and the boat back, 1971 Buick Rivera. The model itself was perfect right down to the perfect gloss black finish. Jessy had also majored in wood shop and was teacher's pet. The choice chrome work he had borrowed and modified from "Revell" kit cars that had once resided on shelves all over his bedroom. The tires were soft rubber model airplane tires that Jessy had bought with real money because the hobby shop had much better security than "New Berry's." Jessy was so very proud of his model and he was sure that it was going to be his launching pad to a career in the auto industry.

The design-class teacher, Mr. De Baca, had a totally different view of Jessy's brilliant creation. They had a running competition going ever since they met in their very first class together. Something inspired Mr. De Baca to single Jessy out and make an example of him at every opportunity. At the time Jessy thought he was just being an asshole. He acted like many of the other teachers in his life who hated him for being the only poor kid in class, or because he didn't have a father and his mother's maiden name was the same as his. This teacher was different somehow. Jessy could feel that in some weird way they were very much alike. Mr. De Baca's mastery of the English language had much to be desired but he was the only mechanical drawing teacher in the entire school system. Good for him, bad for Jessy. It was just a feeling that they had grown up in similar, conditions. Jessy believed the reason his teacher hated him so much was that Jessy was thriving on his not so enviable circumstances while Mr. De Baca was just hanging on to one of the lowest rungs of the ladder in his chosen field. Jessy had gained some popularity based on a level of success in sports and his design teacher noticed the girls who would stop by the classroom to flirt with Jessy before class and he suspected Mr. DeBaca hated him for it. There were a few guys in Jessy's class who had similar feelings but they weren't in the position to give him a failing grade.

When Jessy presented his car design to Mr. De Baca, he took one look at the model and simply said. "No one is ever going to put a (point) on the back of their car." Yeah? Tell that to the people at General Motors, asshole." Neither Jessy nor his teacher knew it at the time but the "boat back, 71 Riviera" would become the car of choice for pimps and drug dealers all across our great nation. Jessy received an "A" on the scale model but only a "C" on the design. Jessy was the only one who knew how devastating this news was. He was expecting nothing but praise for his design and yet still received a "C" for all his hard work. This is a truly important lesson in life for anyone else reading this book. "Life sucks, then you die" …No, wait that's not right. "Things in life happen for a reason" Yep, that's the one. Jessy's entire life would have turned out differently if he had been inspired to become a designer for an industry that one day would export his job to some Asian country we had only recently been at war with. All their cars would have odd looking headlights and would exactly resemble all the other cars from that part of the world. Jessy could have spent years in a white shirt and string tie coming up with ideas that would be instantly stolen by his employer. There would have been that, "Last Straw Moment." The standoff, the police shootout. Things could have indeed gone sideways if Jessy had gotten an "A" on that project. "Thank you, Mr. De Baca. You turned my life around." Jessy would one day say to himself, but that day was a long way down a very twisted and bumpy road.

Note: I have so much respect for the Japanese culture and history. I read both books of "Shike," twice. I am a real fan, however, I'm also an American and until the republicans finally succeed in completely destroying our workers unions, the middle class, voting rights and our Democracy I'm planning to stay and fight for what I believe is the best excuse for a country run by its taxpaying citizens the world has today as far as we know If you believe I'm mistaken please convince me so I can start making travel plans. I could thrive in Jamaica but I would really need to work on my tan, and my bob sledding skills. Following the stunning defeat in design class Jessy felt this sudden urge to upgrade the list of possible opportunities for his immediate future. As luck would have it, Jessy had recently received a letter of eligibility for a partial athletic scholarship to Connecticut State college for wrestling. He was the first district wrestling champion in his school's brief history and was considered this a genuine option. Jessy had to overcome some real demons in life to get this far, and the idea of going to college was virgin territory.

Jessy's young mind up to that point revolved around the very real possibility that he would live the rest of his life with a shovel in his hand earning minimum wage, eating lunch out of a black metal box and dying from some form of cancer while working around toxic chemicals. Now, here he was, contemplating the path of higher education. The problem however, was that his step-dad, Warren, didn't seem all revved up about helping out in any way. Not that he could if he wanted to. Money, or rather, the lack of money was always Jessy's major concern.

For many of you, life before the internet is just a dark hole in history that probably never existed, like dinosaurs to a born again Christian or the civil rights amendment to a Mississippi sheriff. For many of us who can remember TV personalities like "Soupy Sales" and "Mr. Green Jeans," when there was a question like "where can I get some cash to tide me over while I go to some institution of higher learning," you couldn't just "Google" grants and student loans. Young people had to depend on their high school guidance counselors or the wisdom and money from their parents.

Note: Jessy's guidance counselor was a perfectly lovely under achiever who had never even heard of most of her students and least of all Jessy. Her name was miss "I don't give a shit" and she couldn't find her own ass with both hands, a flashlight and a National Geographic ass map. After listening to her advice for an hour, Jessy wanted to slit his throat. She not only didn't have anything of value to contribute but she just couldn't stop rambling off on little personal side trips that involved her kids and her handsome handy man who didn't have a college education but was doing quite well for himself and he stayed in great shape working around her house. Just between you and me. Her handy man was possibly doing a little more than cleaning out her gutters if you get my drift.

Jessy's parents were quite a few links down the food chain when it came to having any extra money laying around. Whenever there was a question about funding, the answer always revolved around a lawnmower, that they didn't have. Jessy mowed plenty of lawns for people who had mowers but didn't earn more than he needed to buy gas and food and the clothes he wore to school. There weren't any "Mc Donald's" or "Wal Marts" back then. Jessy took as many part time jobs as he could find but two thirty-five an hour was the best he could do in those days and that was non-union factory work.

Sometimes his step-dad would lay some book on the bed that he hoped would help guide Jessy down the path of life. "Warren" didn't approve of his choices when it came to reading material. Jessy read "Kon Tiki" when he was in the seventh grade. he was totally fascinated by the adventure of a crew of suicidal Scandinavians who lashed several fifty foot long balsa logs together with "hemp" ropes, and sailed across the Pacific ocean. Warren's imagination was limited only to things that had money or "odds" as the primary subject. He thought several guys alone on a raft must be gay, even if they were the descendants of Vikings. Jessy bit his lip before almost reminding him that Warren had been in the Navy.

Jessy also read the "Autobiography of Lenny Bruce," but again, Warren thought because the book was written by a "junkie," it must be...well... junk. Jessy read "Leon Uris," "George Orwell" "Upton Sinclare," and Sinclair Lewis." His stepfather was reasonably sure that Jessy was going "bat crap crazy." Warren hung up centerfolds from his Playboy magazine collection in Jessy's bedroom to make sure Jessy wasn't batting from the "homo" side of the plate. If Warren really thought he was turning gay he would have been forced to kill Jessy for his own good. The pinups were actually kind of neat and Jessy's guy friends thought It was really cool at the time. Jessy was the only kid in school with pictures of naked girls in his bedroom, who also had parental consent. "Fear of the gay" can be a good thing. Unfortunately Jessy's grandmother was not on board... but she didn't get a vote.

Warren, in an attempt to guide Jessy to a higher plane, once handed him a book and simply said, "You should try to be more like this guy." The name of the book was "The Autobiography of Willy Sutton." This book was written, in prison, by the most successful bank robber of all time. This was before Bernie Madoff blew the wheels off the bank robbery business for like ever. Jessy read that whole damn book from front to back and found it to be quite inspiring. Willy Sutton was the man who, when asked, "Why do you rob banks?" replied "Because that's where the money is." Willy Sutton was a craftsperson at his chosen trade and he was indeed the very best.

Jessy's step father told him "It doesn't matter what you decided to do with your life as long as you're the best at what ever it is." His standard analogy was "I don't care if you become a ditch digger as long as you are the best damn ditch digger you can be." Being the best was all he cared about. Warren meant well in a twisted old school kind of way and Jessy actually got the "Be Best" message without knowing who Malania Trump was. After reading the Willy Sutton book Jessy seriously considered becoming a world class bank robber or a master jewel thief for a while but soon realized that he could never live a life of crime. The whole prison thing never really melted his butter. Some of Jessy's friends who had been awarded the all expenses paid trip to the "free hotel" were usually way more screwed up by the time they got out then they were when they checked in. Their lives were changed for the worse for ever.

Note: Prisons are factories where young 1st. offenders are turned into hardened criminals and let loose on the general public after serving their time. The cost for this process is just stupid. You could have sent these people to Harvard for the cost of their incarceration. If we spent more tax dollars on actual rehab, education and therapy in poor neighborhoods we wouldn't have nearly the need to apprehend and incarcerate young people who fall through the cracks. Yes, violent offenders need to be separated from the general population but "the current way we deal with criminals is a "crime." How can the "Land of the free" have more people locked up in prison than any other country on earth? "They privatized prisons, that's how." It isn't profitable to rehabilitate criminals or help young offenders before they become hardened criminals when someone is going to get richer every time an inmate fails to make it on the outside and returns to the prison system. Plus, felons can't vote so they wrote laws that singled out poor black and brown people and made using crack a felony and coke use a misdemeanor. Crack is cheap, coke is more expensive. Poor people with drug habits go to jail and lose their voting rights while rich yuppies with drug addiction go to rehab and can vote for crooked politicians forever. Hmmm.

The point is, Jessy's sad little family was broke and financially clueless. When it came to funding any thing more expensive than a large anchovy pizza there was a loan involved. The loan was provided by some guy named Veto or Dutch and the terms were...well they could involve the breaking or disappearance of certain body parts if you missed a payment.

While Jessy lived in an upper middle class town his sorry little family was not a member of a class anywhere near the middle. Jessy's family lived on the second floor of a two family home. The first floor was occupied by a really cool Chinese family that was run by an amazing, beautiful single working mother named Asia. Their apartment was twice as large as Jessy's and Asia's two young sons were like Jessy's little brothers. The hundred year old converted duplex house they lived in was about the only rental property in town. Jessy's apartment was maybe 600 square feet tops. His room had a ceiling that was half plaster and half "lath" (wooden slats that support the plaster). The house was built long before someone invented sheet rock. The plaster from the lath side of the ceiling had fallen on Jessy's face while he was sleeping one night causing him to think that the house had been hit by a meteor, they waited for the landlord to make the repairs the whole time Jessy was in high school. Jessy lived in that old house for fourteen years but never met the landlord. The repairs never happened so they used thumb tacks to cover up the hole in the ceiling with a colorful print sheet. It looked like a bad impression of "Genie's bottle." Due to the ramshackle hazardous nature of his home, Jessy didn't invite very many friends to hang out at his crib. The few guys and girls who did come over were treated to pictures of beautiful, naked, women who all had the same first name "Miss" followed by a month of the year. Most of these "friends" never came back.

Jessy's poor mother "was" the bookkeeping department and the office manager for a company owner who believed...correctly, that the less you paid your employees the more you could pay yourself. Never mind that Jessy's mother was running the business and being paid in pocket change. Her boss was a "selfish douche bag." "Capitalism could be a fine idea, but you have to put some controls in place to make sure it works for everyone, not just the white men in nice suits who had the keys to the office." Some business owners understand that well compensated employees are good for the economy. Loyal well paid employees are good for their companies. Jessy's mom's boss didn't understand that the more money in the pockets of the middle class the better it is for everyone. Who do they think buys their products? When super wealthy people put their money in off shore accounts to keep from paying taxes, it doesn't help anyone, except maybe them.

Jessy's step-dad had a county job and Essex County, New jersey is one of the scariest counties in America. Essex county is where Newark was born. Warren was the head cook in the kitchen of a giant, old, red brick (tuberculosis) hospital or "sanitarium" as they called them back then. He earned a crappy pay check and was always getting knives pulled on him by the minimum wage guys from downtown. There were rumors that Warren was a real badass with an iron skillet. He had a nasty attitude toward most minorities and he could go off on just about any race or religion but his own. His spare time was spent sleeping in front of the TV in his underwear or dressing up in his sport coat and slacks, splashing on some lucky "Old Spice" aftershave and heading to the track. Warren wasn't a professional gambler like the rich Texans in one of those stupid poker games on ESPN, which means much of the family spending money was "gone in 60 seconds," or however long it took for his sure thing horse to fall down and break its fucking leg. The money he didn't lose betting on some soon to be dog food named "Peas and Carrots", he spent on his girlfriend. Jessy didn't know about the girlfriend...but his mom did.

Spontaneous rant: Hey ESPN, when did POKER become a freaking sport? I mean the Yankees are playing Boston and you guys have a poker game on, and one of the players is wearing a pair of "X-ray specs" that he got from an add in the back pages of Popular Science. Are you kidding me? You really need to fire some of those "empty suits" you pay to dream up this crap and get back to real sports like...Baseball, Football and (speed-unprotected rock climbing.

Jessy spent his summers working for contractors as a roofer, a landscaper, and a brick mason's assistant. The work was back breaking but he would be in incredible shape by time he showed up for football practice in September. These jobs also had a lot to do with his abilities on the wrestling mat. Most of the other guys on the team spent their summers hanging out at the town swimming pool or bagging groceries down at the "Shop Right, not so super market." In the winter Jessy shoveled snow and put most of the money in a bank account that Warren would borrow from when things got tight. There was a very loose understanding that he would get paid back someday but we all know that you don't pull the mask off the old Lone Ranger, you don't piss into the wind, and you don't lend money to people who spend their spare time at the race track betting on the "ponies." Jessy didn't have a choice in the matter as his parents were cosigners on his bank account. Jessy learned that if he wanted to save his money he would put it in his pocket.

The point to this most recent rant was that Jessy had no visible means of support and if he wanted to attend a school of higher education he would need to find employment in a strange cold place among a totally alien race of people that dress like foreign exchange students and live in the fantasy land of Connecticut. When you grow up in New jersey and have never been further away from your house than the Jersey Shore (yeah that one) you consider places two or more states away as alien as France or Jupiter or... Texas. So much for wrestling his way to the top, or the middle for that matter, besides, if

Jessy ever put on a pair of penny loafers his feet would burst into flames. Those college guys in New England looked like a cross between Richie Cunningham and Pat Boone, and not in a cool way.

Note: Hey kids, some of these references apply to stuff that happened before God invented dirt so please feel free to Google anything that you don't recognize.

The other logical choice in his quest to find the perfect next step in life was an unlikely offer from the New Jersey State senator Krebs to attend the Merchant Marine Academy at Kings Point, New York. Jessy had taken a test at his step-dad's request, scheduled just before a football game that he was supposed to take part in. On this particular Saturday morning Jessy's biggest worry during the exam was what the coach would do to him if he was late for the game. The test was given by the state of New Jersey and the huge auditorium was packed with about a "million" (vast exaggeration) guys with pocket protectors and tape on their glasses. Jessy realized he was competing with the best and the brightest, super smart kids on the planet. You have to remember New Jersey was the same place where Thomas Edison, Albert Einstein, and Yogi Berra hung out. He thought to himself "I am so totally screwed, what the hell am I even doing here."

Jessy nearly got up and walked out but when he started taking the test it was like the lights came on in Yankee Stadium. They had questions on the test for example, if you took this crazy shape with dotted lines all over it and folded it up into something, what would it look like, or what is the next number in this sequence, or if the first gear goes counter clockwise what direction is the thirteenth gear turning. It was like they made the test just for Jessy. Even the algebra problems were easy as they were multiple choice and he didn't need to show how he had arrived at the answer. Jessy could do algebra in his head but could never use the formulas that they forced him to use in high school algebra class. Jessy was always an avid reader and knew the majority of the answers to the history portion. It seemed so easy that it felt like he was cheating.

Jessy completed the test while the other "contestants" were still figuring frantically away with the mechanical concepts section. This was way back before calculators, when smart kids used something called a pocket slide rule to figure out math problems and it was truly a troubling scene. A slide rule wasn't going to help them now. Hundreds of young men doodling problems on scratch paper, erasing, breaking the points off their number two pencils, sweat dripping on answer sheets, bulging zits about to pop, and a lot of muffled cursing. Jessy dropped his completed test in a basket ahead of everyone else and ran for the parking lot, jumped into his two hundred fifty dollar, gold 1952 Caddie, and blasted off to the high school football field. He managed to arrive just in time for the game where he was nearly beaten to death by guys much larger and meaner than him. Jessy only weighed about 145 pounds with rocks in his pockets. Football was a blast and he could catch anything they threw in his general direction but the part where freakishly large psychopaths slam into you at full speed one tenth of a second after you catch the ball..." well that part sucked worse than having your balls gnawed off by a rabid wolverine"

One weekend, several weeks after taking the test, Jessy and some friends were skating at the local ice pond. The town ice rink was just down the street from his duplex, (Jessy was a decent ice skater). By "some friends" I mean just about every teenager in town and a few short people who were probably young children. Jessy was doing his very best to impress an incredibly attractive freshman girl who he was starting to fall in love with...that day. Jessy was a senior and was seventeen and never really considered the legal implications of hitting on a fourteen year old. The little "Lolita" couldn't skate at all but she seemed to enjoy letting Jessy push her around the pond with his hands on her hips. He was enjoying it also and things seemed to be progressing in a very positive direction.

Just then, the spell was broken when Jessy's little sister came running up all out of breath and screamed "Jessy you've got to get home right away." "Oh for crying out loud." Jessy came an inch from telling his sister to go do something horrible to herself, as all he really wanted was to pursue this one sided affair with the attractive little dream girl with the lovely blue green eyes. This fit that his sister was throwing sounded extremely serious. Jessy's first thought was that his mom had finally gotten fed up with all of Warren's stupid racist ravings and had brained him with the three iron from the brand new bag of golf clubs that he had bought with Jessy's money but only used once. This possibility also had a bad side so he made up some totally lame excuse to the fourteen year old package of red hot trouble. After shedding his skates and slipping into a worn out pair of "Pay Less" sneakers, He rushed home to help his mother destroy the evidence.

When Jessy arrived at the apartment he was surprised to find his mom and Warren both standing in the living room, slash master bedroom, slash den, with completely dumbfounded looks on their faces. They were holding a copy of the Newark Star Ledger between them and his step-dad had tears in his eyes. Jessy was partly relieved when he realized that, at least for the time being, there would be no need to mop up blood or pick little pieces of Klan drenched brains off of the already incredibly ugly drapes.

Suddenly fear set in as Jessy pondered as many possibilities as his truly vivid imagination could conjure. Had some creature from another planet visited the Pope and were thousands of bible salesmen and evangelist preachers jumping off bridges and tall buildings all across the globe? Had a plane crashed killing the entire cast of "I Love Lucy"? Possibly peace in Vietnam had broken out forcing the CEO's of McDonnell Douglas and Hughes Aircraft and the rest of the military industrial complex to pack up and move off shore to start hiding all their money. Jessy was just getting warmed up when Warren looked up slowly from the paper and stuttered as he quietly informed Jessy that based on his test scores he had been chosen to attend Kings Point Academy on a full boat scholarship…HUH, WHAT, WAIT, HUH?

Jessy wasn't the best student in school by any means and that was mostly his own fault, but this news really freaked everyone out. I'm quite sure the family dog, Caesar, did a double take and made the

Scooby Doo sound "Wooh?" when he heard the news.

The appointment had been granted by New Jersey state senator Krebs who was going to send Jessy to an academy on state money. Jessy was one of ten students chosen from the entire state to be selected for a free ride to an academy. Sorry girls but this was 1967 and when Jessy took the test he didn't detect one single young woman in the room, he was a healthy horny seventeen year old young man and would have noticed a teenaged girl a mile away if the wind was blowing in his direction.

Kings Point Academy wasn't Jessy's idea but someone had to know someone in a very high place to get into one of the military academies. (West Point, Annapolis, or the Air force Academy.) Unfortunately the most important people Jessy knew were the principles of all the schools he attended whose offices he had spent more than a fair share of his public school career in. I mean his step-dad had his own parking space in front of the school for the many conferences he had to attend on Jessy's behalf. Jessy was freaked out right down to his toes…. that, he was just starting to get the feeling back in… (From the ice skates, remember?) Stay with me, people.

Jessy's entire school experience had been a succession of teachers who put him in the back of the room and saw little need to push him in the direction of college. Jessy had never really excelled in many of his classes save for wood shop, gym, mechanical drawing, and strangely enough geometry. He did fairly well in English and science however algebra was a complete mystery. There was after all always a need for factory workers and roofers. This was back before President Ronald Reagan declared war on the American middle class worker and good union jobs were still there for people who were willing to work for a pay check. In those days you could find jobs in the construction trades and make a decent living, and knowing the Spanish language wasn't a prerequisite. However this latest revelation was coming from so far out in right field you could see Roger Maris. (Old historical Baseball reference). Sorry, get over it.

Jessy was going through changes on several levels as he struggled with the possible options. He realized if he took the sports scholarship and got injured or flunked out, getting drafted into the Army was a real possibility. Jessy was totally gung ho about the whole war thing at the time but the Army? There is nothing wrong with the Army however in 1967 you joined the Navy, you joined the air Force, you joined the Marines, but you got drafted into the Army. "All four of the guys who enlisted in the Army in 1967 thought they were joining the Coast Guard."

While deeply embroiled in decision making Jessy's goofy science teacher suddenly asked "Does that answer your question Jessy?" Jessy really had absolutely no idea because he hadn't listened to a word his teacher had said in the last twenty minutes. Pausing, Jessy asked, earnestly, "If that is true, is the light that we see on the television coming to us as a wave or a series of particles or both?" Jessy figured that if Einstein didn't have a definitive answer for that question than neither would his mentally and morally challenged teacher. He was correct as it turned out and while the teacher attempted to explain quantum physics on a first grade level, his breathing became labored. Jessy smiled and returned to considering his options. Jessy could be a real prick sometimes but this guy deserved it.

Jessy was trying to justify the Merchant Marine academy as a real possibility, but somehow he just couldn't picture himself all dressed up in some lame uniform for four years, getting pushed around by senior classmates, all so that someday he could, at best, wind up as the captain of the Love Boat? (Jessy thought Captain Stubing was a douche) At the very least he would wind up as the captain of a giant dirty oil tanker. A man who hates his job, gets sloppy drunk, and steers his crappy ship into a topless bar on Miami beach by perhaps less than accidental circumstances.

As it turned out Jessy didn't have enough math and would have to take more algebra in summer school to qualify for the scholarship at the Academy. This totally sucked. Algebra sucked, and besides

Jessy was all geared up to enjoy his summer "down the shore" and summer school just wasn't on the radar. By the end of the science class Jessy had totally talked himself out of the whole college thing especially after watching his teacher, with all his education, totally embarrass himself in front of a room full of young people who thought he was giant waste of fresh air, in a very bad suit.

Note: The answer to Jessy's question is both waves and particles by the way, depending on the observer's point of view. You can just ask Einstein when you meet him in the great beyond… someday… maybe…or not.

After returning home from school that day Jessy informed his mother and step-dad that he was considering a third option and told them he was going to look into joining the Marines. Both of them were really very surprised and disappointed but probably for totally different reasons. Jessy's reasoning was based on the fact that he knew more people who had been in prison than those with college educations. Some of his older friends were already "fighting the communist threat" in Southeast Asia. Jessy had spent a few years on a rifle team and could shoot the balls off a fly, if the fly stood still long enough. He would certainly be wasting his talent by attending some school where he was certain that he wouldn't fit in. Back in 1968, people were dodging the draft by getting into college, failing drug tests, or medical exams or pretending to be gay. Of course plenty of the young men and women who were genuinely gay joined the service and thrived. That's a whole other story. There were and are a plethora of gay soldiers and sailors out there but back then "no one was asking and they weren't telling."

Jessy's step-dad had come to realize that once Jessy had made his mind up about something, it was pretty much, written in stone. At this point in their relationship he just didn't have the energy or the inclination to even try to talk him out of his decision. Warren, however was a "ninja" control freak and he chose to use his very last card to influence Jessy in a slightly different direction. The fact that Jessy was still a minor in high school and Warren was his legal guardian would have to sign the paperwork if he wanted to join the service. Warren had been watching the news and he realized that the Marines were getting their asses shot off in Viet Nam, so he said that the only way he would go for the military option was if Jessy agreed to enlist in the Navy.

Jessy really wasn't crazy about Warren's idea but when they went down to the Navy recruiters office they had the coolest poster in the lobby. There was a sailor in a uniform standing on the dock with a wooden sailing ship in the back ground. It looked like an "Old Spice" commercial. The sailor in the picture was wearing a beautifully tailored dress blue uniform with his arm around a beautiful Asian woman. Jessy was impressed and he thought to himself "shit, I could get myself so laid in that outfit." Truly, the reasons young men make the decisions they do is a wonder. Jessy's young ill informed brain also reasoned that with his history as an athlete in football and wrestling, and the expert-rifleman medal, perhaps he could qualify for "Seal" training or some other cool outfit where he would get to see some action in combat... as if that would be a good thing.

After some deliberation Jessy signed off on this option. Warren drove them back down to the recruiters office where Jessy joined up with the US Navy. Yes that US Navy, the one with all the big grey floaty things. They had what they were calling the 120 day program. No money, no car, no free hair cuts for life, just four months peeled off your enlistment. That was cool since three years and eight months was way shorter than the full four years right? Keep in mind Jessy had been totally brain washed by John Wayne, Audie Murphy and Ronald Reagan during his "Wonder years" and to him the military was an obligation and a given destiny for any young man his age. The people Jessy went to school with took for granted that they were college bound and they were much more concerned with whether they would be accepted by Columbia, Yale, or Princeton. Jessy...on the other hand, believed, "The only reason we hadn't won the Viet Nam war was that he hadn't been there yet." Oh my God, he was so fucking stupid, someone should have slapped the shit out of Jessy and then had him sterilized.

Jessy joined the Navy while still in his senior year of high school. Someone really should write a law to prevent stuff like that. There was already a draft in place cranking out Army soldiers like they were M&Ms. Back in 1967 the whole anti war thing hadn't really kicked in yet, at least not in Cedar Grove. This was New Jersey after all, not San Francisco, and the wheels of the peace movement were only just starting to turn up to speed. Jessy's family lived in a very conservative, republican, part of the country where sending other people's kids to a war was all the thing. Jessy had no right whatsoever to be making massively uneducated decisions of this weight at the age of seventeen. He was young and way to deranged to be deciding stuff like this. At this point in his adolescent life Jessy was just starting to get a feel for young woman, so to speak, and trying desperately to get laid, or rather... and much better sounding "he was trying to develop a meaningful relationship with someone special." The armed forces was still just a cool thing to tell your friends and he had no idea that in many parts of the country there was a real stigma attached to being a soldier or a sailor involved in fighting a very unpopular war in a part of the world where we really didn't belong... Does any of this sound just a little familiar?

Places like Chicago and Memphis were less than wonderful when it came to the treatment of America's fighting forces, but California was the worst place ever to be in the service if you wanted to blend in with the local civilian population. I'll get to this later but suffice it to say, "Momma's don't let your babies grow up to be cowboys or soldiers or sailors or airmen if you want them to be accepted by the younger generation in the middle of a bad war." At least cowboys have a horse they can depend on in a pinch." The whole fantasy of wearing a uniform and having women falling all over themselves to get some of that government issue "hardwood" is just that, mostly bullshit. Of course there were service people who had plenty of female companions to get them through the night but they were popular long before they ever joined the service. There were many young enlistees and draftees who did manage to find someone to send them off to war but those relationships became the long distance variety early on and very few made it past the first year of active duty.

During the Viet Nam war the vast majority of high school students weren't keeping up with the news issues of the day, and much like today, the schools weren't doing anything to educate kids on what was actually going on in the world. As trained experts on what a gaggle of dead generals did hundreds of years earlier, Jessy and his schoolmates could match up to any other regulated school system in the land. As for current events they were just a big smelly steaming pile of ignorant douche bags and baguettes wearing lettermen jackets and hanging out at "Bonds" hamburger joint on Friday nights.

There was a discussion beginning in the colleges and universities but then the preppies and penny loafer crowd weren't getting their pink asses drafted as long as they managed to stay in school. If Jessy had been a smarter wiser 17 year old he would have spent more time in the library learning about the history of Viet Nam and less time trying to get to second base.

Note: Hormones, money and religion are the leading causes of war and discontent in the world. Why do young men dress up like friggin GI Joe and run off to some third world country to get their balls shot off? .... Pussy, that's why. How ironic is that. Here you are, sitting in a rice paddy up to your young ass hole in leaches and land mines in some a country that may or may not have oil reserves on it's property. You are starting to realize the whole war is being staged so that the men who run the businesses that sell the planes and tanks and bombs, and fuel, that help to support our huge economy get filthy rich. All the while your girlfriend is boinking your best friend in the back seat of your GTO. This is the very same girl that you were trying to impress by joining the service in the first place. Did that revelation just ring a big old bell in someone's head? I sure as hell hope it did. (This is why I'm writing this book.)

Note Note: Let me clarify what must seem to be a sexist slant in this book. Today there are many young women who fight and die or are wounded fighting for this country's oil interests, but in Viet Nam and the wars before it "combat was for the most part a men's club." There were nurses and women in support rolls who got tangled up in the fighting from time to time but for the most part they weren't fighting in rice paddies, flying helicopters, fighter bombers, or driving trucks in hostile territory. Today's all volunteer armed forces provides many more opportunities for young heroic women to experience the thrill of modern warfare and the awesome recovery wards in our nation's VA hospitals.

"RANT ALERT!!!" The crazy murderous bastards who hijacked jet airliners and flew them into the World Trade Center only did it because some creepy old guy in a dress told them there were all these virgins up there in heaven just waiting to…. well I don't know what. I never understood that part. I must be missing something but what are all these virgins doing in heaven? If you are a female and you are a virgin when you die, you are either old, ugly as a monk fish or you died from some terrible disease or a horrible natural disaster, or some dumb shit wearing a vest stuffed with C4 and marbles blew your ass up. "Either way the last thing you want is to be ghost fucked for all eternity by an endless horde of religious fanatics." Perhaps in countries where men throw tents over their women, looks weren't a big deal, I mean you could have a head that looks like an avocado and it wouldn't matter much if you are wearing a burqa. Those same women could very well be the most beautiful creatures on earth but who the hell would know? I have a problem with the whole not letting people dress and act the way they want thing. The other issue I have with the crazy murdering douche bags who think It's just fine to kill innocent people because some screwed up bearded guy in the sky said so. HEY, crazy murderous douche bags, I only have one question. How good can the heaven sex really be…. "WHEN YOU ARE F#$&ING

DEAD?" I'm no expert but I hear dead people make really crappy lovers. I've never kissed a dead girl, virgin or otherwise but I'm sure not gonna blow myself up so that I can see what it's like. I mean that's just plain wrong... Right?

I personally, feel so bad for the true believers in the Muslim faith. A whole religion was highjacked on 9-11 by a "short bus" load of misguided lunatics. Unfortunately not nearly enough Muslim leaders have had the stainless steel, gold plated balls to stand up and denounce the atrocity for what it was. I may be totally off base on this issue because "I'm smart enough to know that I'm not smart enough to know if there is a heaven or a hell." If there is a hell, however, I'll bet there is a special extra nasty corner of it for people who believe that their god thinks slaughtering innocent women and children gets you a golden merit badge in heaven. No offense, crazy religious zealots, but you guys suck. Truth be told, if I ever need someone to "suck start" my pickup truck, I'm calling one of Osama Bin Laden's followers.

I just had a really cool revelation. The next time one of you crazy ass bastards gets the itch to bang a large group of "ghost virgins in the sky," (potentially huge country hit song title) take this bit of advice. First, you have to dress up in your cutest explosive vest, the one with the woven leather straps and the golden hand grenade accessories would be perfect. Then throw on one of those sweet grey burlap floor length moo moos, and those sweet laced Jesus sandals. (sorry Jesus, that footwear was probably really cool back in the day). Finally invite yourself over to the home of the religious lunatic who drafted you to murder women and children and when he lets you in, just yell "SURPRISE," and press the button on your detonator as hard as you can. You will have to trust me on this but all your dreams will come true. You will get to spend the rest of all eternity with your master and your seventy-two virgins. (once the other martyrs are done with them) You may even get to hang out with his supreme master virgins. If I'm not mistaken that comes to one hundred and forty-four prime grade "A" rosy ripe little virgins. It just doesn't get any better than that. Right? Your crazy assed master will be so surprised, and of course extremely grateful.)

Everything was so very different in the sixties. Religion was just a harmless pass time for most people and church was a damn good babysitter. Sunday morning was the only day of the week that Jessy's parents had sex. Warren dropped him and his sister off at Sunday school and then he hustled back home for God or Ralph only knows what. They had to walk home so Jessy knew something was going on but he tried real hard not to put that picture in his head. Needless to say Jessy walked home from church real slow. Walking in on that shit could drive you nuts.

The evening news was so credible that all the news guy had to do to get people to believe something back then was to say it out loud. They told us that Viet Nam was a "domino" and if the puppet government that we supported lost its power and therefore it's domino then...Well, then...the next domino was California. If you were smart you could have measured Viet Nam on a map and realized that it would take a much larger playing piece to reach all the way across the Pacific Ocean and land on Bakersfield. However the news anchors said it out loud and we swallowed it like a slice of Jersey style pizza. Some of us were raised to defend our sacred shores from foreign invaders, and or, gigantic domino's, whatever the case may be. Think about that for a second. Young men right out of high school were willing to fight and die to protect the American people from DOMINOS. Thank you ABC, NBC, CBS. (That's all there was before cable.) We listened to you and over fifty-eight thousand Americans died. Possibly two million Vietnamese people died along the way but that number never ever gets mentioned in the news because, as everyone knows, American lives are worth at least forty times those of people in third world countries. Don't shrug this last item off because as a country we fall for this shit all the damn time and lots of people die. Most of the people who die are brown and yellow and black but they are all PEOPLE.

So there you have it. The story of how a destitute, relatively normal, if slightly maladjusted high school student chose to turn down a full boat college education and all the fun stuff that goes with it, for a four year all expenses paid trip to Uncle Sammie's, US Navy fun park. They bust kids for smoking pot which has a zero sum effect on the rest of your life except for the whole drug bust part being on your record for ever and ever. (Thank you Mr. Nixon) Cops don't pull you over for joining the service when you are still in high school and have a college scholarship in your pocket. "Yo society! Where are your priorities?"

RANT ALERT: Here is a heads up for all you boys and girls who may feel that the military is a great way to get a free education and health care for life. First read the fine print. These days the free health care usually only applies if you get blown up or shot while serving overseas. If you get blown up or shot in Detroit you are on your own. For some young people the service to your nation is a wondrous and honorable thing but be advised, there are some causes that are fought and died for that are not for you to fight and die for. "The United States lost its innocence at the end of World War II. The Japanese were using wooden bullets by the time we dropped the only two nuclear weapons on them that have ever been dropped on anyone ever, as far as we know. We have not been fighting against any particular enemy as much as we now fight for the monetary interests of the multinational corporations that provide the hardware, supplies and oil that make these wars so profitable."

The word "Plutocracy" comes to mind (rule by the wealthy). Some of you may just have learned something. You shouldn't go starting a war with a country just because some crazy people were trained to be dangerous crazy people on a jungle gym in a desert you can only find if you know how to drive a camel. (Afghanistan) You also can't go to war because your vice president has tons of stock in the company that will get a gigantic contract to rebuild all the shit we blow up. (Iraq)

We were all horrified after the attack on the World Trade Center. We all wanted revenge on the people who did it but they were all as dead as overdone hamburgers. It was frustrating, but eventually we got over it when we realized that going to war would result in countless, needless deaths on both sides with nothing to show for it. When I say we I mean more than half of us. Then there was the fact that at least one and probably several oil producing nations would wind up hating us more than they already did. I must admit that I wasn't at all surprised when we went to war with the wrong countries. The hijackers were mostly Saudi Arabians. None of them were Afghans or Iraqis so naturally the Connecticut cowboy and his Darth Vader vice president decided that it wasn't important what brand of foreigner we "lit up" as long as they were brown....and lived on a different continent where most Americans wouldn't care or notice what we were doing to them. There are a few downsides to the idea that we must be in a constant state of war to make the country prosper, now that multinational corporations run the world.

"The damage these misadventures do to our economy can only really be appreciated by what used to be the American middle class." The point that the corporations are missing here is this. They think that by destroying the working people's unions they are assuring a more profitable future for their shareholders. They are madly in love with the idea that by crushing the life out of the middle class in this country will make them even richer than they are now. Here is the fly in that smelly ointment. Who the hell do they think buys all those cheap Chinese products they are selling. The more money they take out of our pockets, the less we can use to buy their cheap Chinese products. Our entire economy runs on the spare change of the middle class. The less change we have at the end of the week the less we have to spend on things that make our economy work. This is not rocket science people, but politicians and the CEOs they work for are very far from rocket scientists.

The unfortunate truth about what our country has become is that the gears of this great nation are oiled in blood. A fair amount of that blood is shed by brave American service people and a few, much better paid, military contractors. The vast majority of the suffering however is dumped upon the innocent occupants of the third world countries we tend to screw with.

"I love my country but I'm not crazy about the people who are determined to kill it and sell it off for parts."

So there you have it. Chapter one is officially complete. If you read it and understood it you all you get an "A." If you glossed over it...you suck. Do you have any idea how hard it is to write a "God Damned Book?" There is going to be a test.

Sorry about the totally biased history lesson but a good book has a story to tell but it also needs to instill a degree of knowledge. I'm hoping that my readers will feel a need to dig deeper and learn more about this time in our nation's history. Fact checking should be a part of everyone's routine especially now that fake news outlets are being busted for lying to their viewers and listeners.

CHAPTER 2

Blue Navy Blue

Jessy remembers his last day in the "Grove," as he referred to his little piece of paradise in northeast New Jersey. There was no going away party or a big fancy send off of any kind. Jessy and his girlfriend had spent some quality time together to prepare for his last night in town. He wondered how long it would be before he would enjoy the soft touch of a woman. Jessy was beginning to have some serious doubts about the wisdom of his decision. For Jessy it was way too late to turn back now. He didn't sleep much that night, and when he did finally dose off, his dreams were a jumble of old war movies and his reoccurring nightmare about being on a very tall railroad bridge and the train is coming and he has to choose between being squashed by the train or jumping off the bridge to be dashed on the rocks far below. (based on a true story)

Jessy got up early that morning so he could have some breakfast and say goodbye to his Mom. He cooked up a stack of pancakes. They ate those pancakes with maple syrup Jessy had made from hot water, sugar and maple flavoring and slowly sipped on "regular" coffee. They just sat and looked at each other. Jessy couldn't comment on what he was in for because he really had no idea. Jessy's mom didn't voice an opinion on the matter although she probably had more than one. His mother had served in the Navy during World War II. If she was tempted to comment on Jessy's decision, she realized it was pointless to say anything at this stage. There wasn't really much to say and neither of them were any good at making "small talk." It was an awkward moment and then all of a sudden it was time to go. Warren was up now and he was good and ready to finally get Jessy's dumb ass out of the house for good. Jessy said so long to both dogs "Cubby and Caesar." They looked so sad that he wondered if they knew somehow that he was really going away this time, not just leaving for school or work. Jessy's mom had tears in her eyes and that made him tear up a little as well as he followed Warren down the stairs and out to the green Rambler station wagon that happened to be running that day. The adventure of his life was about to begin. Jessy's younger half sister was sleeping in.

The day was extra gloomy, grey, and damp as they drove down route 3 to 1 and 9 over to Jersey City, thru the Holland tunnel, into New York City, down the West Side Highway to the Brooklyn tunnel. Finally after a blinding number of unnecessary turns and detours they pulled into the Brooklyn shipyard where the US Navy had a staging area. Jessy's step-dad was quiet and somber as he got down from the car. Warren said, "Good luck Laddy Buck." Laddy Buck was one of the nicknames he had given Jessy, "Laddy Boy" was another but that one always made Jessy feel like a can of dog food. Warren was adopted and had never met his parents. He was raised by a strict German foster family but he had flaming red hair and was so sure his real parents were Irish that he dressed up in a kilt and marched in the Saint Patrick's Day parade in New York City every year. My honest guess was that he was compensating for his lack of a real heritage by trying to talk like he was from Belfast Ireland.

Jessy was cold and numb as he turned and walked across the huge damp parking lot through a chain link gate and up to the mad house that was the Naval indoctrination center. The building itself was an old red brick auditorium of some kind but it reminded Jessy of a prison. He had glanced down the street that ran in front of the building and noticed several Navy ships docked along the pier. Just then an old destroyer, pouring black smoke, steamed past the docked ships in the harbor and "a reality check cashed itself in the pit of his stomach." This new experience promised to be something, but there was a feeling that this something wasn't going to be anything like Disneyland. As it turned out he was very wrong but it would be a while for Jessy to start enjoying all the government funded Six flags of fun he was in for.

Once inside the building Jessy tried to be friendly toward the other poor, helpless, teenaged, sad sacks as they got their physical examinations. There was the obligatory scene where everyone lined up in their underwear and turned their heads and coughed while some creepy looking corpsman (Navy for doctor but not really a doctor) groped their junk. They filled out some forms, and got yelled at by people they didn't know. Some officers showed up and swore all of them in at once. There was this strange short ceremony where they pledged their allegiance to the nation and their very lives to the armed services of that nation. At this point the gravity of the decision to serve their country very slowly began to sink in. "The sound of hundreds of assholes puckering in unison" is something you don't soon forget. It was like… "quiet thunder."

It didn't seem like a whole lot was getting accomplished during their indoctrination but for some reason it took "ALL Freaking DAY." At one point their handlers fed the enlistees with box lunches of unknown origin but there was a very dry sandwich with something round and pink doing a terrible impersonation of meat centered between two slices of white, stale, bread, and an even drier harder cookie that had live tiny white meal worms in them. Jessy ate the sandwich and passed on the cookie although there was probably more protein in that nasty cookie than the sandwich. Jessy was beginning to think that perhaps prison may have been a better choice than what ever this was that he had signed up for.

Several of Jessy's friend's (let's call them acquaintances) had spent some time (less than ten years) in a state provided, "mandatory apartment complex," and not one of them were as scary as some of the people he observed preparing to serve the country. Jessy was sharing this experience with people who were clearly only there because…they just wanted to kill somebody.

Their superiors lined everybody up and they were marched, or rather shuffled out to the parking lot. No one had been taught how to march yet and what ever it was they were doing sure as hell wasn't marching. There was a look of quiet horror in the eyes of some of the enlistees as they were loaded into one of the beat to shit old grey busses that were quite similar to the busses they use to transport convicts from the court house to the prison. The seats were torn and mended with duct tape. There was a green rubber mat running the length of the bus with holes worn thru. The metal underneath was polished by the shoes of thousands of young recruits.

The young men were driven around the streets of New York city and eventually arrived at a train station where they were divided into groups of fifty or so and then herded onto old scary looking train cars that reminded everyone of something out of a World War II movie. Jessy felt as if he should be wearing a wide brimmed fedora, a grey flannel suit, with a "Lucky Strike" cigarette hanging out of one side of his mouth.

There were roll calls and head counts and several delays that had something to do with a wheel falling off of one of the cars. (Seriously, a truck pulled up with a giant set of steel wheels on it) Jessy calmly took it all in because he figured you can't be late for the Navy when they are doing the driving and you are just riding shotgun. This was their sideshow and Jessy was just a member of the audience. After an hour or so they coupled up to the rest of the train and rolled out of the train station and out into the very heart of America. The train stopped in several large cities along the way, one of which was Philadelphia where they had to pick up some more enlistees. The guys from Philly didn't get into Jessy's car, they were already loaded up in their own little train of two or three cars and after backing up and crashing the couplers that could loosen your teeth, eventually they too were coupled onto the main train and soon the new recruits were all bound for glory, eternity, and a whole steaming pile of other unknown mind bending unknown adventures.

The trip was a long one and some of the guys entertained themselves by playing cards, and throwing dice. Did I mention that these people were from New Jersey and New York? Nothing makes the time fly like a spirited game of "fifty-two pickup" in the aisle of a train on its way to hell. They were just trying to make the best of a bad situation. Jessy felt very alone and totally under someone else's control. Oddly Jessy was comfortably at home here. This was Jessy's wheel house and he knew how to deal with what was in store for him and his fellow travelers. There is a quote from "Hunter Thompson" "When the going gets weird...the weird go pro. Jessy was unique in many ways and those ways included not breaking under stressful situations but rather making the best of what ever test he was faced with. He had survived shit storms his whole life and was able to ride stuff out that many other young white young men could not. The Black guys were just cool. They were listening to transistor radios with ear plugs and jamming out to sixties soul all the way. No smiles no frowns just a smooth layer of pure cool.

Jessy had volunteered and now there was no way out. It wasn't like he was on a city bus and could just pull the cord and get off. Jessy stared out the window of the train car and watched his country speeding by. Now and then he would see people walking or driving somewhere and thought to himself that he wished he was going wherever they were going instead of where he was going. This of course was absurd and he realized that those people wandering around in the middle of the night could very well have totally shitty lives. They could be homeless or on their way to buy drugs with the family's food budget. The kind of lives that drive people over the edge of crazy.

Note: If your life has failed you to the extent that you feel all is lost and that you want to end it all, consider this. No matter how messed up you and your life may be, there are people with flies in their eyes because they don't have the strength to brush them away because they haven't had a decent meal in their entire lives because they live in a place where the people who run their country stole all their nations wealth and kept it. Think about those people and let it sink in. If you still can't find a reason to be thankful for your life...seek professional help there are people out there who were trained to guide people who are dealing with severe depression, and get some sleep. Your brain uses sleep to sort out all the things that are making you feel that you are out of options. You wake up and the answers start to appear one at a time and you can move on. If you still can't find any good reason to live then go off someplace quiet and do what you have to do. Please DO NOT make that same decision for a group of people who you may think made your life suck. It isn't their fault, It's yours. We are all capable of making our lives less "suck-full." (yes it's a word, if it wasn't before it is now so get over it) The best way to make those feelings go away is to help someone less fortunate than you. Of course, first you have to admit that there are people who have less to live for than you do but are still out there plugging away every day trying to make their lives just a little better. This message was a public service announcement...you're welcome.

The point is none of the people on that train really had any idea of what to expect next. They were disoriented, bewildered and missing their friends back home. You start to dream of being in the arms of your girlfriend, or anyone's girlfriend for that matter as long as it meant you weren't on that god damned train. Jessy just sat back and took it all in.

This was the farthest Jessy had ever been away from his apartment in New Jersey and he could feel his lungs starting to clear up halfway across Pennsylvania. The trip lasted all night and most of the next day. The train finally slowed and rolled to a stop on the "back side of South Bum Fuck, Illinois." Again they were herded onto busses and driven even deeper into the dark smelly bowels of America. Eventually they arrived at the gate of an immensely huge, redundantly gigantic Naval base in the exact center of freaking nowhere. There were long lines of large three story buildings as far as you could see and they were situated around giant paved surfaces called "grinders" where they would eventually teach no rank sailors to march around like ants on crack. After being waved in by a gate guard the bus driver drove them to a point where they were completely surrounded by the Great Lakes recruit training center (Navy boot camp) located not far from Chicago, Illinois.

From his first day in the Navy Jessy realized that this experience was going to be less like the recruitment poster and more like a Fellini movie. Great Lakes recruit training center is a city of grey. Grey cars, grey trucks and busses, grey office buildings and mostly grey people except for the new arrivals from Southern California and Florida. Of course by winter they would be as grey as everything else.

The screaming started immediately upon debarking (getting off of) the buses. At this point none of the new recruits didn't know one military rank from another. Instinctively they were sure of only one thing, that literally everyone they met out ranked them. There was a civilian guy wearing ear protectors and using a leaf blower when they were still riding to the barracks and a whole bus load of helpless enlistees realized that he was much more powerful and had more control of his destiny than they did. Jessy would have switched places with that person in a heart beat, even if it meant learning a foreign language.

This new revelation meant that literally everyone who helped run this crazy farm could yell at you and call you all kinds of horrible but really quite creative expletives all day long, which they did. A few of their new labels were "puke" "shit bird" "faggot" "scumbag" and of course the ever popular "stupid, mother fucking, cock sucking, pussy eating, zit faced, shit bag." When someone hollers that at the top of his lungs with a heavy Bostonian accent, it can be really profoundly, stunningly, humorous. Jessy however discovered that laughing when someone is blasting profanities in your face from point blank range just makes them mad.

The list of colorful name tags was endless and varied depending on the region of origin of your superior. The southern chiefs and petty officers were the funniest. They just drew upon their country roots when they came up with insults like "you stupid pig shit suckin, sister loving, toothless, chicken fucker." Who knew joining the Navy would mean learning to curse like a drunken sailor? That question sort of answers itself I suppose. Jessy had come from New Jersey after all so most of the verbal abuse just made him home sick. It was like an inside joke more than it was hurtful, but some of the bible belt guys were in tears as their tormentors zeroed in, on them like they were freshly wounded prey.

Someone with a stripe or two on his sleeve screamed and cursed the group into a line and marched them over to a grey building where they were issued a pile of nasty looking, ill fitting clothes that looked nothing at all like the outfit the sailor was wearing on the enlistment poster. Most average prisoners locked up in county jail got better looking attire than the Navy enlistees. Again, they lined everybody up and shuffled them to the barber shop where they were forced to get all their hair shaved off. When the base barbers were done it looked like a prisoner of war movie or a gathering of Nazi, white supremacist's with a few bewildered black guys looking down at their perfect afro's on the floor. They certainly didn't look like the sailors who were destined to have a woman in every port.

The barbershop scene was humiliating and the haircutters were sadists. They would only cut part of your hair off at first so you could look at yourself in the mirror and see what you looked like with half a "Mohawk" or a "Bozo the Clown" haircut. Everyone suddenly realized that they had been duped and were now utterly screwed and totally fucked. (that was redundant but somehow it just makes more sense)

The Navy lined everyone up once again where the flock of bald seagulls were given a battery of inoculations that made them ten pounds heavier and sick as dogs for days. The make believe doctors used needles, air guns, magic elixirs and pills. The band of hairless brothers were just waiting to be attacked by pigmy's with blow darts. The good news was that these young men were now immune to almost everything, like small pox, measles, plague, berry, malaria, everything that is…. except sexually transmitted diseases. A large number of our young American servicemen learned this particular lesson just a little too late. In Viet Nam they had a strain of VD that could kill Superman, and there was no shot for it. The discussion between a returning service man and his girl friend went something like this.

Her: (after seeing her man naked for the first time after returning home from his tour in Viet Nam)

"Uh…baby. Where did your dick and nuts go?"

Him: "Yeah, well…. about that...They kind of fell off…. you know, …. over in Nam."

Her: "What do you mean they fell off? You look like a friggin Ken doll for Christ sakes. They didn't just fall off all by themselves you dumb fucked up mother fucker. You screwed one of those poison pussy whores in Saigon didn't you? You stupid bastard. Get the fuck out of here before I cut… your…Well never mind that, just go, and for Christ sakes please do not come back…ever."

There was a whole lot more danger in Viet Nam besides the Vietnamese soldiers, land mines, tigers, and deadly snakes. The very fact that our military separates the sexes, to the extent that they do, is a dangerous mistake. First of all, we are talking about high school graduates who may have had their first sexual experience just a short time before getting shipped off to some foreign land where the only local talent they are exposed to were all professionals. Many lives could have been spared If corporal "Fresh Meat" could get off work and hang out with private "Susie Cream Cheese." and maybe have a relatively safe sleep over. This is a personal feeling based on what I learned as a teenager.

Things started to go badly on the second day of boot camp when Jessy was assigned to a barracks run by a chief petty officer named MacQuinton. Chief MacQuinton at first, seemed to be the very definition of the military man's man. He was the guy we had all seen in those propaganda war movies when we were growing up. This crazy son of a bitch was ruggedly handsome, had swagger and he was really loud,...Like scary loud. He was the Robert Duval character in "Apocalypse Now" His confident attitude didn't bother Jessy and he kind of liked the guy at first. The chief seemed to treat Jessy better than the other young men in his charge. When he tried to intimidate the rest of the recruits he scared the piss out of most of them and they obeyed him like he was God. In spite of his brutal tirades no matter how hard he tried, he wasn't able to break Jessy down.

After years of being relentlessly berated by his slightly to the right of Rush Limbaugh and the KKK, step-dad, Jessy had grown very thick skin and verbal abuse had little or no effect. The black, and Hispanic city guys just ignored the chief and went on about their business. Jessy and the chief sort of warmed up to each other and MacQuinton leveled his fury at the weaker minions while he treated a small group of his underlings like family. Coincidently besides Jessy the other chosen few were the big dangerous looking, inner city, African American guys who could have passed for Mike Tyson's body guards. The chief made one of these guys his "sergeant at arms" His name was Jamal and he didn't have a gun but he did have guns, big ones. Jamal was MacQuinton's junk yard dog and looked like he worked out by bench pressing Volkswagens.

The arrangement worked well for the first week or so. Jessy was also able to balance being a teachers pet with maintaining friendships with some of the other young men in his barracks. The truth is there were some people who gravitated towards Jessy in an attempt to escape the cruel wrath of their insanely angry chief.

Soon it became apparent that Chief MacQuinton was slowly going mad before their eyes. Jessy noticed early on that the chief could be either deadly as a pit bull on crack or calm and helpful but you never knew which chief you were going to get and his moods could change in half an instant. He was on the fast track to winning a long all expenses paid vacation to a room with very soft walls. The chief was becoming increasingly mean and abusive towards the slow learners in the barracks. He was punishing everyone for one guys screw up and in turn the vast majority of young recruits would take some form of retribution on that one sorry offender. This is an "old school" technique used by the military, sports coaches, and boy scout leaders alike however when actual physical abuse is encouraged by those in control, things can go sideways in a hurry. In this case someone had been hurt badly and it seemed likely that the crazy Chief was directly involved. By this I mean he beat the shit out of some poor mothers son with his own very large bare hands. The young sailor went to the base hospital and the chief was brought up on charges.

The entire company was put on some kind of hold while the Navy tried to find someone to take up the slack, fill in the crack, complete the stack, cover our back, upgrade the MAC. (Oops... I got off on some kind of rhyming thing there. I probably shouldn't do that, sorry) In the interim the rest of the sea scouts were on a weird vacation. They spent their down time writing some very bewildered letters home.

"Hi everyone, our company commander went bug fuck crazy and almost killed a guy. We may be in boot camp forever. No one knows what's going to happen next. We would all run away but we don't know where we are so we don't know what direction to go. Hope you are all doing well. See you soon...or not. Perhaps I'll be home for Christmas or the 4th of July. Shit we don't know. Say hi to Jimmy. If he is still thinking of going into the military... tell him to talk to me first. Sorry, got to go do some Navy stuff, bye."

It took a couple of weeks for the company to be transferred to a new barracks. Those weeks were tacked on to their boot camp experience and a new first class petty officer was assigned to line them up and teach them how "to be all that they could be." The replacement company commander was skinny and pale and looked as though he could fall down and die at any moment. I believe he came to take over Jessy's company directly from submarine duty and was in dire need of sunshine, vitamin D, and muscle tone as soon a possible. He had permanently watery, bloodshot, eyes that made him look like he was crying all the time. It could have been a bad case of hay fever because exposure to pollen isn't much of an issue on most submarines. As sad and wimpy as this new company commander appeared he still had to be better than that last crazy bastard, right?

The whole "line thing" is a common theme in the service. Just about each and everything you do in boot camp starts and ends buy lining up "nuts to butts" or "rockets to sockets" with hundreds of other "sorry assed, duck fucking, douche bags." (sorry, that's how Navy people talk.) (I'm smart enough not to venture a guess as to how things are expressed in the women's barracks.) They lined you up to eat. They lined you up to use a telephone. They lined you up to take a dump, and they lined you up get your silly sorry pay check every two weeks. In boot camp you spent literally hours a day standing in those stupidly long lines. Of course, the truth is, those lines were every bit as important as the uniforms. They were a necessary part of this giant well oiled machine that is the United States military. "These are the lines of freedom."

Everything you are exposed to in boot camp has a purpose. The young sailors learned that they wore loose fitting bell bottom jeans because in a battle at sea when bombs are tearing your ship into thousands of red hot flaming pieces of metal that can burn right through your clothes, the "bells" let the shrapnel fall to the deck instead of being trapped against your leg forcing you to jump into the ocean. The Navy realized that there would be no "Victory at sea" if all their sailors jumped over board with their pants on fire. Those very same bell bottom trousers could be tied off to make a handy pair of water wings that could keep you afloat when your big grey ship was torpedoed and sank out from under you. This trick only worked if you were lucky enough to be somewhere near the upper deck when your ship suddenly wound up on the wrong side of the surface. Thousands of sailors never got a chance to fashion home made floatation devices during "World War II" because they were trapped below decks when their ship suddenly decided to go on a vertical road trip.

All of this information came in a short amount of time. As a group they were sobered by the thought of being entombed in a solid steel coffin for all of eternity. The Navy assured everyone that death by drowning was by far the very best, most fun, way to die of all the other ways because all you had to do was relax, take a big deep wet breath and fucking die. Thanks Navy, we feel much better now that you cleared that up.

I have to say this for the Navy system. They don't give you much time to sit around feeling sorry for yourself. When you did find a few minutes to write a letter home it might go something like this.

"Hi mom and dad. Can you please get me out of here, these people are crazy. Really I'm serious, you have got to get me out of here now. I think they are trying to kill me so write a letter to president Johnson and tell him I made a terrible mistake. I can't take this much longer. Can you please send me a care package with plenty of gay stuff in it. I'm thinking pink wig, fake eyelashes, lipstick, a pretty blue dress, and, Oops. Sorry I've gotta go and get in line for something very important, don't know what, bye. With love your son (new name) Barbara"

Jessy's bootcamp situation was getting worse yet somehow better by the day. Things were getting so out of control that there were some young American men trying to end their precious lives because of the endless piles of chicken shit they were forced to deal with. While Jessy was settling in nicely. The food wasn't great but...it was there and you could drink all the milk you wanted. For a person who grew up on powdered milk this was a giant plus. Jessy found boot camp life relatively easy to deal with and he simply got in line and did what his superiors told him to do. Sometimes going along with the program is the only choice and learning how to survive and stay calm when things go sideways is a good thing.

Note: To parents of lonely, misfit kids, who are just not getting with the program, for whom you think the military might be the perfect solution. You may want to think a little longer because there is a very real possibility that... "IT'S NOT!" Some people were made to be warriors but many were made to be something very different. Albert Einstein wasn't a warrior but he helped develop the atom bomb. That is an unfortunate example but you get the idea.

One morning as Jessy was making up his bunk, he just happened to look up and see something plummeting past the barracks window. What ever it was...wasn't smiling. Jessy ran to the window and looked down into the concrete area where they hung up their laundry. Poking his head out the window Jessy observed this sorry "shit bird" recruit lying on the ground screaming bloody murder. His reddened face was contorted in pain and he had what appeared to be a very broken leg sticking out from under his body at an angle that you might come across in geometry class but certainly not on a normal human body. There was some blood on the cement and he had a pile of string in his lap. The string was knotted about every five inches and the unseen end seemed to be attached to something somewhere on the floor above.

Everyone had been issued a bundle of eight inch long strings with little metal ends that they used instead of clothes pins. (clothes stops) They were made from very thick strong government issue string. You had to tie your shirts and jeans and "skivvies" (under shorts) on steel cable clothes lines with the little strings and they had to be in perfect rows and the knots had to be perfectly symmetrical. They had a two hour class to learn how to hang up their stupidly ugly ill fitting clothes. This is one of many things the sailors to be, referred to as "chicken shit." The Navy as it turns out is made up of one giant steaming grey boatload of very important chicken shit.

The troubled recruit had spent the whole night after lights out going to every ones locker and stealing all the clothes stops he could find and then he tied them all together. When he was done he tied one end of his "rope" to his "rack" (not his man boobs, but his steel bunk bed) then he tied the other end around his neck and lofted himself out the window. He was on the third floor, Jessy was on the second, so when the young recruit went flying by the window with that puzzled look on his face he was still picking up speed, which he did until the precise second he hit the pavement. He traveled about 30 feet and hit the ground with a terrible thud. I don't know exactly how fast he was going upon impact but you can ask a physics student if you are curious. The sailor's plan was perfect except for his string rope was about a hundred feet too long. This guy was from one of those states down south where his whole family only had about a dozen teeth between them and his cousin was his sister and his other sister was his mother or some such country song. He wasn't real familiar with buildings with two or more floors and way over estimated the number of clothes stops he needed to weave into his plan.

Directly following the human meteorite's fall to earth. By that I mean in a real damn hurry. One minute he was sprawled out on the ground looking like a Picasso, screaming like a monkey with his nuts on fire and the next minute he was completely and utterly gone. In his place there was a detail of recruits cleaning up the blood. The Navy doesn't waste a second in an emergency, situation. My guess is that they carted his dumb country ass off to the base medical facility somewhere that had a fully staffed mental ward. The poor, sorry, broken recruit was never seen again in boot camp. There are rumors that he moved to Texas and was instantly elected governor.

Note: As the writer of this book I feel obligated to mention that I have some issues with Texas, the state of, and many actual Texans, the residents of that flat, tornado magnet. I don't have a problem with all Texans of course. Janis Joplin, Willie Nelson, ZZ Top, Steve Martin, Nora Jones, Beyonce, Lyle Lovett, Meat Loaf, Bonnie and Clyde, Bobby Seale, Selena, and my favorite Eva Longoria. You get the Idea, it's a long list. The other side of that coin are the less lovable residents of the nation's second largest state. And what's with those gigantic cowboy hats? Do you realize how small they make your head look? I'm just kidding, many of my very best friends and relatives are from Texas, I own and wear a big old cowboy hat when I'm working out doors, it's like an umbrella and blocks out the sun better than a solar eclipse but please, just don't get me started on the crooks in Texas politics, that's a whole other book.

The attempted suicide incident helped Jessy adjust to life in the Navy. He figured that there were people around who had problems much scarier than his and he reveled in that fact. From that day on, whenever Jessy noticed some screaming idiot flying past the window...he just smiled to himself, and looked forward to spending just a little less time in that line at the chow hall.

The Navy teaches you absolutely everything you need to survive on board a ship at sea. You had to work in the chow hall, where you learned how to make a tasty breakfast for four thousand men out of real and not so real eggs and a huge shit load of potatoes. You quickly became an expert at cracking eggs and peeling spuds. Most recruits could peel potatoes all day without cutting their fingers to ribbons, but some people were just never born to use anything sharper than a tooth brush. Mashed potatoes aren't meant be pink in color but in boot camp sometimes they were. Similarly some guys couldn't get the hang of breaking four eggs at once, two in each hand. This explained the plethora of egg shells in the scrambled eggs from time to time. There is something special about being in a room with a thousand other mostly grown up people who are all spitting out little pieces of white, crunchy, chicken placenta wrappers. It was kind of like an indoor snow storm, with crunchy sound effects.

The instructors taught Jessy how to put out a compartment fire in a steel room filled with burning oil and so much smoke you couldn't even see the blazing inferno just a few feet ahead of you. The door you came in through is mostly closed behind you with only room for the water hose so that your only choice is to fight the fire until you get it out. That's it, there is no other choice. It's scary but you learn to overcome your fear and let your adrenalin take over. Your hands, face, and lungs are coated in a greasy black glaze when you finally exit the building. One of the recruits showed everyone how not to chew gum during the fire exercise by aspirating his Bazooka bubble gum and choking to death in the fire room. Let's just say the after exercise head count didn't go too well that day.

There were a couple of accidents but the vast majority of our nation's finest made it out of bootcamp alive. All things considered Jessy emerged from the experience smarter, wiser but mostly undamaged by the basic training thing. This made Jessy quite happy. If he had died he wouldn't be unhappy...he would be dead. Like Abraham Lincoln dead but that is a whole other story.

The most rewarding aspect to life in the service and boot camp in particular is the human zoo of people you meet there. One day you are in high school and most of your friends are from the same place you are. When Jessy was young he could have ridden his bike to the front door step of every one of his schoolmates.

When Jessy enlisted he was suddenly surrounded by a huge carnival of characters from all over the country and many places that he never really would have guessed were part of the country. Jessy always knew that Puerto Rico was a protectorate but there was also someone from Guam and a guy from Utah. Most people don't know this but New Mexico is a state and Albuquerque is a real place. Bugs Bunny didn't make that shit up. One guy was from North Dakota. Are you kidding me? Seriously? ... North Dakota? Rumor has it that there is another equally unpopulated state named South Dakota.

Note: North and South Dakota have less than 2,000,000 people combined and together they have 4 senators. California has around 40,000,000 people and only 2 senators...That's it, just something to ponder. Wonder what would happen if California cut itself up into 20 little states with 2 senators each. Like wow, right? The people in China who make our flags would have a hell of a time finding a place for all those stars.

Jessy found that the majority of these fellow recruits were as fascinated by him as he was by them. When they had a little down time the guys would question each other about what it was like to be from Mississippi, Arkansas, or California. Being from New Jersey meant that the very first question everyone asked Jessy was did he know anyone in the "Mafia." Of course Jessy denied knowing anyone "connected" mainly because he didn't want one of the New York guys writing a letter home about the "Jersey douche bag who was spreading rumors about the family." That and the fact that at the age of eighteen Jessy didn't know many gangsters besides a bookie or two and a few street corner hustlers from Paterson. One girl in high school did have a father who tripped and fell on some bullets over in New York one night but it would be years before Jessy met any actual organized crime people. As far as he knew.

Jessy really loved learning about other people and places but some people and their places were much more interesting than others. There was a big strong baseball pitcher from Tennessee who had signed a major league contract but was badly injured while driving a tanker car full of moonshine whiskey. His car was a big Buick with specially welded compartments for his highly flammable product. The bumper had been replaced with six foot sections of railroad track. He told us the story of one get away where his car tore right through a police roadblock and that front bumper turned two cop cars into shredded piles of scrap metal. His accident involved a bridge, a fire, and months of rehab in the hospital. He lost the baseball contract but got to keep the scars. He was a good guy and funny as hell. Jessy liked and respected him as a friend but looking at his face took a little getting used to.

Jessy's closest friend was from Thibedoux Louisiana. His name was Adams and he was a Cajun. That still doesn't explain why French people use so many god damned letters to spell simple words. Adams told stories about working on oil rigs in the Gulf of Mexico and showed our company some Voo Doo tricks including terrorizing our RCPO (recruit petty officer) with a doll that he fashioned from scraps of cloth and some arm hair that he claimed to have shaved from the RCPO in his sleep. The poor guy didn't get any sleep for weeks.

Once while Jessy was sitting on his bunk Adams came over and asked if he could borrow Jessy's high school ring. They were friends and Jessy agreed without giving it a second thought. Adams reached into his pocket and pulled out a two foot long piece of thread and quickly ran the thread through the ring. He pulled the ends together and let the school ring hang suspended for a few seconds and then he softly said watch the ring and only the ring. He spun the ring with his free hand and it twirled perfectly in one place. Then he told Jessy to watch the ring until it turns into a baseball. Jessy played along with the trick and sure enough after ten or fifteen-seconds the spinning ring became a baseball before his eyes. That's all he could remember. Jessy blinked his eyes and the ring was back on his finger. Then Jessy realized that some time had gone by when he noticed that his bell bottom jeans were on backwards and everyone in the barracks were suddenly standing around the bunk and they were all laughing. Jessy had never been hypnotized until then but he knew better than to ask what had gone on while he was "away." Shit like that can screw you up for a long time.

"In this life, the trick to survival and well being is, you have to get in a groove. You can deal with almost anything once you understand the rules that everyday is going to be a mind blowing adventure on some level, the rest is mostly a matter of making the appropriate adjustments. This strategy works well most of the time but some incidents are just so disturbing that it takes a long while to get all the spiders out of your brain."

One overcast afternoon Jessy's company was returning to the barracks after one of their daily marching "drills on the grinder." They had just learned how to perform an "oblique turn" as a unit. This means that eighty men, while marching in step, turn off at a forty-five degree angle at exactly the same time. It took all afternoon to get it perfect but they were all very proud when the drill was over. This maneuver was so cool to see and theirs would be the company to bet on to win the marching competition and the coveted silly little yellow flag of glory. After marching for hours all they wanted to do was jump in the shower and get ready for the march to the chow hall for dinner.

When Jessy entered the huge room where eighty of his new best friends bunked together, He was stunned to find that all of their racks (bunk beds) were flipped over and the lockers were dumped out and everything they were responsible for, clothes, bedding, personnel belongings, everything, was piled in heaps all over the room. No one had the slightest idea what the hell was going on. Jessy had never heard of a tornado forming on and only on the second floor of a building. "What in the high holy hell could have possibly caused all of this destruction Jessy pondered. After a survey of the devastation for ten or fifteen minutes their first-class petty officer, company commander, came barging into the room, all revved up and yelling about the inspection that had been performed while they were gone. He was a man possessed and his face was bright red as he ranted on about the three "gigs" (points off) they had received for violating the skivvy's folding commandment.

Everyone had been issued three pairs of the ugliest, ill fitting, boxer shorts the world has ever seen. They were the kind that puffed out in the back and would make anyone wearing them immune to getting anything close to laid by anyone or anything. Personally I believe that perhaps this was the Navy's way of preventing a sudden outbreak of homosexuality. That and the "saltpeter" that rumor had it was going into the imitation scrambled eggs. There was, after all a practical reason for everything that went on in boot camp. They gave us a training session and we were shown how our ugly shorts had to be folded and stowed in our lockers. Some poor, sorry misguided soul, had accidentally folded his shorts left over right instead of the proper, Christian, American military, right over left approach and one person was responsible for the entire company having failed the barracks inspection.

Jessy's company had spent the entire weekend spit polishing their club house and it was spotless. Everything looked perfect from the floors which they had buffed with wool blankets, to the toilets that they had cleaned with someone's tooth brush. No one told the guy they borrowed the toothbrush from, but somehow I think he knew. Every piece of metal was shined with "Brasso." The windows looked like mirrors and mirrors looked like…well they looked like mirrors too but super clean ones. They dusted every single square inch of wall, giving special attention the tops of the lockers. (the inspectors wore white gloves and locker tops were ground zero) Everyone shoes looked like patten leather and their brass belt buckles shone like the sun. The entire company was so proud of their hard work.

Some ruthless underwear folder had destroyed their perfect inspection and now they would not be able to graduate boot camp with the stupid little yellow flag that you get for passing the inspection. (the stupid little yellow flags you earn for marching and folding underwear are just for bootcamp graduation, you have to give them back after getting your picture taken at the final ceremony) Jessy's company's main competition was a company they had lovingly nicknamed "The Evil Scouts." The Evil scouts had already won every flag and every other meaningless, piece of shit award that you could win. When they marched to the chow hall they looked like a float in the Rose Parade. Many in Jessy's company thought, "How sweet it would be to have just one lousy banner to march around with." Besides that, now they had to spend the rest of the day and evening putting everything back together. Jessy didn't care about flags. He was aware that all this crazy underwear bullshit was just one more way to grind nutty Navy crap into our brains. Despite realizing how incredibly stupid all of this was, he still was forced to deal with the consequences.

The really cruel part of this story was that the company commander chose to inform everyone in the room who the unfortunate person was who had screwed up his shorts and was thus responsible for them not getting to march around with a little yellow flag on a stick. For some unknown reason the vast majority of the company was so outraged at this poor bastard for his crime against underwear that they were determined to exact some level of revenge against him in the most painful way possible. Jessy could not even imagine being that pissed at something so contrived. There must be some form of mental illness that transforms a person into the perfect cut of meat that can be ground up to produce a good obedient military hamburger with extremely shiny shoes. Jessy was immune to this brain ailment and one day it would prove to be his downfall, or salvation depending on your point of view.

Later that night the majority of Jessy's company threw the young sailor a blanket party. For those of you lucky enough to never have experienced or witnessed one, the party boy at a blanket party is held down by several people using his own sturdy, navy issue, wool, blanket. Then he gets to lie restrained and motionless in his bunk while the remainder of the group wails on him with fresh bars of soap wrapped in tube socks. There are undoubtedly variations on this ritual but the outcome is always the same. Some poor unfortunate mothers son winds up all beaten and bruised, for no good reason what so ever.

This particular, tried and convicted, party guest was coincidently also the company religious petty officer. He was a farm boy from Iowa or Nebraska. I don't know but it was one of those flat states you drive through and all you see is corn. The farm boy was from a place with tons and tons and more tons of corn, cows, sheep, chickens, and a 4H club, but no hard rules about proper underwear care. He had come to us from a world where if you got most of the sheep shit raked up before dinner time you were having a good day. The victim kept an old worn bible with him everywhere he could. The poor naive goof would read scriptures to the whole company every night, whether they wanted him to or not. He was really a very nice person and although Jessy could easily have done without all the preaching he enjoyed listening to his farm tales that somehow revolved around how lonely a farm really is and there are all these animals around and how a sheep's vagina looks just like a human one. He never came out and admitted to bestiality so we won't go there.

Jessy tried his best to calm down the mob but they were determined to trash this dastardly fiend with all their self righteous might. Jessy was at least successful at bringing a few of his friends over to the not so dark side and they refused to join in on the beating of the unfortunate childlike "nowhere man." Five or six of them lay in their bunks while the others drummed away for what seemed like hours. When they were done beating the innocent farm boy to the consistency of warm bread pudding they dragged his black and blue ass into the shower room for something called a "GI shower." Someone found a bristle push broom and they used it to remove any dirt along with the top two layers of skin while he lay writhing on the floor. The screaming and yelling were so loud that everyone was sure that someone would come running in at any moment and break it up. No one ever came of course. Their superiors had stationed some third-class petty officer to be on duty in case of a fire or perhaps a revolt, in each of the barracks' facilities. There were people in authority who heard the riot but no one responded. This was all part of some sick plan to put the fear of God into its young sailors and the sacrifice of one helpless eighteen year old was a small price to pay for discipline. God alone knows what would happen if the nation were suddenly attacked by the Russians and one of our brave young sailors had their underwear folded incorrectly. It would surely mean the difference between victory and defeat. The American people would all be eating beet soup, drinking vodka by the quart, and chain smoking incredibly nasty cigarettes if it weren't for all those perfectly folded boxer shorts.

Jessy was concerned that they had killed the unfortunate country boy, but the following day he was still alive, all beat to shit but still alive just the same. Imagine putting someone in a laundry bag and throwing him down the stairs...of the Empire State building. It was sort of like that. Their poor religious petty officer was never quite the same after his special training session and Jessy didn't remember him saying another word other than "yes sir" and "no sir"...ever again. He just went through the motions with his head down and mumbling under his breath what you would assume were bible verses but then it could have been lines from the Rolling Stones song "Paint It Black." Jessy personally was not a big "god guy" but he could have used a few good lines from the book of Rudy or whoever it was who preached that we should forgive those who trespass against us and or those who don't fold their fucking ugly undershorts correctly.

Jessy's tiny crew felt terrible and wondered if there was anything they could have done to prevent this monstrous inhuman act. In retrospect someone could have pulled the fire alarm and would have at least delayed the attack long enough to alert someone in authority to the situation. Of course this particular strategy probably would have backfired and they would have put themselves in jeopardy. When the water dried up, the blood thirsty band of brothers would still have terrorized the lonely recruit. They were still in awe of the mysterious power these people in power had over them. The military is a strange well thought out combination of fear, peer pressure, and meaningless rewards. The stupid little yellow flag that they would never earn or have been allowed to keep even if they had won is the perfect example.

After the blanket party/GI shower incident Jessy was never quite the same either. He realized that this madhouse was something that he would have to either learn to deal with or else start planning a midnight escape from the base. They weren't all that far from Canada but winter was just down the road and they hadn't been issued their sweaters and "Pea coats" yet. One cold morning they found one of the recruits frozen to death. He had died while on watch because he was wearing a light jacket on a night when the temperature was 10 degrees. They found him in an empty dumpster that he thought would keep him warm. Because of some arbitrary rule they weren't allowed to wear their warm winter gear until some arbitrary date had passed. This was clearly no time to go AWOL and risk becoming a blue eyed government issue vanilla popsicle.

Jessy decided to suck it up and stick it out. The good news was that he was gradually getting really good at all this Navy stuff. He had the fastest time on the obstacle course in history. (as far as we know)

Jessy also was getting excellent grades on all the tests and was so totally awesome at the shooting range that when the black Marine sergeant instructor with the prosthetic leg, fresh back from Viet Nam, noticed Jessy was putting all his shots through the same hole in the target he asked, rather strongly "what the fuck are you doing in the fucking Navy dick head? You should be over there sniping the shit out of gooks with the special forces dudes." Jessy wasn't totally clear on what a "gook" was at the time but it meant the sergeant liked Jessy and he wasn't going to hit him in the head with his hickory cane like he did to just about every one else. In boot camp stuff like this was like a promotion and his fellow sailors treated Jessy with a new level of respect from that day forward.

Note: Just for your general information. If you remember the movie "Officer and a Gentleman" the part where Richard Gere gets over on his fellow midshipmen by polishing shoes and belt buckles for a profit. Well, that trick was invented by enlisted men in boot camp well before his dumb ass did it in the movies. Only difference...Jessy didn't get caught.

Note, Note: The finely tuned, if at times misguided, machine that is the US military works because of millions of tiny details. These helpful hints have been learned through out the years by personnel who sometimes payed for those lessons with their lives. Did you know that Chapstick (a petroleum product) and pure oxygen like the kind that is delivered to our pilots through their face masks don't mix? One unfortunate Navy pilot who must have fallen asleep during that class, nearly blew his face off. There must have been a cigarette of some kind involved. This type of explosion requires (oxygen), fuel (Chapstick), and some kind of spark or heat source (joint). Sorry to be so clinical about some pilot's unfortunate mishap but, funny is funny. There was no U-Tube back then but you have to wish there was.

Note, Note, Note: I believe that the education young men and women receive in military boot camps, and service schools, as well as on the job experience should be counted as college credit when they get discharged. No wonder so many ex-military personnel wind up pan handling and living under bridges like well trained trolls when they get out. Few people realize what great employees ex-GI's make. They are just a smelly group of barely educated high school kids when they go into the service. The only thing most of them are really good at is masturbation and...well, that's about it. After the military assigns them a MOS. (military occupation specialty) they are very good at least one more thing. That thing can be driving giant diesel powered vehicles or rebuilding them. Service people are trained to operate nuclear powered submarines as well as giant ships the size of small towns. There are radio, radar and electronics specialists and these days the radar and computer networking people should be guaranteed instant jobs when they get discharged. Unfortunately this is seldom the case. Their training seems so specialized that it is considered worthless when they get out. The part employers miss is that in the military you learn how adapt. You learn to adjust to circumstances that can mean the difference between life and death. These people are trained to take and give orders without question. Treating our veterans like they were candy wrappers should be a crime. They don't start these insane wars. They do their best to finish them.

Jessy easily sailed through boot camp from that point on, and before you know it, the boot camp odyssey was suddenly over. There was a big fancy graduation ceremony with a band and a few high ranking officers dressed up with all their medals and gold braid. Jessy's company proudly showed off their newly acquired marching skills, and even though they never won the little yellow flag on a stick, somehow graduated just the same.

Toward the end of boot camp they made everyone take one last test and Jessy scored high enough to be assigned to attend an "A" school near Memphis Tennessee where he would learn how to work on jet aircraft. This was considered an exceptionally cool school and a "guaranteed path to employment" after the Navy. (Not so much) Jessy was disappointed because he had put in a request to be considered for a slot in special forces, which In his case that meant a

"Seal Team." Jessy was never informed why his requests were ignored but sometimes things happen for a reason and if he had wound up with the Seals the outcome could have turned into a very real genuine tragic opera.

Jessy had many of the skills needed to become a Seal team member but not the temperament and certainly not the politics. By that I mean he was developing political views and felt a need to voice them from time to time. When you are on a special forces team there is no room for politics whatsoever and special forces is another world with no need for personal views of any kind. You must have a mentality like, " An Arab, a Jew, and a white supremacist walk into a bar. It's your job to go in there and eliminate them…and make it look like the Chinese waitress did it…by accident." Jessy just wasn't cut from that cloth. Personally I don't think Jessy could eliminate someone, If it was his job to do such a deed, he would go into the bar and buy the three "targets" plenty of drinks, take a few steps back, and simply wait for them to kill each other.

Seal teams are among the most highly trained and well equipped forces on earth or any other planet as far as we know. Members of these teams work together as one and everyone is an expert in everything. They have to react and improvise. If there is a need to learn a language, they learn a language. They know how to identify and use any weapon they may come across during their mission. If they somehow lose a member of the team, the remaining members pick up the slack on the run. Everyone has to know each others job as well as their own. When the mission is over they start all over and move on to the next hot spot.

These guys get the hardest jobs and perform those jobs flawlessly, as far as we know. There are no other people who are as competent at their jobs than seal team members, as far as we know. Jessy was a real fan. He was also aware of his own limitations. Faced with a situation where he had to end the life of a young boy or girl holding an AK47 attack rifle, he might hesitate to contemplate the motivation of the young combatant. That short hesitation would give the little third world youngster the opportunity to blow his nuts off and that could put the lives of the whole team in jeopardy. That could put the entire operation at risk and that, in turn, could put some of the wealth of the people who sent them on their mission in the first place in the pockets of their enemy's wealthy people. Wars are complicated, the people who fight them are not. Soldiers do what their superiors tell them to do...most of the time. There are times when our young warriors feel the need to go off script but the job at hand always gets done. If this were not the case we Americans would all be driving around town in Japanese and German cars...Wait, that was a really terrible example. The point is that people in the US armed forces are willing to sacrifice their very lives for the better good of their nation. The people in power who send them on endless dangerous adventures all over the world do so for the better good of their Swiss bank accounts. If you feel the need to comment on these opinions you can Email me at www.blowme.com.

CHAPTER 3

J.E.T.S... Jets Jets Jets

When Jessy finished his boot camp training the Navy allowed him a few days leave to go home and pack for his respective school and or ship assignments. The new recruits had a chance to hang out with their friends and girl friends for a couple of days. Jessy visited the high school he had recently graduated from wearing his dress blue uniform and he caused quite a fuss, Jessy was looking good. They kicked him out for creating a disturbance and he realized he wasn't in Kansas anymore. He wasn't in boot camp anymore as well and would be allowed to wear civilian clothes (civvies) off base. Jessy's civilian clothes were nothing to brag about but were still better than the ugly crap he had been issued by the government. That dress blue uniform was pretty cool however. It looked damned good, once you had it tailored. Jessy especially liked the bell bottom slacks with the 13-button flap in front. (one button for each of the original colonies) They were dark Navy blue and made of heavy wool material. One handy feature was that they didn't show the telltale stains if you spilled a drink on yourself. They also came in handy at bars when you had a few too many and couldn't get those thirteen buttons loose in time. Generally, when he was out and about, among the general population, he preferred to dress like someone who had never been near a Navy uniform.

After a brief visit and a few solidifying moments with his ex-wife to be, Jessy boarded a big airplane bound for Tennessee. The "A" school was located in a suburb of Memphis, Tennessee near the town of Millington. (This is a scary idea all on it's own) The base was situated on the grounds of an old Army base that was probably built during the Second World War and the dorms were old fire trap army barracks. The dilapidated two story wooden buildings were built of old, dry, hard as nails, lumber and were structurally very sound but tended to burn up in a matter of minutes when one of them caught on fire. Just such a blaze had taken place sometime before Jessy's arrival, and scores of young sailors had been trapped and died in the middle of a cold dark night on that base. The buildings were wide open on the inside and drafty so that people would bring in cheap electric heaters in the winter. It was a recipe for disaster as the ancient wiring would heat up and ignite the tinder that had accumulated in the walls of the old buildings.

The year was 1968 and they were in Tennessee so they were divided into separate black and white barracks. This sounds incredibly racist when you think about it but it was Tennessee in 1968 for crap sakes and this whole segregation shit was all new to Jessy but those people down south had it down to a science. His mom never brought him up to treat people differently because of race or religion or the color of their sox, but some of these southern folks had a whole other belief system. Southern hospitality means people will be sweet and helpful and charming to you...If you're white and Christian. I'm sure it's totally different down there these days.)

One weekend, Jessy was getting a haircut in the tiny town down the road from the base. The place was sort of like a little, dirty, ugly, Mayberry. In this twilight zone version Andy the sheriff was a fat, loud mouthed, bag made from pure douche. He was sitting in the other chair getting his buzz cut trimmed while spitting nasty brown goo into an old coke bottle as he rattled off these long winded rants accusing the "Jews and the niggers and long haired faggot hippies" of everything that had ever gone wrong with his country...ever. Jessy was not Jewish nor was he African American so right then and there he decided to become a long haired hippy as soon as circumstances would allow. The faggot part was optional so Jessy opted out because he realized there was already an abundance of gay people in the military only most of them didn't know it yet.

Forty years later this very same sheriff could have been a broadcaster for Fox news, or a sit in for now really dead talk radio host Rush Limbaugh. The guy playing "Floyd the barber" was ex-military, with a ridiculous comb over haircut, and didn't understand Jessy when he said, in plain English, "just a little off the top sir." He just kept cutting and cutting and agreeing with everything the sheriff had to say. It was a holy nightmare and was reminiscent of the scene from the movie "Easy Rider" in the diner where Jack Nicholson, Peter Fonda and Dennis Hopper start to realize just how deep in "Southern fried shit" they really were. Jessy hadn't seen that movie yet and was just beginning to notice the loathing and ignorance he was surrounded by, not to mention the shitty, messed up haircut he was exposing himself to.

Jessy hadn't seen the movie "Deliverance" yet either so if someone had suddenly told him to "get on your knees and squeal like a pig" he would have responded with a sincere, heartfelt, "Suck my dick me, ass face!" Jessy did however realize that he was in some kind of dangerous alternate universe where all signs of reason and intelligence were replaced with fear, hate, very bad breath, and not nearly the normal number of teeth. They had strange music coming from an ancient RCA radio that sat on a shelf right between two deer heads that served as hat racks. The music was syrupy sad and all about heartbreak and being broke and drinking too much and ex-girlfriends who just couldn't leave without fucking up your pick up truck and stealing your dog. Sometimes they threw in prison or a train or some current girl friend who banged everyone including your close relatives and hers when you weren't around. It sounded like the blues sung by cowboys, farmers and out of work tractor mechanics.

Before we get off the redneck train Jessy would have loved it if "Billy Jack" had walked in just then and kicked the ever loving shit out of those cracker pricks with his bare feet. Nothing but blood and hair and a tooth or two flying in all different directions would have been just the perfect end to that crappy day. Without going into further details, Jessy never went back to "Dingleberry Ville" ever again. His hair thanked him profusely when he assured it that he was so sorry and that it would never happen again. He of course was lying out of his ass because he was still in the Navy and had a few horror show haircuts in his future. Don't even get me started on what Jessy did to his poor bewildered hair in the 80's. Just think, "White afro" and you will begin to understand what a cruel bastard Jessy was to the top of his head back then. I'm amazed that his hair cut has stayed with him after all this time. Jessy was still pretty cool and his hair knew it. They had a bond.

The "A" school instructors were a combination of Navy and Marine vets who had served in at least a war or two...or three and were killing time while they built up their retirement. After that they would wind up being disgruntled postal workers, or volunteering at a local Veterans Hospital, or possibly shooting at people from the top of a tower somewhere in Texas.

The classes were very technical and the students learned way to much about every screw and nut on the jet engines that powered the carrier based aircraft of the day. The "F-8 Crusader," the "A-4 Sky hawk," and the stupid powerful "F4-J Phantom" among others. They even let Jessy climb into the cock pit of an old Saber jet fighter left over from the Korean war and he learned how to turn up the engine. Sitting in a jet plane and running up the Jet engine to 80 percent is a very real rush as you can imagine, especially when the engine you are turning up is twenty years old and could turn into a blazing fireball at any moment.

There is a lot more to flying a fighter bomber than taking off and landing. There is also the whole bomber part. The more they learned about these weapons systems, the more Jessy began to appreciate what it must be like to be the people on the ground in one of these underdeveloped countries that we decide should be divided up into bomb, don't bomb, maps. Some people are just born in the wrong place at the wrong time. Viet Nam was definitely the wrong place and the 60's and 70's were totally the wrong time.

As for the Navy schools, most of the instructors were very efficient and professional. The huge amount of technical information that they were able to instill in such a short amount of time was astounding. The training was so effective that Jessy can still remember most of the jet engine theory classes and the operation of the fuel control system in those amazing jet engines. That is saying something when you consider all the pot and alcohol and other mind altering substances that he may or may not have consumed since he took those classes and that is indeed another story.

The Navy had to retrain their students in math and science because many recruits came from high schools in parts of the country where science and math were considered superstitions. "If god had really wanted you to know how much 3 X 222 was he would have tattooed the answer on your forehead, right?" Wow I'm starting to get good at this shit. Steven King... you better watch your ass buddy because there is a new "word sheriff" in town.

The math instructor was a Marine combat veteran who made such an impression on Jessy that he literally changed his life forever. I've mentioned that at the time Jessy was totally convinced that the war in Viet Nam was the only thing that was keeping America free from the communist threat and of course those gigantic dominoes. None of these "jet cadets" were quite sure what communism was but they were all sure it was something bad, very bad. They had all been sold a bill of goods by John Wayne, Audie Murphy, Ronald Reagan, and their fathers about how war was this glorious adventure and to become a man you had to baptize yourself in blood, death, honor...and lots of cigarettes.

Jessy's generation had been brainwashed to become righteous brave warriors. They were taught that whoever it was we were fighting must be subhuman evil monsters. The military does a thorough job of dehumanizing the our enemy to make it easier to pull a trigger or push a button that will end a life or a whole town full of lives as the case may be. All feelings are removed from the equation and you are trained to react to orders and not emotions. When soldiers are given the order to attack a village full of other human beings and burn it down with the people still in it, ninety-nine, out of one hundred soldiers will do exactly that, and they will kill anyone who tries to stop them. Occasionally, however, there is someone who says, "Hey, this is fucked up. These are real people we're wasting," and he resists the order he was given and puts himself at odds with the entire military structure that surrounds him. We'll get back to this guy later in this book.

Jessy was assigned to a math class with a tough Marine sergeant named Vogel who had recently returned to the states after three tours of duty as a side door gunner on a Huey helicopter. He was the guy you see in all the Viet Nam movies and news reels blasting away at the jungle as the pilot maneuvers his aircraft just above the tree tops and brass shell casings fly from the ejection port on one side of his M60 machine gun with a tin soup can spot welded to the other side to keep the cartridge belt from jamming. Seriously, you would think with all the money that the American taxpayer pays for these machine guns that they could spot weld the soup can onto the side of gun in the damn factory, right?

The good sergeant's job in Viet Nam was as full of danger as you can imagine. The Viet Cong after years of practice had become very proficient at shooting down our helicopters and the flight crews had an extremely short shelf life as a rule. The ones who lived were lucky and the ones who volunteered for three tours were just plain insanely nuts. Good old sergeant Vogel was one of the craziest Marines of all time. His favorite expression was, "Gun time is better than bed time." This was a person who literally enjoyed ending other peoples lives more than he enjoyed making love. Jessy was "young, dumb, and full of cum" and to him this mindset just didn't register in his nineteen year old brain one little bit.

If you saw this man you could only imagine the quality of the female creatures he was forced to settle for, or more likely pay for.

Perhaps for him blasting people with high velocity bullets was more fun than making love or what ever it was he did to the women in his life. If Jessy had let his vivid imagination wander in the direction of sergeant Vogel's love life it probably would have involved a gun, a knife, handcuffs, duct tape, and a blindfold. Let's stop this drift right here because your writer just threw up in his mouth a little bit.

At first Jessy's sergeant's stories were exciting and interesting to listen to. They gave his students a realistic idea of what it was like over there. His accounts were full of details and color but as his memories unfolded they became so twisted and over the line that Jessy began to feel dirty just being in the same room with this maniac. He told the class of dropping fuel drums from his chopper with incendiary grenades attached with tape and timed to detonate above the thatched huts of a village. When the occupants scrambled out to escape the inferno he would open up on them with his beloved M60. His reasoning was that if they were running away they must be Viet Cong. If they were children they were simply short communists and had to be executed before they could grow up to be taller communists. If they were women they were breeders of the evil menace and they had to be exterminated like cock roaches. This crazy assed instructor hadn't the slightest shred of humanity. To him the people of Viet Nam were merely moving targets like the ones at a carnival arcade only they were much more fun to shoot at than the arcade variety because they were full of blood.

The good sergeant told us the story of a young pregnant farm girl who started waving her wooden rake at his helicopter because the engine noise and rotor wash was scaring all of her animals. He quickly determined that she posed a threat to the American way of life and he cut her in half with several bursts of machine gun fire and her baby was sort of prematurely born in that moment but was instantly shredded to pieces in a cloud of red fog and high velocity ammunition. He was gleeful as he told the gruesome tale and the look in his eyes sent a jarring chill down Jessy's spine. He was a sick, sick man and you couldn't imagine this piece of sub human garbage trying to assimilate back into society with normal people as neighbors and God forbid have an Asian family move in next door to him. As far as Jessy knew he had never met anyone like sergeant Vogel.

Note: The disturbing part is our nation is crawling with veterans of various wars and very few of them want to tell the story of what they saw and did "over there." I wish these people would open up and get that stuff off their chest. Trying to keep memories like that locked up inside is where PTSD comes from. Being the people who get sent to fight our nations wars is hard. Coming home from those wars can be harder.

Note: Note: It is estimated that more than 30% of homeless people are male veterans.

Sergeant Vogel was a raging racist and a war criminal who made Charles Manson look like Jesus so naturally he had the two black marines in class sit in the back of the room which is where Jessy also chose to sit as well. He just wanted to be as far away from this creepy vile scumbag as was humanly possible. The three of them became very close friends and shared jokes under their breath whenever the instructor was facing the blackboard. One day, as Vogel was ranting away on the orgasmic, lustful, pleasures of destroying nonwhite people, one of the black students, "Mike," was drawing something on his scratch pad. The sergeant asked him "hey boy, what the fuck are you drawing in my class." Without hesitation Mike very cooly testified "I'm just drawing a white man." Obviously pissed Vogel exclaimed "a white man? What is your white man doing?" Mike followed with "he's just hanging around," and he paused, "at the end of a rope, like some kind of strange fruit." he exclaimed as he turned his head to the side, sized up the teacher and made a few finishing strokes with his pencil. The teacher didn't get the Billie Holiday reference but he did get the joke.

Jessy froze for a second as he evaluated the situation that Mike had inserted himself into. Sergeant Vogel was a sadistic control freak who held the lives of his students literally in his deadly hands, especially the marines in the class. He was able to decide which students should be passed on to further training in their field and who should be forwarded directly to duty stations overseas. In 1968 this clearly meant an all-expenses paid trip to the sunny and wonderful land of Viet Nam.

Jessy suddenly felt obligated to do something to buffer the wrath that was brewing to the surface before his eyes. He wanted to say something but there was no time to come up with the perfect quip that could quell the wrath of the evil monster in their midst. Jessy did the only thing he could at the moment and began to laugh. He tried to be as sincere and boisterous as possible to deflect the steel cold hate he saw in sergeant Vogel's eyes away from Mike and over to him. The laughter slowly became contagious and soon the whole room was roaring with glee and the insane pressure of the situation started to drift away.

The ploy worked to perfection and Jessy was rewarded with the opportunity to show the entire class how good he was at doing push ups. As it turns out Jessy was very damn good at doing push ups and he even did them the marine way where you clap your hands between each one and catch yourself just before your face kisses the deck (floor). When he was done with some crazy amount of "marine push ups" Jessy jumped back up with a big grin on his face and the sergeant winced and just said, "What in the holy hell are you doing in the Navy, Puke?" Puke was a Marine term of endearment that was bestowed only on the truly outstanding and Jessy smiled and said, "I failed the sadism portion of the Marine test sergeant." More laughter from the class made the bastard start to shake a little bit.

Vogel instinctively hated the black students but now he hated Jessy even more for befriending them. You just didn't do stuff like that back in his dark, unlit, corner of Mississippi. From that day on Jessy got more than the normal amount of practice doing push ups and sit ups and pull ups and just about every kind of "up" you could imagine. The good sergeant and Jessy were at war for the remainder of the class and the tension was so thick at times Jessy could hardly keep himself from blasting Vogel in the mouth whenever he started reciting his racist rants.

Jessy reasoned that if any one should retaliate against this twisted prick it should be Mike or Keith. Keith was the other black guy in the math class. Keith was from Chicago and was a champion swimmer (so much for that stereotype). Keith was also crazy smart and this simple fact pissed off the sergeant to no end. Jessy certainly was not a religious person by any means but he thought if anyone should have a reservation at "Hotel Hell" it was their butt crack math teacher. Jessy was also exposed to a brief but crystal clear view of what life in America must be like for a black man or woman. Jessy could never pretend to fully understand the African American experience but his level of respect increased immensely because of this series of events.

Note: Growing up Jessy didn't have a single African American friend in his little middle class town in New Jersey mainly because there weren't any. That meant he got to be the designated minority because his sorry little family was so ridiculously poor compared to his school mates. In his senior year the first Black family moved to town. They had a son a year younger than Jessy. This is terrible but Jessy thought, "finally someone else can share in the weight of unspoken economic prejudice that existed in town. Jessy didn't get invited to many party's in High school until his senior year. The new kid's dad was a well to do doctor. The son was good looking and an excellent athlete who quickly became one of the most popular guys in school. Oh well it was his turn and Jessy would just have to wait to get a shot of real self confidence. High school sports helped a great deal but the Navy would give him the boost he would need in the years to come.

The experience with his math instructor was a real wake up call. Jessy began to question his own belief system, like what in the holy hell was this war about and how exactly were we helping the people of Viet Nam by blowing them up, setting their villages on fire and murdering their people. He also wondered why was it so easy to justify the destruction of an entire culture as long as that culture was yellow or brown or red or black. Jessy began to study up on the ages old conflicts between Viet Nam and the many other countries who at one time or another had tried to impose their will upon this truly amazing and resilient country. The Chinese, the Japanese, the French among others had attempted to invade and enslave these very brave and resourceful people. Now Uncle Sam was trying to save our god-fearing nation from the scourge of communism by killing as many of the home team as possible with the most expensive weapons the world has ever known. Of course Viet Nam was a convenient place to fight a proxy war against our real cold war enemies, the Russians and the Chinese. The problem was, and this is a fatal flaw in the way the United States views third world nations. When we start dropping bombs on people, we think we are somehow subduing them and turning these unfortunate residents into good, Christian, freedom lovers. In reality we are creating a whole new generation of inspired enemy in the relatives of the people we slaughter in the name of Democracy.

Jessy found himself imagining how he would possibly deal with having his family murdered by a foreign army who had taken over his country. This idea is hard for a young American to get his or her mind around. Slowly Jessy was beginning to sense the feelings of the average citizen in one of these faraway places where we test all of our fancy military hardware. Jessy totally believed in a nations right to defend itself from foreign invaders... only in Viet Nam, The United States was the foreign invader.

The weird thing that freaked Jessy out was that Ho Chi Minh the leader of the people we were fighting, or "Uncle Ho" as he was affectionately known to his friends on the cocktail circuit had been an important ally to the United States. General Douglas McArthur had acknowledged him for helping to save the lives of American fliers who had been shot down by the Japanese in southeast Asia during the Second World War. Uncle Ho, who lived in the United States for a while had also been inspired by the story of the American dream and had studied Jeffersonian democracy to the point that, as rumor has it, he fashioned a document considered by some to be the Vietnamese version of the Declaration of independence as a blue print for his country's future after he chased the French imperialists back to Paris. Ho also lived in China where he became a communist so his politics were a bit complicated.

Unfortunately following the siege of Dien Bien Phu and the brilliant defeat of the French by the out gunned Vietnamese, the United States chose to side with the taller, fair skinned, and much better dressed French. After that war the US began to devise a giant case based loosely on those "giant communist Dominoes." The plan was that the United States would begin dropping thousands of tons of expensive fiery ordinance on every living thing we could see and plenty of stuff we couldn't. Conveniently there were defense contractors lined up around the block to help us do just that.

The main problem our soldiers experienced in Viet Nam was that they couldn't see much of anything at first because of the lush green forests and jungles that existed everywhere. The geniuses at the Pentagon decided to have our super clever chemical companies develop a shit stew referred to as "Agent Orange" that could make all the leaves fall off the trees. This amazingly brilliant strategy would leave nothing but large groups of enemy soldiers standing out in the open with silly looks on their faces and then we could shoot them, lots of times, with our really cool guns and stuff. Looking back the whole idea of naked trees seems like it was thought up by a class of second graders with some unnatural inbred fear of leaves.

This genius plan also assured that any human being exposed to this magical potion would over time develop some form of damage to their central nervous system. The victims included our own troops on the ground, and pregnant Vietnamese women who saw the effects of Agent Orange on their new born children. It amazes me that the people who call an abortion murder are the same people who vote for the maniacs who think this crazy shit up.

Note: To all the self righteous douche bags and douche baguettes. "POST birth abortions are just as bad as the pre-birth variety." Blowing up some pregnant woman by accident while you are trying to kill an enemy soldier in his own country is an abortion as well. This act could also be considered murder by someone related to the unfortunate mother to be, thank you very much.

Agent Orange also worked its magic on the "privates" of privates and corporals and sergeants. Strangely it didn't work nearly as well on Generals but that may have something to do with fact that generals spend more time on golf courses than they do in rice paddies and jungles. Just so you know defoliants and golf courses don't go together as a rule.

Please! Would someone just once try to put yourselves in the shoes...or sandals, of the people whose homes we destroy and the relatives of those people who just happen to be in the proximity of someone that we consider to be our enemy. If our citizens were forced to endure random bombings and our homes and cities were being attacked on a regular basis by a superior fighting force from a country half a world away we would go crazy. I mean rednecks with totally ridiculous arsenals of weapons would rise up and kill every foreign looking person within range of their 50 caliber sniper rifles. (that's really damn far by the way)

The point of this ramble is that after much discussion and research Jessy could find no rational reason for our country sending troops to some other country on the opposite side of the planet that had no way of harming him or his friends and family. Viet Nam had been trying to purge itself of colonial super powers for a very long time and was desperately trying to experiment with self rule the best way it knew how. They had home field advantage and they were very clever at finding ways to defeat much more powerful enemies. They have a perfect record.

Note: governments are a necessary evil and just how evil depends on the character of the residents of the country they represent.

From the day Jessy graduated from the Navy Jet school he decided to seek out a different yet appropriate way to serve his country. Jessy realized that at some point he would need to take a stand against the madness of the war but it would be a while before he figured out exactly how, and just what shape that stand would look like. In the meantime Jessy had another plane to catch. Much like the Beverly Hillbillies he was on his way to sunny California. Unlike the Hillbillies of Beverly Jessy wasn't worth fifty bazillion dollars that they got from shooting a hole in the ground in some hick town down south somewhere. Jessy could shoot at the ground all day long in New Jersey and all he would hit were the corpses of prematurely deceased Italians. (that was a Soprano's joke, sorry.) God I miss that show.

CHAPTER 4

California Dreaming

Note: The flight from New Jersey was long and tiring. This was back in the day when almost all of the "stewardesses" (my computer hates it when I use gender specific words like stewardesses) (sorry MAC) - were women as far as we know. The fact that they didn't ask to see an ID card for service people in uniform back then made the trip an enjoyable one. After one of the scariest approaches you can imagine Jessy's Boeing 727 came in for a landing next to San Diego harbor. They had skimmed just above the roof tops so close to the ground that you could read the license plates on the cars below. Pilots are required to have a special certification before they are allowed to land at the San Diego International Airport.

After debarking from the aircraft Jessy grabbed his sea bag from the luggage carousel and wandered out into the late afternoon warmth of the San Diego bay area. All things considered San Diego must be one of the most perfect places in the country or at least it was in 1968. There were giant, grey, Navy war ships and cute little white sailboats flirting on the water and dense clusters of homes climbing the surrounding hillsides. The first major difference Jessy noticed about southern California was that they have freaking palm trees...everywhere. Back in Jersey the only palm trees were the ones painted on the walls of strip clubs.

Jessy started taking snapshots with his "Brownie Instamatic camera" the second he got off the plane. Every single picture he took had at least one spectacular palm tree in it. Most of the pictures also included a representative of the California State police department, complete with reflective sunglasses and riding boots. You literally couldn't spit without hitting a cop in southern California. You wouldn't want to try it however unless you don't mind being beaten to death with night sticks. The temperature was about 75 degrees in late March and the sky was clear and blue all day long. The brown polluted air of Los Angeles was visible up the coast but it was no way near to San Diego...At the time.

The nights were cool and comfortable. Jessy was totally sold on the climate and the scenery but not the extreme economic requirements of living in California. Even back then home prices were way above normal, and there was the sense of police state in the air but Jessy tried to ignore it in hopes that it would go away... (it didn't)

Jessy's new duty station was the Naval air base at Miramar just north of San Diego. Miramar was, and is, a flight training facility, AKA "Fighter Town." The huge airbase was built for training Navy Pilots how not to kill themselves while taking off and landing on the decks of enormous floating cities like the USS. Constellation and the Enterprise. If you've seen the movie "Top Gun," well than you know a little tiny bit about Miramar. The scene in the movie where Tom Cruise and Val Kilmer fall in love with each other in slow motion during that steamy oily shirtless volley ball game? Yeah, well that was Jessy's barracks in the back ground. In real life the pilots would never be caught dead within a mile of the enlisted men's part of town/quarters. There were, after all, rules that prohibited officers from fraternizing or hanging with enlisted personnel, but in Hollywood anything is possible.

In the real world one of the few times an officer and an enlisted man would interact outside of the confines of a ship at sea or during regular working hours on base was when an officer would arrive home and find his beautiful, darling wife, in a passionate loving embrace with the here to for mentioned enlisted man. This happened quite often and generally involved naked sprinting and sometimes gun play. Jessy personally would never be caught dead in a situation like that...he was much too quick and dodgy. He was also smart enough to know that there were throngs of beautiful young well tanned friendly girls just lying all over the beaches not far away in La Jolla and Pacific beach.

California was just like every beach blanket movie Jessy had ever seen. He imagined Annette Funicello was lying just down the beach with her bikini top untied. (Annette was the first of many Mickey Mouse Club hotties and Jessy had a huge crush on her when he was a young Mouseketeer). From his first day on the base he decided to volunteer for the night shift so that he could spend his downtime enjoying the amazing climate, stunning scenery, and endless sunny days. In the meantime Jessy spent all his weekends in or very near the ocean. Jessy became friends with a surfer named Bob who was once an Olympic prospect swimmer. Bob had this mint condition, yellow, rag top, MG sports car that they rode to the beach in with Bob's surf board hanging out of the back seat. Bob's nose was always coated in zinc oxide to protect it from the sun's rays. That took a lot of zinc oxide because Bob's nose was the size of a door knob. Jessy used Copper Tone SPF 0 to insure a rich dark tan. It also insured lots of peeled flakes that he left behind everywhere he went until his New Jersey skin turned from white to red and finally dark brown. Back then the young people were oblivious to the harmful effects of the sun and the word "melanoma" wasn't part of anyone's vocabulary. Today the list of stuff that young people know nothing about would be endless. No one reads these days unless it's a "text" or the instructions on box of morning after pills.

Jessy's beach was La Jolla shores, a world class destination for ocean lovers. He was totally blown away by the sheer beauty of the place and the atmosphere was incredibly perfect. The long wide beach curved north from a cove and went on forever, from La Jolla all the way to Alaska. Just south of the swimming and surfing beach there was a big fancy hotel where soon to be president Richard Nixon and his family hung out. One of Jessy's beach buddies was always bragging how he was banging Julie Nixon, but this individual had a bad habit of grossly overstating his sexual adventures so Jessy just took his stories with a shaker of salt. Jessy wasn't in the same bedroom with him and Julie so there is no hard evidence that he was really nailing the future president's daughter.

Just southwest of the hotel a sheer cliff rose above a shallow coral reef. This area was alive with every kind and color of fish you could imagine. This natural wonder curved out to a stunningly beautiful cove. The reef had become a snorkelers port of call. Jutting out towards the breaking surf was a natural sandstone arch, back then. That arch is gone now after it was destroyed by giant waves during a storm in 1977. Jessy could barely tear himself away and head back to the base after spending a day in La Jolla. The other guys in his "cube," (Small, separated living area with three bunk beds and six lockers) hated him because there was always sand from the beach and flakes of dead skin on the floor after Jessy's return from one of his all day tanning sessions. The guy in the bunk below Jessy said it was like a sandstorm followed by a snow storm. Jessy was sorry and tried to adjust his habits by showering and applying moisturizer before entering the cube. Jessy enlisted the help of several friendly young women in bikinis to keep his skin well oiled. He was more than happy to return the favor. It was the least that he could do. These concessions weren't nearly as painful as they sound.

The weekends were his own unless Jessy had weekend duty once a month or so. The remainder of Jessy's time was spent swimming, body surfing, and getting to know many of the golden brown California girls who were in complete and total control of the beach. The "Beach Boys" would have you believe that the guys with the bushy blonde haircuts and well worn surfboards were in charge of the sand, but they would be lying. Those girls had cast a spell over the guys and they knew it. Jessy was OK with this dynamic and was just happy to be part of the new amazing life style. Remember, where Jessy came from, the only girls who had a tan all year long in New Jersey had relatives in countries much closer to the equator.

One of Jessy's first California girl friends was a lovely, seventeen year old native American who had the improbable native American name of Judy. Jessy was expecting something more exotic like "Princess who walks on water. (she was a surfer after all) Judy's mom was Navajo and pretty and friendly but her dad was a hard ass Navy commander who Jessy only met once when he went to Judy's home for dinner. He caught Judy and Jessy kissing on the couch and he immediately drove Jessy to the highway and dropped him off in the middle of nowhere. Jessy wound up sleeping under a bush in a school yard. Judy and Jessy remained close friends but he never went back to her house when her dad was home.

This lovely young native American gave Jessy some kind advice early on in their relationship. Judy told him "grow your hair, lose the East coast accent, and don't tell anyone you're in the service if you want to get along down here." Jessy was a little stunned but Judy was an extremely savvy, beautiful young woman and he trusted her judgment. he started wearing a ball cap at work to cover his blond hair that was getting longer and blonder every day. He also dialed back on the "F" bombs and tried to sound like he was born in El Segundo. The phrases, "gnarly dude" surf's up and "cowabunga" became part of his vocabulary. As for the service thing, Jessy was starting to understand the whole antiwar movement and began to feel concerned about the part he might have to play in this very bad idea that was the Viet Nam conflict/police action/ WAR.

Note: Viet Nam was a war. The men who were drafted to go off and fight and die there would agree. Afghanistan was a war. Iraq was a war. Korea was a war. Any time you drop tons of bombs on people's homes it's a war. Whenever you whip out the B-52s it's a war. Young Americans have no idea what it's like to live in a country like Viet Nam, or Iraq, or Afghanistan. For a visual aid try to picture a universe where everyday is September 11, only it goes on for ten years at a time. We lost less than 3000 people on "9-11". The country of Viet Nam lost over two million citizens during that "conflict," Now start counting to two million and take notes on how many times you pass 3000. You can get back to me on this because I'm guessing it will take a while.

Jessy hadn't been in California very long before he met his first "Hippies." Most of the people who frequented the beach were members of the surf crowd but there were always a couple of vans or VW micro busses parked out in the corner of the parking lot with flowers and peace signs painted all over them. They had tie dyed curtains in the windows and there was always a strange sweet aroma whenever you walked near one of them. One fragrance was Patchouli oil, but there was another sweet smell that Jessy would learn much more about in the very near future. There was one particularly outrageous van that had a beer keg strapped to the roof of the cab and a piece of surgical hose running from it down into the driver's side window. There were paintings of naked women dancing around a bonfire, antiwar slogans, and a sign on the back door that said, "Don't laugh, your daughter may be inside." I'm guessing that they would get pulled over by California's finest about every twenty feet if they ever tried to drive that van out of the parking lot.

Jessy was intrigued by the giant brass balls these strange people had. In 1968, California cops made Nazi storm troopers look like Cub Scouts. These people however were unfazed by the police and were flaunting themselves for all to see. It was all so crazy and yet Jessy felt he needed to get to know more about them.

One fine day and quite by accident Jessy met this incredibly beautiful girl who had a band of pink and yellow flowers in her hair. She was wearing a long cotton print dress, there was no evidence she was wearing any other clothing under that dress. She was barefoot with several tiny brass toe rings on her perfect little toes. Several of the guys from the base were tossing a football around and one of them threw the ball and hit the young girl right in her perfect little head. For a brief moment there were flower petals floating around her face and she looked like an angel. Her beautiful green eyes were slightly crossed at that moment. Impulsively Jessy ran over to her and asked her if she was OK. She was a little stunned but she blinked and smiled at Jessy and assured him she was fine and Jessy fell in love a little right there. She told him her name was "Moonbeam."

Jessy picked up the football and threw it in the ocean. The sailor who had beaned his new friend started to give Jessy some shit but Jessy shot him the patented "New Jersey Look," the look that says, "fuck with me ass breath and I'll hit you so hard your dogs nuts will fall off." The guy paused and shook a little and then he backed away and marched off to rescue his ball. Most loud mouths, bullies, and show offs are also cowards. The trick is the ability to figure out which ones are and which ones aren't. In this case Jessy had guessed correctly and therefore would not be forced to battle someone just to impress a beautiful young girl. Jessy was also smart enough to know that those battles usually end badly and the girl who is being fought over is seldom still around by the end of the fight.

Moonbeam and Jessy began talking and she told him she was a model who had a part time job working for the Sears teen catalog. They became instant friends and took a long walk down the beach just talking, smiling and enjoying the ocean and the amazing weather together. They brought along a blanket to relax on at the end of their journey.

They walked way up north past the Scripps pier, almost to "Blacks Beach," where all the naked sunbathers hung out. They found a cave out of the sun, spread out the blanket and set up a little camp site at the entrance to the cave. About then, this lovely young girl pulled a native, painted leather pouch out of her giant woven bag. Then she removed a few items and began to roll up a cigarette. Jessy was naïve but not totally stupid and he surmised that this was going to be his first experience with the dreaded herb, marijuana. Jessy could have refused to join her when she lit up her "fatty," but one look at her innocent face with that silly little grin and he just relaxed and went for it. Did I mention Jessy was nineteen years old and there are times when things are just beyond our control, as they should be.

Jessy had no regrets and some of you may not believe this but he had no craving for heroin, or airplane glue, or spray paint afterwards, however he did have this incredible urge for a Big Mac. Moon Beam, of course, was a vegetarian and Jessy had to keep his need for greasy mystery meat to himself. Moonbeam was on the case and whipped out a bag of "Cheetos Cheese Puffs." The magical snack was gone in a few minutes. They had orange stains on their hands and smiling faces and they laughed every time they looked at each other. Jessy wanted to kiss that orange right off her face but was in fear of being shot down...like Bambi's mother. Jessy's demons prevented him from trying to take a relationship with someone so clearly out of his league to the next level. Jessy grew up in a town where almost everyone was out of his league. The few times he invited a girl to his house they took a look, left and never came back. Jessy was broken and it was going to take time and a shit load of "Crazy Glue" to fix all that.

Jessy was still working on his fear of beautiful women and women in general but he just wasn't there yet. The sad part is Jessy loved women and many of them loved him back. Jessy had a high school sweetheart back in New Jersey but she was...back in New Jersey, thousands of miles away in a very different world. These were confusing times that were getting more confusing by the second.

The whole teen model, marijuana, Cheetos, experience proved to be a profound turning point in his life. For one thing Jessy was crossing a boundary that he had set a long time ago. He had convinced himself in high school, "Never get involved with illegal drugs." Jessy had fallen for all the propaganda. This marijuana stuff however, just seemed so innocent and natural. He hadn't done his homework on this subject yet and all he knew about weed at the time was what he had been told by his teachers and his step dad during one of his crazy tirades. Jessy learned for instance that one of the main reasons for the ban on pot was the direct result of a giant campaign paid for by Patty Hearst's insanely wealthy and influential grand father, William Randolph Hearst. (Patty Hearst was a famous heiress who had inherited some of her grandfathers great wealth and was kidnapped at gunpoint from her college dorm by armed members of the Symbionese Liberation Army in 1974. After some thorough brain washing she helped rob a bank and did some time but President Jimmy Carter would later let her go free. Most of her captors were obliterated and or incinerated in a fiery gun battle with hundreds of LA's finest.

William Randolph Hearst was a newspaper and magazine giant who owned entire forests full of those big tall things they make paper out of. Just for those of you who didn't know, marijuana has another name (hemp) and purpose. Hemp is one of the strongest natural fibers found on earth and was used for thousands of years to make incredibly strong rope and yes... paper. (the original copy of the Declaration of Independence was written on hemp paper. This is one of the main reasons that this important document is still around)

Note: The sentiments of this document were discarded a while back. The phrase "As long as you're white" should have been included but alas it never occurred to our founders that their slaves had any rights at all. The people they owned were like cattle that needed to be fed and protected from the elements but...that was pretty much it.

What does a super rich guy with thousands of acres of trees and a whole lot of wood pulp do when he learns that someone has just come up with a machine that separates hemp fibers at a super fast production rate? This machine was to hemp what the cotton gin was to cheap T shirts. A machine that could put trees out of the paper business for good? Well, for starters Hearst cranked up these crazy but very effective fables about young white teenaged boys who smoked one marijuana cigarette and then instantly turned into mad drooling maniacs who raped and murdered lovely young innocent white girls. Once you smoked that first doobie you were hooked on hard drugs forever. Do you know how he spread the news? Yep you guessed it. (You people are so smart) He printed it in his bullshit newspapers and magazines on his own paper. Reportedly he also used his newspapers to help start the Spanish American war. You can look all this stuff up. There was no "FOX" news back then but they did have William Randolph Hearst, one of the original salesman of fake made up news.

It wasn't long before movies like "Reefer Madness" appeared in theaters across this country of ours. (if you have never seen this huge steaming pile of steaming propaganda, it is a hoot) The United States government fell right in line. (Hearst owned more politicians than the Koch brothers and Vladimir Putin combined) Our sold out politicians passed laws prohibiting the possession and production of this natural substance that can grow "anywhere." The first people to be affected by these laws were of course poor black folks who had smoked reefer for eons and perhaps a few white base players in blues clubs in our nations cities. Once the publicity of the anti marijuana laws began to kick in, the youth of America created a whole new industry that is still alive and well today.

Now of course the illegal drug trade has grown to a point where the murderous capitalist bastards who have taken over the sale and distribution of marijuana and other scarier illegal products have more money than most countries. The least they could do is say thank you to the United States justice department for creating an atmosphere where their enterprise can thrive and grow. It's all tax free, and they didn't have to become a religion or a charity, they simply said, "if you want our stinking taxes, come and get them." The Mexican cops and politicians who tried to end the drug trade in their country are all dead now and no one is lining up to take their place.

Drug rant: The United States is a nation based loosely on the high ideal of personal freedom, and the people of this country think they should be free to do what ever the hell they want, as long as they aren't hurting anyone, and when you tell them suddenly that they can't do something, it makes them crazy and they just want to do it even more. Many times that something never even occurred to them in the first place. Our wise and benevolent government once tried to outlaw alcohol. The result was, they created a huge underworld network of crime families and a giant lawless culture fueled by the immense profits that prohibition provided. They also increased the budget of law enforcement agencies and prison systems all across this great land of ours. Today police show up in armored vehicles wearing flack vests, helmets and AR-15 assault rifles whenever someone calls 911.

Note: Thanks to the war on drugs. We as a nation are going broke trying to enforce unenforceable laws and we now have more people locked up in "for profit prisons" than any other country on earth. We taxpayers pay incredible amounts of money to feed and keep millions of people fed and housed in those for profit cages. When these formerly law abiding, employable, citizens finally pay their debt to society they find that it is nearly impossible to find work with a prison record so many of them return to the drug trade and a life of crime...and the beat goes on. The vast majority of these people are black and Latino and their crimes are considered felonies. Now they don't get to vote. Hmm, a whole bunch of mostly brown and black citizens being deprived of their right to vote. Who could possibly profit from a law like that? Hint: Black and brown voters vote for democrats as a rule, except for that black guy who they put behind Trump at all his rallies. Why don't the networks interview that guy?

Note, Note: learning from the past is not a natural trait here in America. Next time someone asks if you think we should continue this stupid mad adventure known as the war on drugs, "Just say NO." Perhaps if we let the DEA lead us down this road a while longer, Mexico or Columbia could become the next great super power. A super power run by the richest, and scariest bunch of crazy mother fuckers the world has ever seen. I'm just picturing Nazi Germany with dark hair, and nuclear submarines that make shipments of cocaine delivered inside torpedoes and ballistic missiles.

Moon Beam moved on soon after their uplifting experience together. Jessy said she wound up traveling to New York to pursue her modeling career. Jessy should have been sadder but it's not like they were engaged or lovers and there was no shortage of very cool beautiful young women in San Diego. Jessy however, will always be grateful to Moon Beam and her little bag of happy dreams because in many ways she helped to change the general direction of his life. If he could, Jessy would thank her for opening up his mind and for letting him enjoy her beautiful spirit and that wonderful amazing smile for that one brief moment in his life. Oh, and those Cheetos were the best ever, OMG.

Jessy's world was never quite the same after the experience in the cave. It was as if certain people knew his little secret somehow. Those certain people were the ones who were also getting high on the base. Some of Jessy's fellow workers on the flight line started to feel him out and before long they were all best friends and were enjoying a little bit of natural god grown goodness on a fairly regular basis. There was no shortage of good old Mexican weed, and the Navy base was the perfect place to get the more powerful varieties from Panama, Hawaii, and of course Viet Nam and Cambodia. Those sailors were just having the time of their lives. The next couple of years were a series of winding, strange, yet very humorous side trips from the very straight line that had been set before them by the Naval establishment and the United States government.

Back at the base Jessy discovered that there was some kind of parallel universe that, until then, had been invisible to him. Jessy didn't know if it was always this way or if the madness of the Viet Nam war just fostered an atmosphere of rebellion, but those who had begun experimenting with banned substances became part of a very elite and special group of democracy defenders. They didn't hang out at the enlisted men's club on base or the USO downtown in San Diego. They didn't get drunk or get into bar fights. When they did go to a bar it was In Tijuana, and they didn't go to the "donkey show" where women perform unnatural sex acts with animals. (those are the same donkeys that they dress up during the day and people let their kids sit on by the way) (I'll bet most of you didn't know that those cute donkeys could multitask,) Jessy and his friends also didn't go to the clubs in the "red light district" because they didn't relish the idea of getting shots of penicillin for weeks to come, besides the marines were lined up at those places like they were giving away free beer. They only gave free beer to the girls very best customers.

Jessy and his friends spent their "Mexican nights" at the "Oasis club" or the "Blue Note" where they danced all night long. They were in awe of the very talented live bands who couldn't speak much English but could still perform "Proud Mary" on a par with "Tina Turner" and "CCR" as well. This was another defining moment for Jessy. He was just starting to realize that talent of all kinds existed beyond the borders of the United States. As Americans we are brought up to believe that we invented everything worth inventing and produced everything worth producing, but there is a very robust economy out there that we would be forced to deal with in the future. Many people in our country just don't understand this fact. Cultures in countries like China, Japan and Babylon were thriving thousands years before Americans ate their first "Jumbo Jack," or stuck their first flowered, plastic, hat in "Mrs. Potato Head's" plastic head.

Jessy's little extended family attended concerts and a few "love-ins" with groups like "Jefferson Airplane," "Canned Heat," "Richie Havens," "Taj Mahal" and "Buddy Miles," to name a few. Jessy once went to an "Ike and Tina Turner" concert. This was before Tina finally got tired of having the crap beat out of her and took her solo act on the road. Jessy's friend Mario and he were the only white men in the audience. There were many white girls in attendance and it was sort of like an episode of "Soul Train." There weren't any chairs on the floor of the auditorium but that was just fine because everyone in the place danced to every song. They had an amazing time and were treated like family by the others in the crowd all night long. The other people gave Jessy and Mario points just for showing up.

One fun evening Jessy dropped a little acid and went to see Arlo Guthrie. (For those of you who have never tried it, there is no such thing as a little acid) Arlo sang some of his fathers songs and Jessy was close to jumping on a night train to Oklahoma by the end of the concert. Jessy hardly noticed that neither Alice nor her restaurant were represented at the show. That reference requires some research or a serious helping of age.

Note: Google "Woody Guthrie" / the "Great Depression." Don't hurry, I'll wait…………Cool guy, right?

After the performance Jessy returned home to the apartment. Woody only knows how he found his way back. Jessy's "1956" blue and white Buick had an excellent auto pilot. After relaxing for a while Jessy decided to walk down to the local Circle K for something to drink and pick up a greeting card to send to his girlfriend back home. He was about a block from thee store and the store was two blocks from the apartment. I'm sure there is some algebraic equation that would tell you exactly how far he was from their rented house, but it certainly wasn't very far. Jessy was walking slowly with the words to "This Land is Your Land" playing in his head when he heard the siren and was blinded by the search light on the City of San Diego police cruiser. A lone officer exited the vehicle and ordered Jessy to put both hands on the car. He was still a little wired but wisely persuaded himself not to try to escape. Running away from a California cop is simply another term for suicide so Jessy did exactly as he was told. The officer patted him down and asked him to show him some ID. Jessy did his best to explain that his home was a block or so away and that his wallet was back at the apartment and all he had to do was drive him or follow him there so he could show the cop his driver's license and Navy, ID card. That was when the officer started to go a little crazy.

It seems that this police officer had a brother serving in Viet Nam. The cop freaked out when he realized Jessy was in the Navy. The truth is that the person standing before him wasn't dressed like a sea scout. Admittedly Jessy's attire that evening was just a teeny bit over the edge. He had on a pair of tight denim bell bottom jeans with colorful patches and bare feet not to mention a leather vest with long hangy down things decorated with wooden beads, and no shirt. There was a peace sign on a leather string around his neck that stood out against Jessy's perfectly tanned chest. "Jessy had a better tan than Halle Berry." Tilted slightly on Jessy's head was a beat to shit floppy denim cap with some flowers stuck in a hole in the side. The cop's eyes were tearing up as he went off on Jessy for daring to look like he did while his brother was off in a land far away, defending our freedom. Jessy considered pointing out that the way he was dressed was part of the freedom that his brother was defending, but the officer looked and acted like he wanted to shoot Jessy in the face, so he let it go.

The officer radioed in to his dispatch center and told them that he had a sailor who he thought was AWOL, (absent without leave) and to have the shore patrol come and pick Jessy up. Jessy wasn't high any longer, now he was pissed off. This was total bullshit but there were no good options. At this point you have to adhere to the program. The other choices were get brained with a long black night stick, or get shot in the face. Sometimes I think that the whole Hippie movement was just a way for young white people to expose themselves to something similar to the black experience without going through the whole actually being born black thing.

After what seemed like an eternity the shore patrol van showed up and two, fat, nasty smelling, tobacco chewing, red necks from Alabama got down and started in on Jessy...again. You would think these assholes had never seen a stoned hippie, third class petty officer, with some slightly wilted flowers in his cap before. They used their giant arms that looked like legs to literally pick Jessy up and threw him into the back of the grayer than grey, shore cop van, and drove very swiftly downtown to the brig. "Brig" is a big fancy Navy term for jail. They hit every bump and pot hole on the way. There are zero seat belts in the back of a Navy shore patrol van. When they arrived at the brig/jail, Jessy at first expected to be booked or notated in some fashion but it became clear that Jessy was only there for the amusement of the nitwits with the SP armbands on their fat, pork rind enhanced, biceps.

After once again "throwing" Jessy into a large holding cell, one of the guards, whose name was Billy Jimmy Bobby (Jessy guessed that he was named for three men who could have been his daddy) ran to a back office to get a Polaroid camera. He came back all grinning, showing a few of the nastiest teeth most of you have ever seen outside of a zombie movie. The other fat goober started pointing and yelling instructions like he was the director of a "Chuck Norris movie. "Get that there hat, get them pretty flowers, damn get that there peace sign and that there hippie vest." Jessy felt like Brad Pitt with all the flash cube bulbs going off in his face. They taunted Jessy for a while but ran out of words early on and had to start repeating themselves. "Hey peace freak faggot, you sure look awful nice in that fag hat you stupid fag peace loving faggot." Jessy was tempted to ask the dumb turd if he had some kind of issue with his own personal sexuality but once again he thought better of it and just stayed quiet. Jessy showed so much restraint that night he could have been the center fold in the latest copy of Buddhist monk magazine.

His brain free tormentors grew tired after way to long and left Jessy alone to consider his situation. As it turned out Jessy wasn't exactly alone. There was a black sailor sitting silently in a corner wearing his neatly pressed, dress blue uniform, sharing the oversized holding cell with him. Jessy was locked up for being out of uniform while off duty on a Saturday night. His roommate was there for being black, in uniform, on "Alabama night." Jessy and his new friend had a lot in common but they wisely kept the chit chat to a minimum because the tooth deprived duo from dixie had started doing shots of Bourbon and it seemed this would be a real bad time to start expressing their feelings out loud.

Ship board sailors were required to take turns being on shore patrol duty when in port and our "southern fried heroes" had paired up to raise a little government supported mayhem upon hippies and minorities who also were serving their country. For them, it was just like being back home...except they weren't allowed to burn crosses or hang people from trees for looking at white women. The following morning Jessy and his cell mate were both released. The charges against them weren't dropped based on the simple fact that there never had been any charges.

Back at the base Jessy was about to discover a brave new world that he never dreamed existed. The strict Naval environment was evident on base. There were American flags flying everywhere as well as cannons, and a few retired jet aircraft were adorning the grassy parks that were scattered around the campus. The underground was less pronounced however, and secret. There was a building right on the flight line where the sailors who loaded the rockets and bombs on aircraft showed up for work. The grey "ordinance shack" was a three room quancet hut, and the ordinance technicians or "ordies" were feared and respected by everyone. You didn't want to piss off people who could blow up your car, your dog, or your hat...while you were still wearing it.

Jessy was invited into the "ordies shack" one day by some new friends who he had recently smoked a joint with down in "Happy Valley," near the base. They entered the building and the front room was all very clean and ship shape. There were pictures of aircraft loaded with bombs, flying over the jungle. There was the obligatory picture of then President Nixon and plenty of grey furniture and of course an ash tray made from a bomb casing with a squadron insignia painted on the side. The room was well guarded by a sailor with a neatly pressed uniform and very shiny shoes. After checking Jessy out and getting the OK from his new friends they continued through a heavy blue wool curtain into a second store room of some kind. Every thing was in perfect order and ready for inspection.

Just outside the window, less than fifty feet away, there was an F4-J Phantom jet taxiing out to the runway. The deadly looking plane was loaded down with bombs and rockets, all ready for a practice run at the Arizona bomb range. They stepped down a short hall way and came upon what appeared to be a pad locked back door but when they went through the door (the pad lock was a fake) there was another heavy black curtain and a bead door. They pushed the curtain and beads aside and entered a third room. It was dark, but as his eyes adjusted, Jessy could make out pillows and people lounging all over the floor. The strong smell of grass was almost overpowering. There was a filtered exhaust fan that some mechanics had fashioned that worked quite well. The strong smell of pot smoke could not be detected outside the building.

This was a mind blowing scene and Jessy couldn't believe his watering eyes. There was a huge water pipe with smoke rising from a full bowl and someone invited Jessy to hit on one of the three tubes attached to the base of the pipe. Jessy settled onto one of the pillows and after breathing in a couple of deep tokes of the sweet smoke he coughed a couple of times and settled in for the afternoon. There were posters of "Janis Joplin" and "Jim Morrison of the Doors" and brightly colored Peter Max posters and peace signs all around the room. Jessy noticed a red light on the wall, it was off. The light was connected by a wire to a button under the counter at the far end of the building. If an officer came to visit the guy at the front desk hit the button and someone in the back turned the music down. I mean this little building was in the epicenter of one of the most famous Naval air stations in the country and here they were, stoned, listening to "Frank Zappa," and munching on potato chips and "Milk Duds". It makes one wonder how Alice would have handled the scene if there was a place like this in Wonderland. I think the Cheshire Cat would have been cool with it.

Note: Jessy learned that this kind of unauthorized recreation was common in the military. On board Navy ships there are spaces called voids that were created when the ships were built. The rooms inside most ships are square but the ships themselves are not. Consequently there are many voids of various shapes and sizes on all Navy ships and the bigger the ship the bigger the voids. Many voids had their own doors and could be used to store or hide items that you didn't want out in the open during inspections like folding card tables, stills, and water pipes. There are many things you didn't learn from watching Ronald Reagan war movies.

Jessy started to get to know some of the other sailors in the room, at least the ones who were awake and this was when he first met "Smacks." There was this tall, athletic looking African American with a huge, fully blown, perfectly round, "Afro" and a tie dyed scarf wrapped around his forehead. He had on an extra large pair of dark sunglasses and looked a lot like "Sly Stone," of "Sly and the family Stone," a musical group that was very popular at the time. Jessy smiled and exchanged introductions, fist bump, high handshake, and a five on the side just to seal the deal. Smacks was a little hard to communicate with at first as he tended to drift off track from time to time. Jessy could tell that Smacks was under the influence of more than just some grass. They talked and laughed and soon both had big stupid grins on their faces. Jessy kept wondering how Smacks was able to function within the boundaries of military life. He learned his new friend with the spectacular "fro" had been discharged months before and was residing on the base when he wasn't living down in a Tijuana whorehouse with several of his girlfriends. He somehow managed to hide the natural haircut beneath an oversized, navy issue baseball cap when he was wandering around the flight line or the barracks. Just in case any of you were wondering, afros are retractable.

Smacks was sleeping in a spare bunk in the barracks and eating at the chow hall but no one in authority knew he was still around. His government funded free accommodations came to a sudden end one day when a fleet of shore patrol trucks pulled up to the barracks and a dozen "turtle heads" (how sailors lovingly referred to the navy police in their tiny grey plastic helmets) poured into the building. Jessy and his friends had just rolled into the parking lot after downing a few Big Macs over In Claremont, a small town just south of the base, when all the excitement started. They instantly decided to hold off on going inside and opted to wait and see what would happen next. The building itself was three stories tall with large ledges that ran the length of the building above the first and second floors. (as seen in the aforementioned movie Top Gun) The ledges made frequent window washing relatively safe and easy. As the drama unfolded, everyone realized what was going on. Someone had "dropped a dime" on our friend Smacks. (this was back in the day when a pay phone call cost a dime) (This was also back in the day when there were in fact pay phones with coin slots)

Jessy and his crew sat in the big Buick Road Master, like they were at the drive in movies, passing around a big fat doobie. Jessy had carefully parked downwind and was being very discreet since there were pissed off men in little grey helmets and "Billy clubs" running all over the place. As they watched the scene play out before their eyes. Jessy and his crew all looked up to the third floor just as Smacks, wearing only a pair of bell bottoms climbed out of one of the windows and onto the wide concrete ledge. Looking cool and relaxed he backed up to the edge of the ledge and took one short step back. At first everyone thought he was committing suicide but as he dropped he simply and gracefully caught the edge of the ledge with both hands as if he did shit like this every day. He then dropped him self gently onto the second floor level where he repeated all the same moves again and deposited himself into the garden at the corner of the building. At this point their friend just simply disappeared. Jessy had played football with Smacks at the beach and he was scary fast and could just jump right over the guys who tried to tackle him so he wasn't surprised when Smacks was there one moment and gone the next. The sad silly shore cops searched for an hour before giving up in disgust, and what you had assume ended with some vengeful retribution against the misguided snitch who had ratted out their unwelcome but quite talented house guest.

The incident with Smacks made Jessy realize that the crushing weight of power and control, that until that moment, everyone thought the Navy had over them, had a few cracks in it's red white and blue veneer. If there had been a big red curtain handy they could have cast it aside and there would be the base commander standing in his underwear with food on his face screaming for everyone to ignore the man behind the curtain. As they watched the mob of Navy police depart in their sad little grey pickups all they could do was smile. Truth be told, after all the pot they had recently disposed of, the earth could have been on fire and the most they could have done about it was perhaps cook up some "Jiffy Pop Popcorn" by sticking it out the window of the car.

Note: Who ever invented Jiffy Pop Popcorn or snacks in general...had to have considered the effects of smoking pot when they were coming up with their tasty treats. I would have loved to be on the stoner camping trip when "Smores" were invented.

CHAPTER 5

The Job

After some serious studying Jessy took a jet aircraft related proficiency test that was all about the million or so things that you could do wrong that would ultimately result in a very expensive flying machine falling from the sky with a perfectly good, well trained pilot on board. Jessy must have done well on that test because he was promoted to "Plane Captain" about four minutes after completing it. Being a plane captain means that you are trained to know every thing there is to know about your plane. Jessy didn't just know his plane, He was madly in love with that plane. The aircraft was the super powerful F4-J Phantom jet fighter bomber made by our friends at McDonald Douglas. Some attractive lobbyist representing the McDonald Douglass company blew some old white guy way at top of our government and got a huge contract to build a shit load of these incredibly scary flying destroyers of other peoples stuff. Jessy thought It was by far the coolest combination of metal and fire that we had at this point in human evolution. The Phantom could burn up more JP-5 jet fuel in a few seconds than any other aircraft of its kind. This made the oil people happy and that is, after all, what it was all about.

The F4-J Phantom jet held all kinds of records in it's day. It could fly faster and higher than any other combat aircraft in the world back then...as far as we knew. It was as close to the SR-71 (space ship that looks like a jet) as you could get, at the time...as far as we knew. For those of you not familiar with really cool stuff this means that the Phantom was just a few thrust pounds short of being able to fly into outer space. The F4-J was just plain bad and it knew it. If a machine can have attitude this one had a real severe case. It also could take a licking and keep on ticking. These crazy stupidly well built planes would come back to the same ship they left from with all kinds of bullet holes and stuff shot off of them and they were still ready to take off and fly more missions.

The pilots were ready to get back up there as well. Combat is indeed a drug and the more dangerous the mission, the greater the need to return to the action. The veteran pilots were amazing and had bravery stenciled in their underwear. They also had a way of dealing with what they were doing that was a tiny bit disturbing. Jessy once asked one of his veteran pilots how he could drop napalm bombs on a village full of human beings only some of whom may be the enemy…or not. He looked Jessy right in the eyes and told him. "I make believe there is nobody down there. It's the only way any of us can deal with the power of life and death that we have when we climb into that cockpit." This brief interaction with a "superior officer" made Jessy realize that, "he was his enabler, his accomplice." "Jessy was the mechanic tuning up the get away car for a crime against humanity."

"War is madness on steroids, with a super fat wallet" The Viet Nam war was heavily financed by the most powerful nation the world has ever known. (At the time) The Vietnamese people never had a chance in hell to survive victorious…except for the part where they didn't know how to loose a war. These very same people had turned back the Chinese, they had kept the Japanese at bay during World War II and they had kicked the shit out of the French who had attempted to enslave the Vietnamese people to help harvest their huge rubber plantations that France was betting on to make them a super power again. This of course was just on the very cusp of the plastics revolution that would soon turn all that rubber into clay.

Note: "The French conundrum" How can a country so full of themselves and so hostile towards any poor bastards who don't speak French be so good at stuff like health care, and eating food the rest of the world would never even think of? I mean sautéed snails? Are you kidding me? Yes, I'm just screwing with you France. I love French cooking and I am crazy about "quiche." I remember back in the day there was this author named Bruce who wrote a book titled "Real Men Don't Eat Quiche." He published his book in the early 1980s and He used examples like "John Wayne," and said that the "Duke" would never eat "Quiche" because he was a real man. "Hey America! Now hear this." If you are a real man you eat any fucking thing that tastes good. You can eat "quiche Burritos" with a spoon if you want because real men don't give a shit what four foot tall "Munchkins" in "Buddy Holly" glasses, say, or think, or do. So there, blow me. (note: call my lawyer and see if I can get sued for any of that) (just kidding Bruce. I'm sure your very popular book was written purely in jest and that you also thought that John Wayne was a Hollywood, government, front man, who was being used to sell patriotism to the youth of a nation whose leaders (the uber rich, and their paid for politicians) had decided that perpetual war was the best way to proceed into the twenty-first century. George Orwell was off by a few years but he had it right. (google 1984) Then read the book...please.

Jessy's Navy job revolved around these super cool, super dangerous birds of prey. The F4-J Phantom jet fighter bomber was the sexiest airplane built since World War two. It was his purpose in life to know how they worked and how to make sure that if one of them did happen to fall out of the sky...his name wasn't on the paperwork. As a plane captain it was your job to inspect the Phantoms before their missions and sign a form that roughly said if the plane blew up it was your fault. The pilot could drink a bottle of Southern Comfort and fly his plane into the side of a mountain and it would still be the plane captain's fault. The idea of plumbing was adopted by the military. Shit does indeed flow downhill and as a plane captain it was Jessy's mission to stand at the bottom of the hill and dodge all the huge, giant, flaming, stinking, turds that were headed in his direction.

One of the other functions of a plane captain on the flight line was to climb onto the wing of the aircraft and make sure that the pilot had strapped himself into the cockpit correctly before take off. If you found your pilot had slid himself into his ejection seat facing the tail of the plane it was your job, indeed, it was your duty to turn his dumb ass around. The next thing plane captains had to do was to pull all thirteen safety pins from the ejection seat and place them in a red plastic bag and show them to the pilot so that he knew that his seat was armed and "HOT." The giant, J79 jet engines, were already running so everything they did was translated by hand signals.

One morning, an (EID) "extra intelligence deprived" rookie pilot, who was trying way to hard to look like he had a clue, jumped onto the wing of one of Jessy's jets. He stepped up into the cockpit using the spring loaded shoe door ladder. Then, the pilot to be, ducked his head to avoid braining himself on the canopy and slid down into the seat (facing forward) and Jessy began to get the straps and buckles ready to fasten him into the plane. After securing the pilot safely in his seat he removed all thirteen safety pins from the ejection seat and placed them in the red bag. Then Jessy tapped the pilot on his flight helmet and showed him the bag. the pilot nodded like he knew what had just been communicated to him. About then he started playing with all the cool dials and buttons. Jessy watched in horror as the shit head began to pull on the ejection seat handle. This is quite similar to playing with the trigger of a 44 magnum while the muzzle is in your mouth. Jessy was leaning over the pilot at the time and if the seat had fired he would have launched himself one thousand feet into the air... with Jessy's severed head and shoulders in his lap. Jessy recoiled the best way he knew how. He slammed the pilots head into the other side of the canopy with both hands and arched his back and fell backwards onto the wing. The pilots flight helmeted head banged back and forth like a bell clapper and this dramatic move put him into a state of shock. An enlisted man had just put his hands on a superior officer in an aggressive manner. By all rights Jessy could have, should have been on his way to the brig, but the expression on Jessy's face made it clear that if this particular superior officer considered turning

Jessy in...something very bad could happen. There was a look of fear in the pilots eyes as he sheepishly settled back down into his rocket seat and tried real hard not to look at anything especially that yellow and black striped ejection seat handle.

Jessy finished prepping the pilot for his mission and then jumped down onto the runway and went through a set of hand signals to test the various components before take off, as if nothing had happened. Jessy expected to be court marshaled for assaulting a superior officer but no such order was ever issued. Possibly after some time in the air with the image of a bloody face in his lap, the pilot must have decided that discretion was the better part of valor, and he let Jessy go on about his business. This was probably a very wise move on his part. Jessy was beginning to get really tired of all this toy soldier crap and his patience with officers was wearing quite thin indeed.

One beautiful southern California day, Jessy and some friends were seated in their countries finest military restaurant enjoying an amazing lunch of steak or lobster or possibly both. Miramar really did have the best damn military chow hall in the world. Seriously, on lobster days it was all you could eat and some guys went freaking nuts. Empty claws and broken shells were flying everywhere. Melted butter sprayed in all directions and sailors were sliding across the floor while trying to get more sea spiders on their plates. It was sheer delicious madness.

Jessy was doing all he could to keep from falling into a dark pool of guilt while also enjoying every last savory bite of his wonderful, tax payer provided, feast. There were certainly people in near and far away places, starving to death at that very moment, and here they were stuffing their faces with perfectly prepared deep sea delights. They were all blissfully enjoying their seafood heaven when the whole building suddenly shook. Within a second there was the unmistakable sound of a thunderous series of loud explosions. Jessy glanced around the chow hall to see a giant room full of people who had no idea what was happening. In southern California earth quakes are as common as breast implants but this was something very different.

Everyone rushed out of the dining hall and into the parking lot just in time to see a small dark object blast through the roof of the now fully engulfed hanger number three. No one knew what it was at the time but there was this terrible feeling that the flying object had a face and a name. The hanger was situated on the flight line up the road from where they were standing. Giant bright orange flames bellowed out of the east and west doors of the hanger as that small dark object arched over the hot desert landscape and landed in a puff of dust. That object turned out to be some one's young son. He was a sailor who had been working on the ejection seat of one of the F4 aircraft when an F8 crusader jet came blasting in through the open doors of the hanger. Somehow the seat fired during the first explosion and launched the young sailor right through the steel roof of the building. He may have activated the seat himself to escape the flames.

The stunned sailors watched in horror as the deadly inferno grew more intense. As they took in the whole scene someone noticed there was one single parachute with what you had to assume was a college graduate in a flight suit hanging from the straps. The parachute floated safely to the ground at the end of the runway. Small explosions continued to tear up the inside of the huge metal structure. The hanger was awash in smoke and flames and death.

There was no immediate means of transportation available and Jessy's big Buick was parked back at the barracks parking lot. All at once everyone started running toward the plume of smoke in their loose fitting navy issue work boots (boon dockers). The hanger was more than a half mile away and it took them four or five minutes for most of them to reach the flight line. The Navy teaches it's sailors to be excellent fire fighters. On board a ship at sea, every second counts and every sailor assumes his job as a firefighter in a heartbeat. By the time the chow hall people arrived a small army of men who survived the initial fireball and the subsequent explosions had gotten fire hoses up and they had the worst of the fires under control. The young brave sailors were performing rescue missions into the smoking aftermath. There had been sixty sailors working in or around the hanger when the F-8 came flying through the doors and crashed into the planes inside.

There were several stories about what exactly had happened. One of Jessy's friends said that the plane's engine was running at full throttle as it entered the building and it sucked a mechanic through its engine just as it hit the ground. There was a cloud of red vapor just before the first giant explosion. That friend fell to the ground when he saw the plane coming directly at him and this is what saved his life. He was just out side the hanger and the screaming, pilotless, jet passed just over him before tearing into the line of parked aircraft and working sailors.

There were so many sailors who showed up all at once that the shore patrol had to hold them back to prevent more people from getting hurt. Soon helicopters arrived to transport the injured to Balboa Naval hospital. Jessy felt helpless and noticed that there were a few blackened corpses laying on the pavement. Most of the dead sailors were people Jessy knew. One of them had slept in the next bunk in Jessy's cube in the barracks.

All the sailors were wondering what in holy hell they had just witnessed. Eleven young men died that sunny day in Miramar and not many people outside the base ever heard about the horrible event. The news was tightly controlled during the Viet Nam war. Everything on base had to go through the government. Jessy didn't watch much TV back then but he asked some of his civilian friends from off base if they had heard about the accident and they hadn't. There is of course the possibility that the story made the nightly news but most of Jessy's friends were busy getting high and had totally missed it. There were some newspaper articles written at the time but not nearly enough to cover the scope of this "accident." I say accident because I don't think the pilot deliberately flew his plane into a hanger full of very expensive military aircraft and other associated support equipment, not to mention the young offspring of ten American families (two of the eleven fatalities were brothers) from all over the country.

They estimated the damage at around twenty-five million 1969 dollars. This was a fairly large amount of money back in 1969. The most expensive jets lost that day only cost two or three million each. Today our military fighter aircraft go for fifty times that amount.

There was some sort of formal military inquiry and the pilot made a statement and testified that his aircraft had shut down after his engine flamed out and had lost all power, forcing him to eject. In theory a pilot isn't supposed to bail out of a running aircraft if they are flying over a populated area but rather they should try to direct their plane away from buildings and people and try to land the best way they can. If the pilot happens to get killed in the process at least his family knows he died trying to spare the lives of those on the ground.

This pilot's memory of what happened could have been clouded by a sense of self preservation. The enlisted people on the ground knew his story about his jet engine shutting down was possibly slightly askew and had little sympathy for his less than heroic deed that day. The Navy didn't take the statements of the line crew under consideration since the word of an officer always trumps that of an enlisted man...always. The pilot was transferred to a new duty station for his own good and was rumored to have caused another costly "accident" when he clipped the wing of another plane while flying in formation. This time however only two planes were turned to rubbish and no one was killed as far as we know. No one knows what happened to the pilot after that.

Jessy was slowly developing a deep seated dislike for the "Roger Ramjets" of the world. "Rogers" was a nickname Jessy had given to the pilots. Jessy arrived at this catch phrase based on one particularly "assholeified" jet jockey that the ground crews had all learned to live with.

This pilot bravely sauntered around the flight line in a pair of custom made suede flight boots. He was a character in his own war movie and he always had a silk scarf wrapped around his neck with the tail hanging down the back of a very cool decked out flight jacket. He looked and acted like a movie star but treated his flight crew like they were his key grips. Jessy was his plane captain one day and "sky pilot" began ordering the ground crew around with a look of distain on his chiseled face. This is like pissing off your waiter on a busy night in your favorite restaurant. If you don't want someone spitting on your mashed potatoes or jerking off in your soup… always respect the wait staff. Jessy was more familiar with this plane than the pilot and the Jet Jockey knew it, but he tried extra hard to look like he knew what he was doing in the cockpit so he tapped on all the gages with authority and played around with the joy stick between his legs like it was his "Johnson."

The pilot had heard the story through the grape vine about Jessy and the other misguided pilot who had played around with one to many brightly painted gadgets in the cockpit so he knew not to go near that ejection seat handle. Jessy caught his eye at one point and glanced over to the handle as if daring him to grab that black and yellow baby just once. The pilot blinked a couple of times and he knew that Jessy was now the one in the drivers seat. Jessy swiftly showed him the red bag of safety pins and stowed them down beside his seat then tapped him on his glossy flight helmet with the cool screaming eagle decal. The pilot gave Jessy a thumbs up and nodded. Then Jessy jumped down off the wing, grabbed his light wands, and took up his position about thirty feet from the nose of the F4-J Phantom.

At Jessy's signal the pilot ran up the engines slightly and they went through the preflight dance all in particular order. First he was instructed to turn on his running lights then another signal and the wing flaps raised and lowered and Jessy swiftly ran from one side to the other to verify their correct operation. The crew of two scampered beneath the belly of the jet and checked the belly gages to verify that the hydraulic lines were fully charged. That means 10,000 pounds of pressure by the way. DO NOT have your hand or head inside a hydraulic door when it snaps shut. This would be let us say... bad...very bad. Lastly Jessy had the pilot drop and raise the tail hook. In case you were wondering Southwest 737 airliners don't have tail hooks. To be fair 737 airliners don't often land on aircraft carriers. Every thing was working as expected because all of Jessy's planes had been inspected by Jessy. He may have had a problem with the whole war thing but his job was his job and Jessy took his job seriously.

After a couple of minutes all the tests were complete and Jessy's guys pulled the wooden chocks from the tires and they all stood back to allow the plane to taxi out to the runway. On this occasion however Jessy made sure his crew was all lined up perfectly at attention and they began to sing the theme song from the cartoon show "Roger Ramjet." They were singing quite loudly "Roger Ramjet he's our man hero of our nation etc.") but of course no one could hear a thing over the roar of the two General Electric J-79 engines. The pilot looked down at them in wonder, waiting for the signal for him to continue to the runway.

Jessy finally sent him on his way and they all snapped a perfect salute as he pulled away. He probably knew they were "goosing" him and so did everyone else on the flight line but there was really nothing he could do. At any rate, that is where the term "Roger" came from when referring to their beloved pilots. Small victories were rare for enlisted personnel but Jessy gained a few points among the other plane captains that day. As it turns out he also drew some wrath from one particular second class petty officer.

CHAPTER 6

Crime And Punishment

There was a small building called the "Line shack" situated just across from the flight line where the Phantom aircraft were parked, ready for inspection and launch. The line shack was there for the plane captains and their crews to hang out between launches. There was a dispatch area in the front of the building where plane captains received their assignments and flight times. They were expected to have all of their "birds" inspected and ready to fly. As plane captains, they signed off on each flyable jet. The signature meant that if anything at all went wrong with the plane it was your ass. There was a whiteboard with each days plane numbers and columns where they checked off the status of each aircraft. If the plane captain detected any kind of leak or damage to the skin of the plane, excessive wear of a tire, loose or missing screws or rivets, a crack in a canopy among many other things that plane would be gigged (noted as un-flyable) and repaired before being reinspected and sent back to the flight line.

On a typical shift each plane captain would get two or three aircraft to inspect. They would launch their "birds" that same day as long as the flight wasn't cancelled or if they decided to have a night launch. Everything was very organized and ran better than the New York City subway system most of the time. Plane captains and ground crews spent their down time in the line shack, drinking coffee and listening to record albums on Jessy's GE stereo portable record player. They played The Beatles, Neal Simon, Simon and Garfunkel, the Rolling Stones and Sly and the Family Stone. Country music was against the law in California back then, although Johnny Cash was just starting to gain some popularity, probably because of the whole Folsom prison thing. Willie Nelson was sort of a crossover artist and had a certain amount of "street cred" on the left coast because of the whole pot smoking thing.

As plane captains they found it necessary to come up with some games to play to pass the time after launching their birds. Jessy didn't play cards so he rummaged through the spare junk area and found some three foot long pieces of half inch tubing and fashioned some very effective blowguns. Jessy made the darts from sharpened sheet metal screws and duct tape. The next step was to choose items around the office to use as targets. The ugly black and white picture of President Nixon never had a chance. One evening after an exceptionally vigorous game of blow darts everyone was surprised by the sudden dramatic entrance of petty officer Billy. Billy was his last name, not his first, and he came from the swampland in a state somewhere.... where they have swamps. There were swamps back in Jersey but they were full of people. The people may not have been alive but they were people just the same. They called the swamps Meadowlands so they could fill them in and build sport complexes on them. Mr. Billy came from a swamp that had actual prehistoric creatures twelve feet long that enjoyed eating pets and stray children.

Petty officer Billy was a second class petty officer (he out ranked Jessy by one class) and he went absolutely bug fuck crazy when he saw the "Tricky Dick" picture with a big hole where the center of the face used to be. He acted like he was going to start killing people. Billy began screaming and just wouldn't stop. He stormed about the room, waving his arms like a mad man. He must have been secretly in love with president Nixon and he started speaking in tongues there for a while. After way to much time, out on the dark side, he settled down long enough to take all of his pent up rage out on his favorite red headed stepchild. He knew damed well who had instigated this horrid act against his beloved war criminal. His face was about an inch from Jessy's as he told him to be back at work at zero seven hundred hours sharp (That's 7:00 AM) for special duty. Jessy's eyes were stinging from dragon breath. After Billy stormed out of the room Jessy tried to wipe the smelly spit from his face. Billy's teeth were spaced like a picket fence and he always had a hard time keeping the nasty stuff in his mouth where it belonged.

Jessy spent that night trying to figure out what he had done that was so wrong. President Nixon was a monster and a war criminal as far as he was concerned. Many of the sailors on base hated the fact that such a huge flaming asshole was running our country, but not petty officer Billy. Billy had a real serious crush on Nixon and all things Republican. If he is still alive Billy's probably at a Tea Party rally wearing a MAGA hat carrying a sign claiming that president Obama is a communist, gay, Nazi, Muslim, Mexican, illegal alien, eskimo, who was born in Kenya. That last statement actually makes sense to almost 40% of American voters today. The kind of people who can lose an election by 8 million votes and still think they won.

When Jessy showed up for duty the next day Petty officer Billy was standing in front of the line shack with several cans of sort of green and sort of grey paint. He also had an old wooden milk crate filled with brushes, rollers, red rags, and a gallon can of turpentine. The paint was left over from World War II and had the skull and crossed bones sign on the label with a long list of ways the fumes from this deadly potion could kill you or leave you permanently brain damaged. The EPA hadn't really kicked in yet. To be fair Nixon had a decent record when it came to the environment. He created the EPA. Today he would have been run out of the republican party like Al Sharpton at a Klan meeting.

Jessy caught on right away and realized that he would be spending the rest of the day painting the line shack and perhaps the rest of his life if he wasn't real careful with the whole ventilation issue. Jessy didn't argue and resigned himself to the punishment and began planning out the project in his head when petty officer Billy started off on him again. He had several hours to compose a speech and he gave Jessy the swamp version of the Declaration of Independence and accused him of being a communist and a fascist pacifist. Jessy probably had a few socialist views at this point. Social Security and Medicare sounded like good ideas. Having a fire department when your space heater sets your house on fire is a plus as are roads and bridges. The peace sign that he wore on his jacket was a dead giveaway but fascist, communist? That seemed just a little on the harsh side.

Note: Damn it people. Before you start accusing people of being this or that, read a god damned book for Christ sakes, or these days all you have to do is Google the crap you are calling someone so you don't sound so fucking stupid. Just so you know, like in case you live in a swamp. Fascists believe in corporatism, where corporations rule the state and wars are a means of keeping the country strong and the investors money coming in. Sort of like what we have today. Actual communists believe that we are all responsible for each other and we need to work as one for the common good. like in "It takes a village" Nothing like what anyone has today.

Jessy tried to explain all this to petty officer Billy but his eyes were starting to bulge and glaze over in a fit of righteous indignation and he screamed "just shut the fuck up and start painting, you stupid fucking commie, faggot, bastard." This was a classic last straw situation and Petty officer Billy had finally pissed the other person in the room all the way off.

After petty officer Billy stormed off Jessy began to devise a plan of attack that would be appropriate to this level of "Swamp thing behavior." There was a one inch piece of molding about four feet up the wall of the line shack that ran all the way around the room and the room was sort of green above the molding and sort of grey below it. His orders were quite clear. Petty officer Billy had said during his rant that he wanted every thing above the line to be green and every thing below the line must be grey. He planned to be gone all day and warned Jessy that, "You had better be done when I get back or there will be all kinds of holy fucked up hell to pay."

This last statement was disturbing considering that the person who was going to make his life "HELL", came from a swamp. Hell is a relative thing and when you had to live with snakes, ticks, alligators, spiders the size of catchers mitts and close relatives who were only connected to the human race by a thread. A place where teeth were optional. Hell must be a really scary place indeed. Right then and there, Jessy resolved to paint that damn building EXACTLY as he was told and that is what he proceeded to do. Not only did Jessy follow his orders to a tee, he finished with time to spare, including cleanup.

When petty officer Billy returned late that afternoon, he marched into the line shack with a big shit eating grin on his face thinking there was no way Jessy had completed his mission on schedule but when he took one look inside the building his eyes got as big as hub caps. Jessy had painted every inch of the room grey or green just as he was told. Everything below the line was grey including the table, the chairs, the floor, half the door including the door knob and, the bottom four feet of the refrigerator, front and back. Jessy had painted the trash bucket as well as the salt and pepper shakers on the now all grey table. Above the line he didn't miss a thing. The windows were green now and the room was quite a bit darker during the day as a result. The clock on the now green wall was green but it was still seventeen thirty (5:30 PM) under that green paint. At least Jessy was reasonably confident it was, but you sure couldn't tell by looking at that fucking clock. He had painted the clip boards that hung from little green hooks, as well as the papers clipped to the clip boards. At one time those papers contained more than enough useless government gibberish that some douche bags in Washington had deemed so terribly important that no one ever read, with the obvious exception of petty officer Billy. Jessy's crowning glory was the brand new picture of President Richard M. Nixon that had been hung that very morning to replace the one with the big hole where Nixon's big old nose had been. That creepy picture got three coats. In case you were wondering the molding was perfect and correctly two tone.

Jessy was just as proud as can be. There was a knowing smile on his face because he had followed his orders to the letter, without question or hesitation. Finally Jessy turned to face petty officer Billy and was shocked to see his face nearing critical mass. Billy was turning bright red and he had a huge vein bulging out of his pimply forehead. Billy's eyes were darting around the room like he was counting mosquitoes and Jessy backed up a step just in case that big old ugly head of his exploded. This time there was no speech, "Swamp Thing "just stuttered something, not words by any means, just odd sounding noises, grunts, and a gag or two. and then he suddenly turned walked into the door frame, bounced back and forth and then staggered out of the kind of green kind of grey line shack.

Jessy was positive he was totally going to get sent off to "Ice Station Zebra" or some other government facility near the arctic circle. Jessy had opted "to push the envelope all the way back to the post office," and now would have to pay the price for his futile gesture. Jessy spent that evening trying to imagine all the horrible, possible duty stations he could be carted off to, not the least of which was of course an aircraft carrier stationed off the coast of Viet Nam. As a trained plane captain, his job aboard ship would be to help launch planes, loaded down with bombs. The bombs themselves were a potpourri of death and destruction. There were bombs filled with high explosives to blow shit up. There were bombs filled with napalm to burn shit down. There were bombs that were filled with hundreds of little baby bombs that sometimes didn't explode until some child came along and thinking it was a toy and played with it. The village clinics had to handle a shit load of unfortunate civilians mostly young kids who made this deadly mistake. One particularly nasty prick of a bomb was invented by a scientist of the sadist faith and was filled with pure white phosphorus. The phosphorus bomb, when exploded sent white hot droplets in all directions. When these droplets of burning liquid metal landed on a human being they burned into his or her skin and just kept right on burning. (those last three were later declared illegal) but some nations still use them.

Note: Bombs don't have feelings or a conscience but the people who decide who we drop them on are supposed to. For the first time Jessy began to contemplate what he would have to do if his orders came in. He clearly had to give his decision some serious thought because to disobey an order while in the service to your country could very well involve prison time. The kind of prison time where the keys to your cell get lost forever and your relatives get a letter saying you died serving your country. This may be an exaggeration but no one knew exactly what would happen if they refused an order to deploy once it was given.

Jessy showed up for duty the next morning expecting the absolute worst. He just knew petty officer Billy would be there with an officer of some sort and probably some men in tiny grey helmets with side arms. When Jessy arrived at the line shack there were cheers and handshakes and plenty of laughter as guys from all over the base showed up to check out his artwork, but there were absolutely zero swamp people. It seems petty officer Billy had some sort of giant break down and was being sedated downtown at the Balboa Naval hospital by the park. He didn't have many (any) friends and everyone else was just happy to see him gone. As for Jessy, he was suddenly a hero and the other guys on the line treated him like he was Dorothy and had just squashed the wicked witch with his sort of green, sort of grey line shack. The remainder of that day went surprisingly smoothly, mainly because the line crew didn't have a supervisor trying to tell them how to do their job. They all knew how to do their God damned job.

The following day, just like Voo Doo, there was a brand new first class petty officer running operations on the flight line. The new supervisor's name was, coincidently, Doobie. Jessy didn't know if that was his first name, his last name, or just a very tricked out nick name but he figured anyone was better than petty officer Billy. Doobie, as it turned out, was an extremely cool supervisor. Doobie didn't hassle his subordinates at all because he was smart enough to know, that they knew, that his crew could perform their duties perfectly well without his supervision. This is the sign of a superior manager. He also knew that his experience was mostly on aircraft with propellers in an entirely different war (Korea) and his hands on supervision would probably result in some level of pain and or death, and lots of severely bent aircraft. From that day on they lived in peace and harmony.

Note: Management is the tool that people in power use to keep track of the people who work for them. "Seldom do managers need to manage anything if their people are properly trained and experienced. Unfortunately this doesn't stop some of them from trying."

The new boss was one hundred percent better than the last, but he was just a tiny bit off plumb. By that we mean he was as crazy as a monkey on heroine. There was this very weird habit that Doobie had where he would tell his young male tribe that if they took off their shirts and let him pop out the blackheads on their backs he would let them have the afternoon off. Jessy thought this was more than a little creepy, but it was California and the beach was so close, and besides it was comforting to know that there was nothing but tan on your back while you were getting to know your new best friends in their bikini's. As for the whole "gays in the military" thing. There always was, there is now, and there always will be. It's probably just closer to the surface now than it was back then.

Note: People are people and those who have the biggest problem with other peoples sexual preferences, usually have serious issues with their own sexuality i.e. Mike Pence. Good old Doobie was gayer than an Easter basket, or queer as a football bat as they say, he just didn't know it yet. Note: As a country the United States has been "dragging" (sorry) it's feet on the LGBTQ (lesbian Gay bisexual transgender queer) issue. People are people and all people deserve the same rights and privileges as all the other SCREW (Straight

Christian racist extremist white) people. Gender neutral bathrooms for all y'all.

Jessy for one wasn't going to be the one to tell him. It's hard to understand how someone who has denied his feelings for a lifetime comes to that kind of realization. Perhaps when you are going through your record/CD collection and there are mostly soundtracks from Broadway shows, or maybe you notice that you have ten to many pairs of colorful cowboy boots in your closet. At any rate it must come as a shock to some military men's-men who wake up one morning with a giant hard on and a really strong urge to rub some sun tan oil all over the cute recruit in the next bunk. There are as many views on how to live a life as there are people on earth. I love the fact that we are all different and we can all live side by side once we learn to cut each other an inch or two of slack. All to many people aren't smart enough to see diversity as a positive thing…To bad.

CHAPTER 7

The "A" Team

People in the military have friends, or at least know people who are so dependably scary that the guy from the "Elm Street" movies wouldn't screw with them. While serving in the military Jessy was friends with several of these people and looked upon them with great respect. He also knew enough not get anywhere near their bad side.

The most obvious of these awesome mutant ninjas was a not so gentle giant we will refer to as Stan. Stan was a stocky heavyweight Golden Glove boxing champion from Montana who was one big solid muscle with a head and a great haircut. When Stan worked out on the heavy bag at the gym the whole building shook as each devastating blow lifted the 150 pound bag several inches with either hand and then came crashing back down on its chain that was suspended from the roof of the metal frame muscle barn. The first time Jessy walked past the gym while Stan was working out he thought they were having another earth quake.

Jessy first met Stan when Jessy pulled a night watch in the barracks. Everyone took turns minding their home away from home and saw to it that everyone was awake for their shift at the appropriate time. If the place caught fire it was someone's job to wake everyone up and make sure they all got out of the building. In an ideal situation the night watch was the last man to get out alive. They worked from a wake up sheet on a clipboard that everyone who needed to be disturbed from their wet dreams had filled out the previous day. Jessy took over his first ever graveyard shift at midnight and the guy who he was relieving handed him the clip board with all the names of each sailor and their wakeup time. He then handed Jessy a mop handle minus the mop. "What's this for?" Jessy asked, with an unknowing look on his face. "That...is for Stan, my friend." He was careful to let Jessy know just how important this nugget of information really was. "Stan is on the first floor, cube six, bottom bunk, on the left. You use this mop handle to wake him up. Just be out of sight when he opens his eyes."

"Are you just messing with me?" Jessy asked. "Is this guy someone who I need to be concerned about"

Jessy's mentor advised him that the last poor unfortunate person who neglected to use the wooden mop handle found himself sleeping in the garden outside Stan's cube covered with shards of glass and a broken jaw.

"So, you want me to poke the monster with a stick?" Jessy asked in disbelief.

"It's either that or Stan will hit you so hard when he wakes up, your grandmothers tits will fall off."

Jessy had been warned and was careful to use the mop handle as he was told. At the dreaded moment that was noted on the wake up sheet Jessy leaned around the corner of the cube doorway and peered at the darkened bunk that held the sleeping hulk of the deadly giant, Stan. Jessy noticed that Stan's back was easily twice the size of any other normal human being he had ever seen. His back could have been used to project movies on, although you wouldn't advise this option to anyone.

Carefully Jessy took the mop handle and gently tapped Stan on his ridiculously huge shoulder. Nothing happened so he tried again a little harder than the first time but again Stan did not stir an inch. The third and forth tries were increasingly violent in nature but were still not providing the desired results. This was truly a predicament that had to be overcome. It was a Monday morning, Stan had spent the previous evening at the "EM (enlisted men) club, over drinking and if he was late for his shift it was going to be Jessy's ass that would pay for it. Jessy decided he needed to take some sort of aggressive action and it had to be sooner than later. Jessy took the stick in both hands and after calculating the proper velocity and angle he hit Stan squarely in the head with a blow that could have killed a lesser man. At first he thought Stan might not wake up ever again but Stan soon stirred and after rubbing his head he turned and looked Jessy in the eye and simply said, "Thanks man, you really know how to wake a guy up." They became friends soon after because Stan was well aware of his own reputation and he knew that Jessy was taking his life in his hands when he hit him that hard in the skull with a stick...Guys are weird.

Soon Stan and Jessy were drinking Red Mountain wine by the gallon and cooking "Jiffy Pop" popcorn over a campfire down at La Jolla shores with some of the girls who spent the better part of their lives at the beach. This is Californian for what you did while waiting for the morning fog to burn off. As it turned out Stan was a poet as well as a deadly fighting machine and while it has been way to many years ago to try to remember any of his poems, they were very heartfelt and stirring. Jessy could make something up but it just wouldn't be right, besides Stan could still be alive and Jessy wouldn't want to do anything to piss him off. Jessy does remember shedding a tear or two after hearing Stan recite one of his poems. His voice was oil well deep that sent a chill way down your spine. Jessy wiped a few tears from his eyes innocently but Stan noticed and he lowered his eyes and broke out with the least bit of a proud smile. Jessy has never told anyone this story before this writing. It was like that warm man-moment between the Japanese scientist and Godzilla.

One quiet night Jessy was wandering back to the barracks from the bank of pay phones where he had just spent a pocketful of quarters talking to his girlfriend back in New Jersey. As he approached the barracks Jessy noticed a loud conversation coming from the far end of the building. Jessy jogged to the corner of the barracks where he found Stan getting yelled at by a huge loud person with a thick southern accent wearing a super big cowboy hat. Stan was a big man but not all that tall, perhaps six feet with his shoes on. The southern gentleman was six or seven inches taller and was brawny and dangerous looking. Stan stood his ground as the cowboy got louder and his twangy voice was scaring the chickens. Jessy personally didn't see any actual chickens but if there were any chickens nearby he was sure they were shitting all over themselves. The one sided discussion revolved around something Stan may or may not have done with his own mother. Jessy was starting to get interested because he was aware of how this particular conversation was going to end. Stan could take a certain amount of bad mouthing but you just couldn't say anything that involved his mother, that was the rule.

Just then the Corona beer bottle in Stan's hand dropped to the ground. When the first right uppercut landed on the offender's square jaw his big old cowboy hat shot straight up into the cool night air. The guy's chin shot up also, just like in a "Popeye" cartoon. He was looking straight at the sky but I doubt he could see the full moon that night. The next four blows sounded like a short burst from a machine gun. The poor stupid bastard was sound asleep in a twisted bloody pile before his goofy hat came back down. When it did Stan ground it into the dirt with his BF Goodrich sandal and hurried off into the night. Jessy also didn't wait for the shore patrol to arrive because of the bag of weed in his pocket. Jessy didn't pay to see that brief fight...but he sure as hell would have.

Another person on Jessy's "people never to fuck with list" was Larry. Jessy met Larry at the beach at La Jolla shores one beautiful sunny day while jogging near the waters edge. The surf was high and Jessy was just trying to keep a step away from the waves as they came ashore. The wet sand was firm and easy to run on. All at once some guy went blasting by Jessy like he was made of extra strength slow motion. Being young and competitive Jessy stepped up his pace to try to keep up. Jessy slowly caught up but was feeling the burn in his lungs when he noticed something that freaked him all the way out.

This runner who wasn't even breathing heavy was kicking a "pinky ball" between his feet as he ran. Shit, Jessy was about to have a stroke and this guy was bouncing this little pink ball perfectly with every stride. Jessy was astounded and stammered something stupid like "Where are you from, Mars?" It was the best he could do at the time because his brain was about to shut down. The mystery runner slowed to a trot and laughed at Jessy's feeble attempt to match his stride. Want to try it, he asked as he kicked the stick ball in Jessy's direction. The ball flew past him but he caught up with it and was able to pass it between his feet a few times and that was at little more than a jog. Jessy was tired and discouraged as he kicked the ball back to this Zen master of beach runners.

"Larry" was also stationed at Miramar and was a mechanic in Jessy's squadron. Jessy was fairly new on base at the time and didn't know many of the guys who worked in the hanger on the other shifts. They walked and talked briefly and Larry told Jessy his name but not much of his story.

They ran together back to the park and Jessy stopped but Larry just kept right on going. Jessy was cooling down when one of the plane captains he worked with came up and asked him how he knew Larry. Jessy told him that they had just met and that he seemed like good guy. "Jesus man do you know who that guy is?" his friend exclaimed. "How would I know who he is? We just met." He told Jessy that, Larry was the most dangerous sailor on base." This was sobering news because he had seen "Stan" in action and that was a thing of terrifying beauty. Jessy's coworker explained that Larry was some kind of martial arts expert who could kill you with nothing but his feet. He had trained in the art of "savate" or French foot fighting for eight years. He was a master and everyone knew him by his reputation.

As the story goes Larry traveled to Tijuana one night with a couple of sailors from the base. Larry's buddies got drunk in a bar and started a fight with a superior number of Marines. The argument moved out to the street where Larry's comrades ran off like scared school girls, leaving a quiet but very aware sailor in the center of a circle of eight or nine pissed off "jar heads." The two cowardly seamen got to a corner and turned around just in time to see the first Marine's head fly back violently followed directly by the rest of his body. One by one the highly trained soldiers lunged toward Larry and one by one they were dealt a blindingly swift foot to the head. At some point Larry had removed his shoes and stood on one bare foot while he spun like a top and put all but one of the Marines to sleep on that dirty Tijuana sidewalk. The last guy just took off.

The story was hard to believe mainly because of Larry himself. This guy was so calm, and he always had a cool subdued smile for those who he considered friends. Jessy did some homework and verified the story with some very convincing eye witnesses. Stan was the one who sold the story for good when he told Jessy that he made it a habit to never mess around with Larry. Stan didn't stay clear of anybody but Larry was his one and only exception. Larry and Jessy hung out with many of the same people and when they were together they got along great, however Jessy knew enough not to push his button. He wasn't totally clear where Larry's button was but he sure as hell didn't push it or anything that looked like a button when he was around Larry. That would have been a huge mistake. "Huge." "Like trying to use a hair drier in the shower Huge."

Commentary on violence:

Jessy had only been in a few fights in his life and they were all purely defensive. Sometimes he was defending himself, and sometimes he was defending someone else but he never picked a fight with anyone. Jessy came out on top in all his battles when he was a teenager but when he was younger not so much. On one occasion Jessy got his eleven year old ass kicked by three friends who all knew him separately but none of them were aware that the other two also knew him and considered Jessy a friend, until that day. If this doesn't make sense please read it over until it does. Thank you.

It was a crazy cold winter day and Jessy was dragging his beat to shit, second hand, "Flexible Flyer" sled back home after a day of "hair on fire" sleigh riding on a local iced over hill on "Morgans farm" that was only a little less steep than a sheer cliff. He was tired and wet and cold and could have taken a shorter route home but instead took the long way because he was in stupid love with an impossibly unattainable girl who lived on Bordick Road. Linda was Jessy's dream girl at the time and he always took every possible opportunity to walk past her house. Linda was dating a guy in the Navy when she was in sixth grade. You see where I'm going here.

Jessy dragged his sorry sled a half mile out of the way for a chance to possibly see Linda in her yard but of course that did not happen. he just kept on going when he passed her house because of "fear and loathing" of what would happen if he was ever brave enough to walk up to Lynn's door and ask the people inside if she was at home. After trudging past the house of the girl he had this mad, ridiculous crush on, Jessy continued down the hill toward the old two family house that was his home. "Young boys have serious brain damage caused by young girls who are perfectly aware of this medical condition that they have caused. The girls love this power and use it at every turn."

Jessy was probably about a half mile or so from the relative warmth of his home when he saw three guys walking in his direction. You need to consider the fact that this town was small enough that everyone in town knew almost everyone else. Jessy knew these people and they knew him. At first Jessy recognized "Marty" who he considered a very close friend. They had spent countless hours watching the "Three Stooges" on the TV in Marty's parlor together with Marty's brothers. They played baseball in the large lot next door to Marty's dad's bar. They hung out with his big Italian family and Jessy had helped Marty build his two story clubhouse on a piece of his family's property along side of their home with the town tavern on the first floor. Next was "Nando" who was more of an acquaintance but still someone who Jessy considered a friend.

"Nando" was a small person who held a certain amount of respect because he came across as cool in a "James Dean, Fonzy" kind of way, except for the cowardly punk part. Nando wore black everything. His shirt was black his pants and shoes were black, and I'm guessing his underwear was black but Jessy didn't really know him that well. He was wearing a black leather jacket with the collar turned up like Marlon Brando in "The wild One." (ask your parents).

Last but far from least there was a fat, loud Jewish guy named Scott who had a big fat chip on his shoulder that had something to do with him being big, and fat, and Jewish. He was always blaming everyone for the "Holocaust" and because Jessy had blond hair and blue eyes and I'm fairly sure he thought Jessy was of Nazi decent. Jessy was English-Irish but that didn't matter on this day. Scott was clearly in charge of his small band of brothers and Jessy was all alone and had no clue what was about to happen next.

As they came closer to each other Jessy noticed the three were talking amongst themselves but looking at him slyly as they approached. When they were at arms length Scott moved around behind Jessy and grabbed him around the chest pinning his arms to his sides. Suddenly Marty and "Nando" started punching Jessy in the face and stomach. Scott was twice his size and Jessy was helpless to defend myself so he resigned himself to the beating. The good news was that besides being cowardly punks, Marty and Nando were also weak and sucked at punching stuff, like Jessy's face. Jessy was wearing a heavy winter coat that absorbed the body shots nicely and by moving his head from side to side he was able to make most of the blows to his face glance off without much damage. There is a trick or two involved in getting beat up and this was Jessy's first lesson. If you are able to outlast your tormentors they eventually get tired. Punching someone repeatedly is lot of work and when your victim doesn't cry or scream for help it takes much of the fun out of the experience.

After the beating Scott let Jessy go and the three misguided assholes marched off like they had just defeated the Germans in

WWII. Jessy used some snow to wash much of the blood from his face and to sooth the pain in his swollen cheeks. The journey home was a long and lonesome walk of shame. All Jessy wanted to do when he got to the house was to take a warm shower and eat something, anything. Somehow getting his ass kicked had made him extremely hungry.

As he slowly climbed the stairs to their tiny apartment his step dad saw him and immediately noticed the smeared blood and bruises on his face. He sternly looked Jessy in the eye and asked "What the hell happened to you?" Jessy started to explain how three guys had beaten the shit out of him when Warren instantly grabbed his coat and he exclaimed "Let's go." "What? Go where? Can't I just take a shower and try to forget this ever happened?" "No" his stepdad roared. "We have to find them god damn it, NOW." Jessy never made it to the top of the stairs. Warren grabbed the collar of his ugly, green, hooded, blood spattered, winter coat and pushed him down the steps and out the front door. Warren disappeared around the side of the house and all to soon he came back with an eight foot long 2X4 white pine stud that he had brought home for some reason but he never figured out what to do with it. Warren wasn't a carpenter. Warren wasn't a plumber or an electrician either but that didn't stop him from trying and he very nearly killed himself on several occasions. So now they had a big long piece of wood sticking out the back of the Rambler station wagon while Warren had some twisted idea that they would find the guys who had beat Jessy up and he was going to hold them while Jessy hit them over and over with a beam. This made zero sense to Jessy but it made perfect sense to Warren and he was driving.

Warren drove around for an hour and they passed several groups of guys including the very same kids who had trashed Jessy. Each time Warren asked "Is that them? Jessy just said, "Nope." He was pissed and sore and hurt in more ways than he wanted to think about, but these guys were still school mates and he couldn't imagine showing up at homeroom on Monday after putting three of his classmates in the hospital, with a 2X4 stud. That just wasn't something Jessy was prepared to deal with.

They continued their search for what seemed like a lifetime but they were almost out of gas and Warren, thankfully, had forgotten his wallet. They finally drove home and Jessy stumbled out of the Rambler and headed for the shower and a cold plate of spaghetti from a can, (microwave) wasn't a word at the time. Warren took the 2X4 and put it away for...next time?

Jessy didn't have very many good days when he was young and this certainly wasn't one of the good ones. Now he had to deal with what to do about the fact that three people he knew had beaten him like a drum. Two of these people he could expect to see in school on Monday. His options were limited because everyone knew and liked Marty and Nando. Briefly Jessy thought about calling his friends in Patterson but they were much to dangerous to let loose on these douche bags. Jessy was considering some sort of revenge but the boys from Paterson might kill someone and that would be a wee bit over the top. Jessy was dealing with some very real anger issues at this point but he wasn't homicidal.

Jessy decided on the course of least resistance. Jessy knew Marty and Nando were afraid of him now and they say that a coward dies a thousand deaths. The plan was simple. Whenever Jessy passed Marty or Nando in the hall he just looked them in the eye, frowned, and shook his head, or he would ignore them until the last second and then would smile knowingly and walk on by. It didn't mean anything but they didn't know that. They knew they had fucked up and now they would have to wait to see if Jessy had a plan to deal with them. Marty and Nando became aware that Jessy was friendly with a really scary crew from Patterson and that alone was enough to give them ulcers. The best part was that the big fat kid, Scott, had disappeared. His parents had moved him to a better town somewhere and no one ever saw him again. This was fine with Jessy, Scott was an asshole and now his partners in crime had no one to defend them. Marty and Nando stayed out of his way from then on and Jessy felt no need to escalate the situation. War was averted and the threat of destruction was all he needed to sleep at night.

Jessy's friends in Paterson would have called up their troops and his two remaining tormentors could have spent the next three months in the intensive care unit. The Paterson boys had put some poor kid in a drier at the local laundromat for two dimes (twenty minutes) on HOT just for visiting some girl from their neighborhood. Jessy never really fit in with those guys but his stepdad Warren was lifelong friends with the father of one of the guys from the "corner candy store." Literally they all hung around the same corner store that sold a variety of things that included hamburgers, shakes, candy, and they had a real soda fountain that made the best black and white sodas and egg creams. They also sold airplane glue but you needed a note from your parents to buy it. Jessy was the best athlete in the group when they played baseball, stickball, and street football. There was a game called "hot leather" that involved a thick black belt, some running, and of course red welts on the person who finally got cornered by the guy who found the belt.

Jessy mostly minded his own business and hardly ever got into fights, although he had to jump in to prevent someone from being severely damaged on several occasions. Once in a while he just stood back and let one of those someone's take a beating when they deserved it. If you provoke a bigger, more dangerous person into kicking your butt, you shouldn't expect others to jump in and get their knuckles all bloody because of your large, loud mouth.

"Violence is forever," and people tend to seek revenge upon those who do them, or their loved ones harm. This is not always the case but the "turn the other cheek crowd, is a small and select one.

Note: People who believe that peace is the answer, (John Lennon is dead, that leaves Jessy, Yoko and some guy named Lenny). People who believe that peace is the answer should never be confused with

Christians, or people of any major religion for that matter. Buddhists seem peaceful enough but I think it's because they fast all the time and don't have enough energy at the end of the day to do much harm. Give one of those bald guys in the saffron robes a couple of hamburgers and a few six packs and I'll bet they would go all "Kung Fu" on anyone who gets in their face. And forget the Jews and Muslims. That Old Testament god was a real prick.

Some of today's Christians, define hypocrisy. More people have died in the name of Jesus than anyone else ever. The New Testament is loaded down with stories of Jesus doing good for the weak and the poor and the sick.

Many of todays Christians have become selfish assholes who don't believe in paying taxes for education, welfare, or health care. These very same people don't seem to have any problem with military funding. Is this just a little contrary to the stuff Jesus was trying to teach his followers. or am I missing something?

I simply must remember to ask Glen Beck the next time we're doing shots of "Patron" together. "Glen, if Jesus was in the Air force what color bombs would he drop on his children? This question would probably make his crazy little eyes spin around and his head would explode all over the inside of that oversized NAZI helmet that he wears when he is downing shots with his progressive friends. Of course this is a trick question on many levels. First, Jesus could never actually get into the US. Air force because of the whole beard and long hair thing, not to mention his views regarding the bombs v. children issue. As for the color of the bombs, everyone knows that you drop blue bombs on little boys and pink bombs on little girls...duh.

Note: I Wrote that screed on Glen Beck years ago and he may have had an epiphany since then. I'm going to cut him some slack and hope he found his way out of the darkness. Alas Glen has been replaced by much crazier people like that orange ex-president guy, what's his name? And Alex Jones? OMG There are legions of nut cases driving around in giant, smoky, black pickup trucks with "American flags" and "Fuck Obama" or "Fuck Hillary" or "Fuck Biden and Harris" flags who listen to Fox who are afraid to let teachers tell kids that America was built on the backs of slaves.

CHAPTER 8

Jessy's Transformation

All was quiet on the western front (coast) for the time being and things were going smoothly on the flight line and off base as well. Jessy had a girl friend back in New Jersey who was as close to a fiancé as you could get. She would one day become his ex-wife, but he was nineteen she was three thousand miles away, more or less...and did I mention Jessy was nineteen. There were many conflicted feelings when he met and dated California girls. A man can rationalize anything when there is a beautiful young girl in a tiny swimsuit in desperate need of a fresh coat of suntan lotion. For the first time in his life Jessy was at ease around these young women and he was comfortable talking to and getting to know them. The most astonishing part was they really wanted to get to know him as well. Jessy didn't take this newborn popularity lightly. He realized how fleeting something like this could be and that set him apart from the chosen few who had been created to be loved by women no matter what they did. The best part was that Jessy really enjoyed the company of the young women he was meeting. The California girls were very different from the "Jersey girls" Jessy had grown up around. Not better just different, Jessy was slowly maturing and learning how to be attentive and enjoy their stories and their feelings.

It was around this time in his development that Jessy met a beautiful and smart young girl named Aileen. Aileen was visiting her wealthy dentist uncle and was in town for the summer. She was only sixteen and Jessy was careful not to let their relationship get out of hand but she had an old soul and was very deep in her understanding of the world around her. They sat on the sand and talked for hours and she told Jessy how she felt about the war and of how she would often cry while she watched the evening news. She was so sincere when she spoke from her heart. Jessy could see these feelings in her eyes. Jessy had never met anyone like her before.

Jessy was enchanted with Aileen and he began to try to enhance his knowledge of the world events going on around him. He was a little crazy about her in spite of the huge difference in their ages. When you are nineteen and a wonderful young girl of sixteen comes along there are laws in place that make those three years a real "Border Wall." Jessy was aware of this and refrained from committing a "statutory crime" with Aileen but from that point on he began to read the newspapers and started watching the news on TV. Slowly he began developing a deeper understanding of the mess we had gotten ourselves into in southeast Asia. Aileen was gone by the end of the summer but Jessy will always be thankful for the influence she had on his life and his world view. He would like to say "Thank you Aileen, I hope you've had a wonderful life and I sometimes regret not trying to follow up but, partly thanks to you, my life became very complicated after you went back home."

Jessy started showing up at concerts and rallies for the causes of the day. He went to Caesar Chavez rallies for the farm workers union. He gave his spare change to the Black panthers, and the socialist workers party. One night he attended a concert put on by the "Viet Nam Veterans against the war" and for the first time was sincerely hooked on the whole peace movement. Jessy really had no choice since Jane Fonda was one of the entertainers and he was a big fan ever since her movie Barbarella. Dick Gregory, Peter Boyle, and Donald Sutherland also made impressive appearances. There was also gorilla theatre and music that altogether made him feel for the first time feel like he wasn't the only one who shared his feelings. The following day there was a huge march in down town San Diego and several people in the crowd tried to urinate on veterans with purple hearts in wheel chairs. Unfortunately brains come in all sizes. Jessy didn't agree with those who spat on returning soldiers and called them baby killers. There is the fact that we were killing babies in Viet Nam. Wars kill babies and anything else that gets in their way. Wars suck but the young guys who got drafted to go and get their nuts shot off didn't deserve to be treated like criminals when they got home...unless they were.

Jessy's friends were partiers and pot smokers but none of them were politically minded by any stretch. Jessy seemed to be the only one on the base that was venturing off in this direction, with the possible exception of "Smacks" who he would run into quite "by accident" at these gatherings. Smacks was an enigma and he lived in some kind of parallel universe. There were times when Jessy secretly suspected that Smacks was some kind of super, deep cover, agent. There was no real explanation for the fact that he never got busted for any of his outrageous behavior other than blind luck. Of course people must have thought the same thing about Jessy who really liked Smacks partly because when they were hanging out it was like having some kind of crazy, magic, get out of jail free card. Looking back Smacks could have been hanging out with Jessy for the same reason. Jessy realized however that when the time came for him to make his stand against all this military madness, he would be totally on his own.

Jessy was already working the night shift when he was promoted to third class petty officer. This promotion gave him the option of moving off the base and into an apartment with a couple of roommates and one of their girlfriends. (it's not like he was going to buy a house on four hundred fifty a month) Jessy's friends were both fellow east coast guys who liked to smoke a little pot and party in Mexico. Mario was a cool Italian guy from Trenton, New Jersey and Eric was from Boston.

Mario's girlfriend was a native American from the "Nez Perce" tribe. Her name was Sunny and she was a wonderfully wild native

American girl. She was all about "whites and reds" (uppers and downers) Sunny was so much fun to be around, and when she was speeding her personality was just magnified. Sonny was very cute and she really had a cool sense of humor. Her laugh was infectious and she was the life of every party. She was the kind of person who could get everyone at a funeral to jump up and start singing and dancing. They all loved Sunny, even when she was a little "amped up.

There was only one little problem with Sunny" You really didn't want to be around when she was doing "reds". She was a totally different person on downers. Her eyes looked like they were nearly closed and she would loose her temper with no warning or provocation. No one was safe from her wrath when she was "droopy." Sunny wouldn't do downers very often but she seemed to use them to give her the courage to go off on the people she was pissed at. When she was really mad at someone she wasn't afraid to call in the troops from the res. Sunny could summon up some very scary native American gangsters when she needed them.

Sunny had taught Jessy all about her tribe and their history. The most interesting part was the story of Chief Joseph and his running battle with the US cavalry in the late 1870s There is a whole movie about him so we won't bother you with a history lesson, however Chief Joseph was one of America's greatest military minds. (if you google him his occupation is listed as warrior) He was a truly brilliant military leader but you probably will never read about him in school books unless you attend West point.

Note: We Americans may not get to read about Thomas Jefferson either if the "Christian Cracker Barrel Congress" down in Texas has anything to say about it. They want to write Jefferson out of the history books because he believed in the separation of church and state. Just so you know, a large amount of this countries school books come from Texas. The same state that gave us George Bush, Dick Cheney, Tom Delay, Enron, Halliburton, and the wars in Iraq and Afghanistan is in charge of dishing out faith based education to the youth of America. "There is good reason that there just happened to be a school book depository in Dallas in 1963." If this last reference went over your head I apologize. There may be some young people out there who don't know who John F. Kennedy was and that he went down to Dallas one day to smile and wave at people and was blasted into eternity by several very bad people in front of a school book depository.

Note: Elizabeth Warren (or whoever is president by the time I publish this damned book. The next time Texas threatens to secede from the union.... Let them.) I would help the Mexican workers build THAT fence.

Back at the apartment Jessy had a sweet little household going on. All of them had different schedules so there wasn't much of a problem with the fact that there was only one bathroom. There was only one bedroom as well. Mario and Sunny got the queen sized bed, Eric and Jessy took the bunk bed, with Jessy in the bottom bunk and Eric in the upper bunk. Sometimes Eric would have a sleep over with one of his girl friends. Jessy was OK with the bunk thing, he'd been sleeping in one since boot camp and this was still a much better deal than living in the barracks on the base. There was a certain fear factor however when Eric was pounding away with his girl friend and Jessy was trying desperately to get some sleep while fearing that the bed was going to collapse on his face.

While Jessy was working at the base at night in the hot brakes area on the flight line he noticed that there were three guys pulling and packing drogue chutes after the Phantoms returned from their training flights. Jessy had worked with the hot breaks crew while working the day shift and had grown quite proficient at the job. No one could pack chutes faster and his chutes always opened when they were called upon. Many of the chutes packed by less talented line crew members just popped out in a tangled mess or never made it out of the bag. Jessy fashioned a deal with his chief, he would do the job of the three men allowing them to return to the flight line as plane crew members and in return he could go home when all the birds were on the ground and the chutes packed.

The job was a challenge but it kept Jessy busy and the time just flew by. The returning jets would land and the crews watched to make sure the drogue chute had popped out of the tail cone and opened properly. The chute helped slow the plane enough to remain on the two mile long runway before turning back up the taxi way on it's way back to the flight line. If the chute didn't open the pilot had to use extra brakes to slow the speeding aircraft. After one of these landings the brakes could get so hot they might cause the magnesium wheels to catch fire. Magnesium fires don't go out, they burn out, and you don't want to be the person who tries to put out a magnesium wheel fire with water. The resulting explosion will send you to heaven or hell or France for ever.

As the one and only member of the hot brake crew Jessy was by default his own crew chief. Jessy gave the rest of his crew, and by that we mean Jessy a large number of fringe benefits. Whenever they (he) landed a flight of phantoms and packed their chutes Jessy let his crew (him) take a nap. A packed drogue chute makes a perfectly soft pillow and the concrete runway was like sleeping on a cloud for someone as tired as Jessy usually was.

The F-4s made plenty of noise when they came in for a landing. When he heard the scream of those J79 engines Jessy would turn his head toward the runway, open one eye, and watch the tail of the incoming jet to be sure that the chute door opened, the pilot chute popped out, and the main chute deployed. If these things happened in the correct order most pilots could slow the plane down without burning up the brakes. Most but not all. After the aircraft taxied back from the end of the runway

It was Jessy's job to stop the plane by crossing his light wands so the pilot could see them. Once the plane stopped rolling he would dart under the fuselage and tap each wheel with the back of his hand. If the brakes were safe the skin on the back of his hand would still be on his hand. If they were to hot some of that skin would be stuck to the wheel with strands of smoke that smelled like, well...fried flesh. If the brakes were really hot they would glow red and Jessy would bail out from under the plane in a very big hurry. Those wheels could go off like bombs and kill anyone near the plane.

Note: Jet aircraft tires are inflated to 320 psi (that's 10 times the pressure in your car tires) and when they get really hot that extra pressure can cause the wheel to explode. Usually the wheel will fail before the tire.

The wings, were where the landing gear (wheels) were mounted, and also the fuel tanks so they had to evacuate the plane to the "hot break area." The hot brake area was several hundred yards from the flight line and Jessy would signal the pilot to get his plane over there ASAP. The pilot would alert the base fire team from the radio in the cock pit. Sirens would sound and the fire truck would arrive in a minute or two to lay down a special fire retardant foam and the pilot, and the RIO could be rescued if things got out of hand. The pilot (Maverick) is the one in front and he flies the plane. The RIO (Goose) is the radar intelligence officer, he sits in the back and flies the bombs and rockets to their targets. It takes both of these people working in perfect unison to perform a successful mission.

Note: A successful mission is one where a group of people on the ground who were alive yesterday are, let us say, somewhat less alive today. This also applies to their pigs, chickens and water buffalo.

If the returning jet's brakes passes the skin test Jessy would run to the rear of the plane and grab a few of the cords of the drogue chute and pull it to one side. Then he would wave his wands to signal the pilot to release the chute and gun the engines to pop open the spring loaded chute clamp. This maneuver worked usually but there were times when you had to pull the chute loose by grabbing several of the chute cords while standing directly in the Phantoms powerful jet wash. Then you would pull with all your might to free the "D" ring from its clamp. The "D" ring was a heavy piece of metal that was attached to all the chute cords and you had to be careful to get out of its way when it came loose and flew directly at your face. Jessy saw a sailor get hit square in the forehead with the "D" ring and the chute wrapped around his body while the jet wash rolled him down the runway like an unconscious nylon burrito.

While Jessy was dashing around the Phantom's running jet engines he was exposing himself to high frequency sound that was damaging his overly large ears and all the important ear stuff that makes hearing sounds possible. The Navy should have issued Jessy proper ear protection like the plane captains and their crews on the aircraft carriers wear that was a padded cloth helmet with a chin strap. The ear protection that Jessy was given were the same as the Micky Mouse ears that you wear at the shooting range. No padding, no cloth, no chin strap. These protectors went flying down the runway as soon as someone got into the jet wash of a running jet engine. They were totally useless but the Navy only had so many of the correct ear protectors and those were all on those big assed ships with all the planes on the roof. Jessy wound up with severe hearing loss and a bad case of tinnitus. Tinnitus is constant ringing in the ears that goes on forever and doesn't get better it only gets worse.

Note: Military personnel don't earn enough money and they deserve a much larger benefits package when they leave the service. The men in suits who work for the corporations, and by that I mean our politicians in Washington will line up a bunch of uniformed service people and stand there with them during election season but they don't appreciate the young men and women who loyally serve our country. They constantly come up with new and totally useless reasons to put our service people in harms way. Even the non combat jobs are dangerous and people get injured or die all the time and OSHA isn't there to insure they get a safe workplace environment. The people in Washington are there to make money and give tax breaks to the people who paid extremely huge amounts of cash to get them elected. These very same people don't give a shit who has to die to ensure we sell more ships, jets, bombs, rockets and tanks. We fight wars to secure access to someone else's oil reserves. If the sons and daughters of families across the country get killed or wounded in those misadventures it doesn't concern them as long as the shareholders are collecting dividends and pay as little tax on those dividends as possible. Most enlisted military families live below the poverty line. Go figure.

Jessy had to find himself a part time job as a greens keeper on the base golf course. He also had a job working down at the port of San Diego as a part time non union longshoreman. (He was the only non management Anglo worker) Usually during the week he was only at the apartment long enough to sleep and shower. On the weekends Jessy and his roommates would go dancing in Mexico, or sometimes they would attend reasonably priced concerts in Balboa stadium and afterwards hang out in Balboa Park. Across the road from Balboa Naval hospital.

Note: For a ships captain who sailed around the world "discovering" places that already had people living on them. (Sunny's tribe was thriving in Oregon long before Balboa "discovered" the West coast.) Vasco Balboa sure had way more than enough stuff named after him. I'm just making an informed observation here. I'm not judging the guy, although for a man, he sure wore some silly looking outfits. In the paintings I've seen he looked like an Easter basket with skinny legs in black tights and a hat that resembled a fancy French pastry.

Short Colonialism Rant: A typical communication between an explorer and his King would go something like this. Assuming, of course, that the King and his explorer both had cell phones.

Explorer: "Um, uh, hi, your majesty, I sort of just discovered a totally new world while on my way to India.

King: That's great Vasco, did you find any gold? We sent your sorry ass over there to find a shit load of gold and bring it back to me, your king.

Explorer: Yes there is gold here. But there is one small problem as I see it. There are millions of brownishly colored people living here already and they have all your gold."

King: Uh yeah, that is a common issue. "Can't you just kill them?"

Usually we just kill them and the problem isn't as much of a problem in the morning.

    Explorer: "We can't kill all of them, did I mention there is like a million of these darkly shaded, mostly naked, indigenous people all over the freaking place? They are deadly accurate with their bows and arrows. We would need a lot more of that grey powdery stuff that my soldiers put in their long shooty things and a shit load of those little round metal balls." (This particular explorer had majored in business.)

King: "OK, how about this for a plan B. Just kill a few of them. Start with the strongest and smartest ones so there won't be any "Mandingo's" (look it up) to muck things up. Enslave everyone else and send me all the really young attractive ones on the next ship. Boys, girls, whatever. I'm really not to particular. Oh yes, and this is very important. Shove the church as far up their ass as it will go. Nothing subdues a native population faster than a pissed off deity. And by the way, you're welcome. That's why I'm King. Well, I've got to go now, you're breaking up, mainly because they haven't invented cell phones yet. I shouldn't have to say this but please don't forget to bring back all the gold your ship can carry on your way home or you don't need to bother coming home…ever. Thanks."

CHAPTER 9

Favorite Destinations

While living in the San Diego one bedroom mansion, Mexico was by far the grand daddy of all their favorite haunts. After one of these infamous adventures in "TJ" (Tijuana) some serious down time was required after the ride home. A typical trip to Mexico involved Jessy and his roommates jumping into his Buick and heading for the border. They would cross the magic, not so invisible line with all the agents, cops and federales. The Mexicans checked you on the way in, the Americans checked you on the way out. They would then drive to the down town area of Tijuana. This was a short but visually stunning excursion where Jessy was always astounded by the stark difference between the United Stated and a real, hard core, third world nation. This was saying something as Jessy had grown up running the streets of Paterson New Jersey. They would drive past piles of oddly shaped structures assembled from a variety of building materials that included plywood, corrugated steel, cardboard, tar paper, and discarded cinderblocks. A few random telephone poles here and there provided power for television, hair driers, and toasters.

Fires were frequent and often deadly. Within these piled up shacks there were no real streets but simply hundreds of dirt alleys that wandered off in various directions. One of Jessy's friends who had joined them on a Mexico trip for the first time once asked "how do these people get their mail?" Sonny shook her head and responded with her sly grin. "You're kidding, right? Do you see a fucking mailbox, like anywhere?" His question was reasonable coming from someone who had grown up in a country where the government could mail a late tax bill, or Ed McMahon could send an entry form from the publishers clearing house to just about anyone, anywhere.

While exploring the back streets and side roads on the poor side of Tijuana they would often notice children in rags running down the alleys on their way to beg quarters on the busy streets downtown. Sometimes a simply beautiful young women with long raven hair and dark brown eyes dressed in simple yet lovely white, black or red dresses would emerge from the rubble on their way to work in the bars downtown. It reminded Jessy of the song "A rose in Spanish Harlem."

They would gently roll down the torn up pavement on not quite bald, $5.00 used tires, onto a side street and park a few blocks from the center of town. Jessy would then unload any long haired hippies who were hiding in the trunk. These travelers were mostly hitchhikers who would have been denied admittance into Mexico without some kind of help. The Mexican government had a big stick up their ass when it came to hippies. They didn't like any Americans who didn't have enough money to spend in the clubs or pay off the police. Jessy never accepted any payment for his taxi service...That would have been a crime but Jessy had to be one of the only people on the planet to smuggle young white people into the sad country of Mexico. Were they breaking the law? That subject was up for debate. This is what some would call a "grey area." Dark grey perhaps but the crimes being committed by our government at the time were much more harmful to humanity than someone getting free transportation in the trunk of a Buick. "Rationalization is a gift from the gods and Jessy was always quite religious in that respect. If Jesus had owned a big fat Buick I'm sure he would have done the same damn thing. Amen."

After debarking the riders they would walk down to the "Blue Note" or the "Oasis club" and dance and drink cheap beer all night long. Sunny and Jessy loved to dance and Mario and Eric liked to drink beer and listen to the music. Sunny knew her way around town and she would hook us up with a friendly cab driver who would supply us with a "roll of whites" (mild speed tablets). Sort of like real strong coffee but you didn't need to go to the bathroom as often. For a couple of US dollars a tin foil roll of tabs would last them all night. They often stayed well into the morning and just as often there would be a frantic search for the car afterwards. The beat to shit back streets all looked alike in the daylight. Nothing looked the same in the bright morning sun as it did in the dark of night when they had parked the giant nasty pig of a car. Once when they finally found their ride in some shady area off the main drag, they had to excuse themselves to the young Mexican couple in the front seat who were trying to steal the radio.

A typical road trip to Mexico usually ended with an affordable breakfast of Huevos Rancheros and plenty of coffee at the "Chock full of Nuts" all day all night restaurant In downtown TJ. By 11:00 AM they would be wide awake and ready for the trip back to San Diego. After the drive they would arrive safely back at the apartment. Sleep was the only cure for the way they felt after the all night ordeal. Jessy would shower when they got back just to get the smell of beer, cigarettes and burnt tires out of his hair. The sky's of Mexican border towns are generally brown with the smoke from tires and cable insulation. Fire is the easiest way to get at the steel cords in the tires and the copper in the cable. You didn't see many documentary pieces about air pollution on "Telemundo." At least not back before they started to notice that it was always twilight in Tijuana no matter what time of day it was. The same could be said for Los Angeles at the time but that bad air was caused by millions of cars stuck in traffic.

Jessy and his friends had another downtime destination back then and that was Los Angeles. The trip would take somewhere between one and three hours depending on how lost they got along the way. Jessy's Buick Road master was always the mode of transportation and in 1968 it didn't have a GPS system. The president of the United States didn't have GPS back then either. Jessy would take care to visit the junk yard in Murphy Canyon before a long road trip. The tires were used but they had plenty of rubber and he generally only paid about five dollars each. Jessy didn't mention this fact to his passengers. They would chip in for gas but he figured that the overall safety of the Buick should be kept on a need to know basis, and they didn't really need to know.

One memorable trip to LA began when a friend told them about a big concert being held at the Shrine Auditorium featuring the monster group of the day, "Iron Butterfly." Their excitement grew throughout the week as the prepared for the road trip. They made a short list of stuff to buy and things to do. There wasn't a Ticket master back then so Mario asked around to see if anyone had scored extra tickets but no one had even heard about the concert yet. They were undeterred and decided that worse case they should be able to get tickets at the door. The Shrine was a huge old venue that was built before Columbus discovered America. They had been there before and cheap tickets had never been an issue.

Someone would need to scare up a baggie of "Mexican mind widener" for the road. Eric hooked up with the local "Pot Mart" distributor and ten bucks later they were all ready to listen to some good old fashioned rock and roll. It wasn't old fashioned at the time but whatever it was they were ready to get down to it. Jessy stopped by a small local bodega and picked up the chips, Cheetos, and little white doughnuts that were an important part of the journey. There were also couple of quarts of "Superman Orange drink" in the bag of goodies that evening. They never drank alcohol on road trips.

Everyone got off early from work that Friday and threw on their concert attire. Jessy generally wore a broke in denim cap and tight brown plaid bell bottom slacks and a black print silk shirt. Today this kind of outfit might be considered a little on the hairdresser side, or something out of Saturday Night Fever, but in those days people thought he looked cool. The hippy culture was everywhere at the time. The girls would be wearing long print dresses of cotton and lace with colorful floppy hats, tie dyed scarves, and sandals. There would be a few mini skirts and just the right amount of tube tops, see thru blouses and very short shorts. Denim bell bottom jeans and T-shirts were of course always in style for either gender.

Everyone helped load up the big car and after stopping to fill the tank with twenty-five gallons of regular, or about $7.50. Gas was going for about $0.30 per gallon. What in the holy hell happened?

Rant alert! In those days most of the oil came from places like Texas, North Dakota, New Mexico, Colorado, Alaska, and California, in that order and it still does but not nearly as much. Instead we get most of our oil from Cana da and Mexico today. We do get oil from the middle east and Russia but not as much as they would have you believe. I still don't understand what all the fuss about the middle east is about. Other than it being a great excuse to crank up prices every time there is unrest in places like Libya or Iraq. This translates to every other day for those of you keeping score. Wall street and the oil cartels have screwed us so hard and in so many ways we should all feel like rape victims by now. The "price of oil" scam could bring this country to its knees, and some politicians want to give these vandals more tax cuts? seriously? People this corrupt used to go to federal prison and now they get millions of dollars in bonuses. What in the holy hell happened? Oh yeah, right, we started electing bad actors and oil men from Houston and their friends to run our country. As far as the "oil shortages" we hear about on the news every other day...when was the last time you drove up to a gas station to buy over priced gas and they were "ALL OUT?" Like 1973 or 1978 right? It's a scam.

Soon Jessy and his crew were on route 5 and headed north toward Los Angeles at a good rate of speed. Because of the fact that the tires were all different sizes there is no way to tell you exactly how fast they were going but the speed limit was 55 miles per hour so best guess is somewhere between 75 and 80. They had a plan to attend to. This plan involved smoking up all the reefer before they got any where near LA. Everyone on board respected the police in San Diego but the cops in Los Angeles were like something out of a horror movie. A guy named Rodney King had an opinion on this subject. You would have to go all the way to New Orleans to find scarier police than the "blue crew" they had in Los Angeles at the time.

Someone brought a pocket size rolling machine and the guys in the back seat were turning out joints like union workers in a Carolina cigarette factory. Before long they had to roll down the windows to see the highway because of all the thick sweet smoke in the car. Cheech and Chong would have been proud of them as they cruised north with a white fog pouring out the windows. Jessy's copilots had carefully stashed a couple of doobies for the ride home as they rolled into the land of hopes and dreams.

Note: Jessy doesn't condone smoking pot and driving. He did it, He was wrong, and he's sorry but it's a good thing he wasn't drinking Bourbon that night or this story could have had a very different, sadder ending.

After a few wrong turns and a few requests for directions they arrived in front of the famous Shrine Auditorium. They were amazed that they hadn't wound up in Arizona or Alaska. Jessy was getting excited but something seemed very wrong as he circled the parking lot looking for a large space to park his car. Everyone they saw was dressed up in black suits and gowns like they were going to the "Oscars." Jessy found the answer as they passed the bill board that announced in big red letters that the butterfly showing that night turned out to be a Madame and not an Iron one. Jessy spun around and glared at Mike who had told everyone about the "Iron Butterfly" concert. The boys all yelled at Mike in unison as they loudly declared "Madame Butterfly? Are you fucking kidding me?"

They were stupefied! After having just driven a huge amount of miles, stoned, and now they had no where to go in a really scary city, a town without pity, this was so shitty. (sorry) At first Jessy was really pissed off at the situation and the absurd nature of Mike's error but before they knew it, slowly they started to smile and soon were all lost in a sea of ridiculous, pot induced, laughter. This went on for a while until everyone had snot bubbles on their noses. All was good with the world.

Slowly it was decided that someone had to come up with another plan. They were way to wasted to consider driving back to San Diego. Driving wasn't the problem but the car was so ridiculous it was a moving target for the state troopers and Jessy just wasn't looking forward to having an extremely uncomfortable conversation with one of California's finest at that moment.

The first bright idea came from Jessy and he said lets go find a party. It seemed reasonable at the time but this was LA. and they were lost, like in "where the hell are we" lost. They drove around for a while and wound up in a part of town called "Watts." The windows were rolled down and they could hear music so Jessy just followed the sound until they were outside a large building with a stairway leading up to a second floor club of some kind. Everyone was yelling at him to keep going but Jessy saw several very attractive young women going up the stairs and he was driving. They exited the blue and white Buick starship and climbed the stairs. The music was getting louder but Jessy still couldn't say he had heard any of the songs before. Fact was, he couldn't understand any of the words either. When they got to the top there was a landing with a very large man in a suit taking money at the door. He had a thin black mustache. The door man asked for ten dollars each in a very heavy Spanish accent. They all noticed at about the same time that they were the only Anglo faces at this party and a crowd of young well dressed young Spanish teenagers had gathered near the door waiting to see if they were going to let them in. They also noticed that the girls were all very young and a big neon sign that said, "TROUBLE" was blinking in their heads. They calmly retreated and lived to tell the story. Of all the lessons I may try to impart in this writing the most important of all is knowing how to identify and avoid a no-win situation.

As a group, all five in the traveling side show had suddenly become incredibly hungry so the decision was made to find a sit down restaurant and chow down for a while and wait for the effects of the marijuana to wear off.

After getting lost, or rather, even more lost, they came across a little diner beside the road called "FOOD." Please don't ask me "what road?" Don't ask me what planet for that matter. The "Food diner" was not destined to become a nation wide franchise.

This somewhat less than earthly diner was completely out of context in California and looked like it belonged along the docks in Baltimore, or Camden, but certainly not in the suburbs Los Angeles. In New Jersey the chrome would have been polished and all the neon lights would have been working but this was SoCal and the place looked like a scene from an apocalypse movie. As they entered the old run down diner, possibly where the expression "greasy spoon" came from. A chill ran down Jessy's spine all the way down to his rapidly shrinking nut sack. If you have ever seen an old black and white episode of "The Twilight Zone," it was sort of like that. Just imagine walking into a diner with a cast of fat zombies at the counter. They all tried to act natural but everyone in the diner was staring at them with looks of disgust on their bloated, scarred, pock marked, faces. Mike suggested they make a run for it but they were starved and Jessy said, optimistically "how bad can they screw up a hamburger anyway." Mike looked at Jessy and whispered "did you see those scary bastards at the counter? They got that way by eating here, man."

They shyly slid into a booth and waited for Mario who had gone missing somewhere. The menu was predictable with hamburgers, meat loaf, liver and onions, and some kind of stew that looked like it had been prepared with, "Out of town customer meat." Jessy decided on the hamburger with a side of onion rings and a vanilla shake. Mario quietly slipped into the booth and started checking out the menu. Mario was quite toasted and seemed extremely distracted but fascinated by the choices before him. He finally went with the grilled cheese. Mike ordered a chili dog. Frenchy had the tuna melt and Eric, ever cautious, just ordered apple pie and black coffee. Our waitress was a stone cold nightmare. Judging from the name tag on her discolored waitress attire, her name was Marge. Marge had a half smoked Chesterfield hanging from her dry cracked lips. She treated Jessy and his crew like five steaming piles goat shit but she took the order without a fuss. No smile no fuss.

They just sat there waiting for the food and Mike decides to tell a new joke he had just heard. In a really loud voice that you could hear out on the highway he says, "How do you get a dog to stop humping your leg?" No one had heard this one yet so they all asked in equally loud voices "I don't know Mike how do you get a dog to stop humping your leg?" After a well timed pause Mike exclaims "You just pick him up and give him a blow job." Another pause as the punch line sunk in and we all started laughing like lunatics including Mike and the cook, way back in the kitchen. This joke may not be funny by todays standards but it really helped relieve the tension. The other dinner guests glared at them like they were Satin's actual grand kids. At this point the comfort level was plunging rapidly but they wanted to eat so badly they would have stayed in that booth if a swat team had suddenly burst through the door launching tear gas canisters while blasting holes in all the ugly customers at the counter.

It seemed like it was going to take forever for the orders to arrive and Mike was freaking out so Jessy had to assure him that the cook wasn't done jerking off on his chili dog. Mike chuckled and relaxed because he thought Jessy was kidding...he wasn't. Just then the waitperson arrived with a giant dark brown fiberglass tray with some of the stuff they had ordered but mostly things they hadn't. She said, "Who ordered the chicken fried steak?" Jessy shook his head and said it was his because he couldn't stand to wait one more minute for some food, plus he didn't have the balls to send the order back to the kitchen in a place like this. They all settled for what ever wound up on the table and after a few trades dug into the meal before them like it was their last. Mike enjoyed his corn dogs but Eric was pissed off that they had given him pecan pie instead of apple and hot chocolate not black coffee. Jessy begged Eric to just relax and eat, and he would buy him anything he wanted when they got back to San Diego.

It was just then that a shrill voice started calling loudly for someone, or something named "Buttercup." The voice was coming from a very large woman in a print dress and a red, gravy stained, apron with the word "FOOD" in white letters on the front. They guessed this her place and she was calling a pet of some sort. She started asking everyone in the place if they had seen her cat "Buttercup." Jessy looked at his crew and everyone just shook their heads back and forth in a negative manner. Everyone that is except Mario who was looking around like he was reading a "Playboy magazine" in church. Jessy glared at him and shrugged his shoulders to gesture "hey man, what the hell did you do?" Mario rolled his eyes toward the front window and the big blue and white car parked right outside. This was when Jessy saw the giant black furry animal on his dashboard staring back at him. "Shit" Jessy thought to himself but he said it so loud inside his head he just knew someone had heard it. Mario did some weird stuff when he was stoned but he had crossed over the weird line this time and he knew it.

Jessy took one last bite of white sausage gravy covered, deep fried mystery meat and grabbed the check and signaled the boys that they were getting ready to hit the road. They quickly gathered up enough money to pay the check with a modest tip and hurried out the door to the car. Without being obvious Jessy opened the drivers side door and the huge black feline disappeared into the dark night. They jumped into the monster mobile and made a speedy retreat without spraying too many rocks on the pickup trucks and choppers in the parking lot. Less than a minute later they were back on the freeway and cruising at a high rate of speed toward South America...or San Diego, which ever came first.

They were a band of very relieved travelers after the escape from the horror show diner and the possible "catnapping" charges. Jessy was feeling confident that it would be clear sailing from here on. He had spent five dollars on a new tire and the spare was as good as any of the others they were riding on so they were home free. Mike whipped out a couple of joints he had cleverly hidden under the ashtray and lit them up. They passed the doobies around the car and soon everyone had a "smile on" in spite of the twisted turns the evening had taken up to that point.

The music was turned up, the windows rolled down and all Jessy had to do now was stay awake and get them all back home alive. The air felt good as the mile markers flew past at an alarming rate of speed. Jessy wondered why with all this wind blowing around the car was there so much smoke. About then his question was answered when everyone started screaming "FIRE, FIRE, the damn car is on Fire."

Yep, they were ablaze and the flames were coming from the back seat. Mike, Eric and Frenchy were back there so Jessy yelled "PUT IT OUT GOD DAMN IT."

Now. I must explain something. Mike was the 189 pound state wrestling champ in high school back in New Jersey. He was also pound for pound the strongest human being Jessy had ever met. They had wrestled each other at the park in La Jolla and Jessy found it was easier to grapple with a bridge than Mike. When Mike heard Jessy yelling "put it out" without waiting to consider other options he kicked the door open ripped up the back seat and started to shove it out of the car. This strategy had a simple charm to it except for the part where there were still two screaming idiots on the seat at the time. Jessy yelled for Mike to stop and put the fire out not the seat. The terror in the eyes of Jessy's passengers was making Jessy very uncomfortable but he spotted a road side gas station up ahead and he guided the flaming beast over to a water hose in the back of the parking lot. everyone jumped out and Jessy got the hose going and the fire was out in less than a minute. There was still some smoke but no one had been burned, thank God or Frank or who ever was on duty that evening. Did we mention that the writer is not a religious person? Besides, if there is a god he probably had bigger fish to fry than a minor foam rubber fire in the back seat of a sixty-five dollar 1956 Buick, or who is going to win the next Texas, Oklahoma football game for that matter.

One of Jessy's guests had dropped a lit "fatty" on the seat and had almost burned his car to the ground. No one would admit to the crime and Jessy wasn't going to call the cops. After some cleanup and swabbing out the water with an old shirt they found in the trunk everyone got back in the poor beat to shit car and headed on down the road. Someone started whining about the wet seats but Jessy wheeled around and warned them to just shut the fuck up or they could damn well walk back to town. Frenchy, who was deathly afraid of coyotes, was extremely quiet all the way back to the apartment.

All you could say about the good part of their strange journey that night is that no one riding in that magical car was killed, seriously injured or arrested. Jessy was reasonably certain that there were the same number of passengers when they got back to San Diego as there were when they had set off to Los Angeles.

CHAPTER 10

"And now, THE NEWS"

Mario and Jessy went out one day and scored a cheap, second hand TV set at the used stuff store. With the help of some free rabbit ears they found in the alley, a couple of rolled up wads of tin foil and a "slinky" they were able to get a fairly decent signal. None of the people in the apartment were big television fans at the time, however they did like to watch "Rowan & Martin's Laugh In" and Jessy loved the "Smothers Brothers" before they crossed the line in some idiot TV executives head and did one to many skits about current events and were thrown off TV forever. Back then some things were considered out of bounds. Commenting on the war in Viet Nam, or marijuana use, or of course sex were what the younger audience was craving at the time. The bad news was, when someone grew balls big enough to swim into those forbidden waters they would instantly be eaten by one of the sharks in your favorite network's headquarters. Sort of like it is now except for the sex, and the number of networks. Today the primetime shows are a lot sexier than in the sixties. Couples in sitcoms usually slept in separate beds back then.

Jessy was getting hooked on news about the war and he considered Walter Cronkite one hell of a news man. There were nightly updates on some of that days battles and the losses we were taking. We were loosing young people at a terrible rate and the Vietnamese were simply getting slaughtered. We were told the kill ratio was ten to one but by the end of the war our losses were around 56,000 as opposed to possibly over 2 Million Vietnamese. (that's closer to 36 to one) Way too many of the Vietnamese losses were innocent civilians. The army we were fighting at the end of the war was huge compared to the tiny band of gorillas we started out trying to defeat back when Eisenhower was president.

Note: This of course was before the complete corporate take over of the airwaves and you could get some fairly good reporting from the front lines back in the day. There were no Hooters girls from "Fox fake news" giving us the corporate spin on everything. I have nothing at all against the actual Hooters franchise. I'm very fond of the "Boneless wings." They also have an outstanding food delivery system. I however am really not a fan of the stuff that passes for news on the Fox network, or many of the new news networks these days. You can google Rupert Murdoch and see where that goes. Hint: Australia.

Jessy was beginning to see what his friend Aileen was trying to tell him when she conveyed her deep sadness about the war and its terrible effect on our country, plus the effect it was having on the country of Viet Nam and it's population was just unimaginable. Our military was destroying unknown numbers of lives of people we had never met, not to mention the lives of the soldiers we were shipping over there for mostly political and economic reasons. This was as we were just learning of our bombing of Cambodia, Kent State, and the Mi Lai massacre, when all holy hell broke loose. (Please Google these references if you aren't familiar with them.) The pot was just beginning to boil, so to speak. Jessy knew he had to do something very soon to make a statement but he was still trying to decide just how, and when, and where that statement should be made.

CHAPTER 11

The Letter

Fate was about to make its grand entrance, and something as innocent as a simple letter from the war zone would have a profound affect on Jessy's life forever. One warm evening as he was walking back to the line shack after a launch Jessy saw his friend Bobby who seemed to be very upset over the letter he was reading. He asked Bobby if everything was OK and then noticed there were tears in Bobby's eyes. Jessy also noticed that his letter had no stamp on the envelope. He told Jessy that the letter was from his brother who was serving in Viet Nam. His brother was a marine and was stationed at a small airbase near Saigon. He had smuggled the letter back to bobby by way of a sailor who was being rotated back to the states. The mail is a sacred trust here in the USA but you give up all of that shit when you join up. Letters were censored, and some mail just never showed up if the wrong sentiments were being expressed. This was one of those letters. At first Bobby was hesitant about telling Jessy what was in his letter but he realized that if anyone would understand what he was feeling it would be Jessy. By now the other sailors Jessy worked with knew how he felt about the war and Bobby really needed to share this story with another person who cared.

In this particular letter, Bobby's brother was describing a mission aboard a Chinook helicopter. His squad had been ordered to capture, detain and question some villagers from a hamlet that was suspected of hiding some number of enemy soldiers. He was the new guy among a group of old hands and he was expected to go along with the program. He was told this was going to be a routine mission. The team flew into the village and promptly rounded everyone up without a fight. Men, women and children were lined up in a kneeling position on the ground and searched. These people were simple farmers and no enemy troops could be found.

Historical note: The Viet Cong played a dangerous game with the poor rice farmers and simple villagers of their own country. They would march into one of the thousands of small hamlets that dotted the landscape and set up shop for a few days while they rested and stocked up on rice and other free supplies that they could appropriate from the helpless "village people" (No not them). "The home team" would leave after a short visit followed almost immediately by the uninvited guests from the magical kingdom far away where Levi's come from. Naturally the Americans would assume that the villagers were guilty of harboring the enemy and they would have to pay in some profound way for their crimes. Our Army would exact justice of one form or another and in at least some cases with war crimes of their own. Often the easy way was to whip out some "Zippo" Lighters and just torch the village. Sometimes someone with a medium amount of power would make a decision to do something to leave a more lasting impression on the people we were trying to protect from the "Red Menace." One such incident was the "My Lai Massacre," where Lt. Calley and his men murdered, raped, and tortured an entire village during the war. Calley was given a life sentence for premeditated murder but he only served three years of house arrest before being pardoned by president Richard Nixon. "Nice move Dick." What if two of the girls who were raped and machine gunned that day had been Julie and Trish? Would you have pardoned Calley then? Look at me, I'm getting all down on some dead president who can't defend himself because of the whole dead thing. That is just plain wrong on so many levels but that crooked prick always pissed me off. I'm sorry.

After a careful decision making process, the American soldiers singled out five villagers at random, sort of. There were three young teenaged boys, one old man, and an attractive, young girl, perhaps fifteen or sixteen years old. The soldiers tied their prisoners hands and shoved them into the helicopter, and then they lifted off. The pilot took them up to one thousand feet and hovered while the soldiers began to "question" the villagers. They asked the old man a few questions about the location of the Viet Cong enemy forces and so on but got no answers just a long winded speech in Vietnamese spoken out of fear and desperation that none of the Americans understood. The soldiers got really pissed off and grabbed the old man and threw him out the door, screaming, still in Vietnamese. Bobby's brother freaked out and yelled at the others to stop, but it was way past late now.

The other guys told him he'd better "Shut the fuck up and get up to speed." or he would be next. One by one they grabbed another poor villager, rattled off some bullshit questions and when they didn't get a proper answer in English. Fooom, another poor farmer in black PJ's went skydiving without a parachute. Finally, when they were down to the young girl, they didn't even go through the formality of interrogating her. They simply took turns holding her down and raping her. When they were done she was crying and screaming for her life but that didn't stop them from tossing her, mostly naked, out of the open chopper door. Her cries of terror faded as she vanished into the forest canopy far below. Bobby's brother wanted to jump out after her but he didn't. He just flew back to base in silence and wrote his brother a letter.

Bobby's brother was truly forever damaged by the experience and getting the letter out to the real world was a form of penance. Poor Bobby was horrified and really didn't know what to do with the information. He looked up to his older sibling and this news was stuck half way into his brain and there just wasn't any room for the other half. After reading the letter both young men had tears in their eyes. Jessy felt so bad for Bobby and tried to imagine what it would be like to find out someone he was so close to had that kind of weight to bear for the rest of their lives. Later in his life Jessy worked for several years in a Veterans hospital and spoke to a number of veterans who had similar tales and has seen that look in their eyes as if a part of their life was lost over there. Some call it the "thousand mile stare." These guys look off into the distance at nothing at all and that stare is like an open window to the pain in their heart and the incurable wound in their soul. It's like they are trying to reach out but most of them can never bring themselves to expose the horror of what they did or witnessed over there. "Over there" is all the same. Viet Nam, Cambodia, Panama, Somalia, Iraq, Afghanistan, it doesn't matter. War is a special kind of hell and the only thing that changes is the shade of brown the people you are paying your tax money to have eliminated.

This whole story came back on Jessy and the horror of what we were doing to the Vietnamese people started to sink in. Jessy recalled some of the gruesome stories that his crazy assed marine math instructor had told him back in "A" school. He thought to himself what if he had been born and raised in Viet Nam and that was his sister or daughter who was raped and murdered by those murdering assholes on the helicopter. You could bet that the next time an American chopper or jet or truck or American soldier came anywhere near him, and he had access to a weapon, he would be shooting it in their direction. Jessy had a personal connection to all of this. Jessy had grown up in the same house with a Chinese family living down stairs. The mom was beautiful and very smart and they became close friends. Jessy would watch her two sons when she went out and the boys were like his little brothers. They were both athletic and smart and would become successful in their lives to come. Because of this Jessy had a real hard time when his fellow sailors would go off on a racist rant about "slants" and "slopes" and "gooks." After a while the people who used those words and other hurtful shit knew not to do it around Jessy. Those people weren't all from Alabama, Mississippi, and Texas. Many of the worst offenders were from the northeast states of New York, Pennsylvania, Massachusetts, and of course New Jersey. Hate comes in all colors but once you realize that fact you can choose not to be an asshole.

In retrospect there is no mystery to the fact that the North Vietnamese army was a thousand times larger at the end of the war than it was when we first sent advisors over there in the late fifty's. President Eisenhower was the first to sound the alarm about the "Red menace" and the "Giant dominoes" fairy tail, as reasons to wage war in southeast Asia, but at least he was a cautious man and was also the first to warn the American people to the dangers of the "military industrial complex, and to beware of a world based on perpetual war." John F. Kennedy saw the war as a tool that he could use to show the world how dedicated we were to stopping communist aggression. However, Kennedy was a very smart guy and he came to realize that continuing to send more money and young lives to Viet Nam was a horrible misadventure. Personally I believe that is why, more than anything else, he became a "dead Kennedy."

Note: War should always be the option of last resort unless of course you are the CEO of a company that makes fighter jets, bombs, rockets, tanks, military warships, or killer laser beams mounted on 747 aircraft.

Jessy spent the next few days letting the letter sink in. I'm sure he smoked a fair amount of pot that weekend, He really couldn't remember. Then of course if he could remember, than he didn't smoke nearly enough pot. Somehow he was able to come up with a plan. It was a two part plan. The first part of the plan was drive the big fat Buick over to "Mickey Dee's" and get a couple of Big Mac's, and a big bag of salty fries at the drive up. Thinking back it's quite possible that he washed it down with a vanilla shake and a couple of greasy tacos from "Jack in the Box." Jessy can still remember a way to long conversation with that stupid clown head that sounded like it was three feet under water. This was his "last meal," like the one you get in prison before they walk you down the hall, because the second part of his plan took his breath away when he first considered it.

Jessy was fully aware that some time soon he would be getting an order to report to some big assed floating airfield for his tour in Viet Nam. He also knew that he wouldn't be able to obey that order.

His mind kept flashing on the news footage of our F4's coming in low over some village and letting loose with "napalm" canisters and watching as someone's sad little town went up in a giant ball of orange flames and black smoke. Children on fire running for their lives. Jessy just could not let himself be part of that insane picture. So Jessy developed his plan. He figured that you couldn't go to jail for disobeying an order he had never been given. Jessy made the decision to protest the order before receiving it.

The following night Jessy showed up for his late shift at about 15:30 or (3:30 in the afternoon) There was a short inspection that went badly for him, due to the "Peace Sign" he had artfully painted on his olive drab foul weather jacket. After failing inspection, he strolled into the sort of green sort of grey line shack and grabbed a request form from a plastic holder on the wall. The holder was above the molding so it was sort of green. An enlisted man only had access to one "form" no matter what it was that he needed or wanted. If you wished to take a vacation, or needed a new pair of "boon dockers," (feet killing low cut boots) or a request to be transferred to a new duty station, you had to fill out the same 4" X 6" request form or "chit" as it was called.

Jessy filled out the "request chit" and walked it into his supervisor's office. This person was an "old salt" who had been in the navy since the Navy stopped using oars to power their ships. He was still only a first class petty officer which meant that he probably had been a chief at least once or twice but had been busted back down to first class because of some drunken brawl or perhaps he got caught skin to skin with some officer's lonely spouse. At any rate he was nearing retirement and was simply trying to stay out of trouble long enough to keep a decent pension that he could collect while working for the post office.

As Jessy quietly handed the chit to his supervisor he took a step back as the first class P.O. read it. Jessy was prepared to make a run for it if it looked like his superior petty officer was going to blow a vein in his neck or something. He was old but still quite deadly and there were several heavy objects in the office that could come flying in Jessy's direction in an instant. Jessy was on all his toes as he eyed the disarmed hand grenade on the desk. The first class petty officer finished reading the form and he shook a little before throwing the thing to the floor. Then, quietly he said, "Now son, you pick that up and walk it into the lieutenant's office...I never saw it." He raised his voice one precise octave and said, "Do you understand me?" Jessy nodded and bent down picked up the paper and walked up to the wooden door with the frosted glass window and knocked on it three times, like a secret code knock. Very slow, very precise and deliberate, as if his life depended on the way he knocked on that door. The lieutenant's voice was calm and cool as he gave Jessy his permission to enter his office. Jessy carefully opened the door and stepped through the doorway and into the darkened room where the officer behind the desk started to size him up. From what Jessy knew of him he was a good, fair, and honest man and a boy scout who hopefully could be trusted. He was a straight shooter and in a way Jessy hated doing to him what he was about to do. Jessy paused when he took in what was going down and how this would affect his young Lieutenants life. Jessy handed him the request chit and he took it calmly and began to read the short but deadly words.

The request form had a place for your name and the date and line for your service number and a few lines for the actual request followed by a line for your signature followed by a line for the signature of your superior officer. The exact verbiage is a little fuzzy after all this time, but basically Jessy had written that he was requesting he be reassigned a non-critical roll in the Navy due to his own personal beliefs and that he would not be available to help kill any more of the people of Viet Nam. The Lieutenant took a deep breath and sat back in his chair and just looked at Jessy as if to say, "Do you realize what you are doing to me?" Jessy just nodded to acknowledge that he did. The Lieutenant shook his head and asked Jessy to please leave his office. Jessy turned and slowly walked out into the warm California sun. The Lieutenant was bound buy the rules. He could have easily torn up the stupid little piece of paper and told Jessy to fuck off as was tradition in the service but he was an honorable man and he chose to process Jessy's request. He knew all to well the implications that went with it. Jessy's brave lieutenant made the decision to process the request, and was transferred to sea duty in Viet Nam a week later. It could have been worse.

Jessy really had no idea what would happen next. No one that he knew had ever done anything like this before and Portsmouth naval prison is full of people who had committed less severe crimes than refusing to fight the war. As it turns out, no one that anybody knew, knew somebody that had done something exactly like this in the history of, well...history. Of course Mormons, and Amish, and Black Muslims had been pulling out the ever popular conscientious objector card for a long time, but Jessy's case was different. He didn't have any objection to defending the country from foreign invaders. He had no religious objections whatsoever. This had nothing to do with some deep belief in God or any of his close or distant relatives.

Jessy did however have a problem with invading another country on what turned out to be false pretenses. He still does have a problem with that idea to this day." Ahem, Mr. Cheney, and your dopey little hand puppet George. What in holy hell were you guys thinking? ... Iraq? ... Afghanistan? ... Seriously?"

The very next day Jessy was transferred back to the day shift. No more sunny days at the beach observing the wonderful effect that the sun's rays have on the female body. The next day after that Jessy was walking out to his big Buick for lunch with a couple of guys from the line. It was really hot and as they approached the car they noticed that there were two men in dark suits climbing all over the interior. There was this rather large ass pushed up against the rear window and they could see someone else all upside down under the steering wheel. Instantly Jessy decided that they walk to the chow hall and take a very long lunch. Something was obviously going sideways and he needed some time to figure out exactly what it was. Jessy and his two friends agreed that the suits rummaging around in Jessy's car were agents from CID or NCIS. Jessy never locked his car. There was nothing to steal including the car and he could always use the zero security feature as a defense against illegal search and seizure.

Note: When you are in the military ALL searches are legal. You don't have any normal legal rights especially on base.

The Criminal Investigation Division (CID) is a little recognized and hardly ever heard of part of the military while NCIS (Naval Criminal Investigation service) gets all the glory and cool TV shows. The guys who bravely serve in the CID must ponder how they wound up where they were and not in the FBI. Jessy and his mates took an extra long time eating and properly digesting their first class steak lunch and returned to the car about two hours later. By that time the two guys who were "Rousting Jessy's Ride" were all spent and sweaty. The sun was high and hot. The agents had long since lost the dark jackets and their ties were all loose and pulled to one side like they had just helped some fat lady give birth to twins in the back seat of a Gremlin. Jessy told his friends to get back to work and then he wandered up to the old car like he was completely surprised to see two grown men all tired and sweaty leaning on his Buick. The two burned out men identified themselves as CID agents and they said that they had found evidence in his car. That evidence was going to get Jessy in "some kind of very bad trouble." The detectives held up this extra super large evidence envelope that was about sixteen inches wide and twenty-four inches long and told Jessy to get in their piece of shit, grey Ford Pinto. Jessy had only paid sixty-five dollars for his Buick and he could have gotten four or five of those Pinto's for his car on a flat trade.

They all carefully climbed into that awful, tiny, cramped, grey, turd of a car and the two detectives drove to a small grey concrete building over by the front gate of the base. They had hand cuffed Jessy because he was clearly a threat to the American way of life. He slowly emerged from the back seat. (not an easy chore when your hands are handcuffed behind you) then he followed one of the agents into this embarrassingly small office with the traditional two tone paint job only this one was dark grey on the bottom and light grey on the top. Jessy was about to make some free decorating suggestions when they introduced him to a tall scary looking officer.

He was wearing a commanders uniform and looked like he was about to do some business on Jessy. This process was worrisome for two reasons. First, these people, such as they were, had great power over Jessy. then there was the part where they were waving this giant envelope in his face as they began their questioning.

Jessy's car was clean, he knew, because he had cleaned that two ton piece of American steel and was sure that he had cleansed the beast of all the roaches and stray joints after that last road trip. Of course there had been a fire, and sure Jerry the state wrestler from New Jersey had tried to throw the whole flaming back seat out of the car while they were doing eighty miles per hour on the freeway coming back from the "not a concert." Sure, there were two screaming friends sitting on that seat at the time but after the madness Jessy gave the monster a real good working over. He knew there wasn't any pot in the glove compartment because they had smoked it all on the way home.

The still sweaty agents made their case to the commander that they had found evidence and that they wanted to open a case against Jessy. The commander asked them to produce their evidence and they proceeded to open the evidence envelope and turned it up side down over a large piece of paper on the desk. They shook it, they wiggled it, they tapped it on the side, they tapped it on the top, and so on for a few minutes. Jessy looked at the commander and shrugged his shoulders. The commander looked back and raised his up turned hands and shook his head like "who the fuck are these ass holes?" Just then they all heard a faint but absolute sound. Something had finally fallen out of the envelope. It was very small and round and black. One glance and Jessy recognized it as a pot seed. The black color meant it was probably involved in the seat fire and was likely imbedded in the melted foam rubber which explained why he had missed it when he did his house cleaning. Jessy felt much better now that the huge mystery had been solved.

The commander hesitated and finally said "Are you people fucking serious? Do you really expect me to charge this man with drug possession over THAT?" and he glared at the tiny pitiful charred shred of toasted greenery on the desk. The detectives said "It's what we found." They both walked to his end of the room and whispered something to the commander so that Jessy couldn't hear. He knew by now what was going on and they were pleading their case based on the fact that Jessy was a dirty war resisting communist and had to be stopped before he brought down the entire democratic system as they knew it. Jessy was a public menace and would have to be incarcerated, shot, hung and then spend the rest of his life in the electric chair. All they could do for the time being however was reassign him to a non-critical job while they built a case against him. As it turned out this was a huge stroke of luck and Jessy's Naval career was about to take a really sharp turn to the weird.

There was a process to all of this crazy bullshit and Jessy was instructed to go to the legal department on base and have them assign a military lawyer to handle his defense.

Jessy was provided with government issue legal counsel. (Lawyer, beige, 5'9", cheap grey suit, one each) His legal counsel would have reminded Jessy of the public defender in the movie "My Cousin Vinny" but it didn't because that movie wouldn't come out until 1992 and this was 1969. This guy was constantly uncomfortable and repeated himself so often one might think perhaps he was experiencing some kind of stroke. The two very different men had a short sit down meeting where the lawyer took some notes and told Jessy he would need to be patient and that it may take a while for him to get their case together. Jessy didn't see that dumb little sorry lawyer ever again. Rather than prolong the agony I'll tell you now that the government had zero evidence against him. The poor sad little seed was burned up so badly that there wasn't anything to run through the lab, either that or some clumsy military cop had accidentally dropped the seed down the sink. One way or another Jessy was eventually going to be cleared of his terrible crime only he wouldn't know it for nearly two years and this had absolutely nothing to do with him having a government issue lawyer paid for by taxpayers. For the remainder of his enlistment Jessy would be under a very expensive taxpayer funded investigation including some kind of surveillance.

Note: American people who get up and go to work every day, pay taxes on the money they earn. The elected officials of our nation decide how to spend those taxes, hopefully, for the benefit of the people. Things that benefit the people: schools and universities, hospitals and clinics, public welfare services, fire and police departments, infrastructure, roads and bridges, water/sewerage networks, electrical grids, parks, libraries and many more fine ways to spend taxpayer dollars. Things that don't benefit the people: an out of control military industrial complex and for some reason paying government agencies to follow Jessy around.

The government assigned a team of agents to try to find out who Jessy was and why he didn't want to kill people for them. It is truly unbelievable... the crazy assed shit that the feds spent our money on, especially when you had a real live paranoid lunatic like Nixon in the White House. The FBI sent a few agents to Jessy's home town in New Jersey and they proceeded to question everyone from his parents to his football coach. To this very day there are people who don't communicate with him because of those agents and their dark suits and sunglasses. Thanks FBI, and thanks to the poor taxpayers of who...most of us are. The worst part was and still is that the people we should be keeping an eye on are running the country. The sad truth is that the people who decide who gets their phones tapped and who gets to have people follow us around all day are the very people we should be locking in a little concrete rooms for ever and ever Amen.

Almost immediately after his interview with the lawyer Jessy began to notice strangers in cheap suits who were just across the street or down the block, or following him two cars back as he drove to and from the base. Remember this "It isn't paranoia when they really are out to get you." One morning Jessy was about to leave for work when he noticed a dirty white Chevy Nova with no hub caps parked just down the street from the apartment. There was someone in the in the car reading, or pretending to read a newspaper. He didn't know for sure if this was his tail because they switched agents all the time. Just for fun Jessy decided to confront him in the most unexpected way possible. He made some coffee and poured two cups with cream and sugar, then carried them both down the sidewalk. As Jessy approached the car all he could see was the news paper, but up close he noticed a cigarette hole burned right in the middle. He walked over to the drivers side window and tapped on the glass. The driver set the paper aside and rolled down the window and Jessy handed him one of the coffees. The agent just looked at him like he was from another planet. Jessy simply said. "Have a good day pal, enjoy your coffee, sorry but we are all out of doughnuts" Then he smiled, walked to his car, got in, started up the big Buick, and with a couple of back fires and a cloud of smoke he was on his way to see what they had in store for him back at the base.

CHAPTER 12

Special Services

Overnight Jessy had been transferred to a new department on base called "Special Services." Never to be confused with "Special Forces." He reported to an office, just off the lobby of the base movie theatre. There were no inspections in special services. There were no rules in special services or much of any organized structure at all for that matter. Jessy soon found that everyone assigned to special services had "royally screwed the pooch" in one form or another. The year was 1969 and most of the other guys in this group had been charged with pot possession. This meant that the strange little "band of busted brothers" had been pulled over with some amount of grass or another. In this case,... his case,... revolved loosely around a little burned up seed, while the guy who operated the base bowling alley got stopped trying to cross the border with thirty-two kilo's of weed.

People usually didn't get busted for LSD or THC or mescaline, mostly because they were the kind of thing you could swallow at the last second when you noticed the circus of city cops chasing you down the freeway. However a bag of weed went down real slow, especially when you were trying to answer questions fired at you by the police or the shore patrol. Jessy however was a special case because his status was considered political, that and the fact that his legal issue hadn't even gone to trial so he was still a third class petty officer. Third class PO is way down next to the bottom of a very tall flag pole. Not the bottom of the pole but pretty damn close and yet Jessy had rank over the other sailors in the unit. Ironic is just a word but this was "Dead clown ironic." Jessy was in way deeper shit than almost anyone else and yet he was more or less in charge. Jessy realized how lucky he was, being in charge of other people and not in a military prison yard. Not that any of this was a good thing but somehow was still kind of cool.

Because he was sort of the new kid on the block Jessy had to depend on a few people who he could trust to show him the ropes. There was a tall skinny guy named Dave who Jessy instantly became friends with. Dave was always smiling and laughing. Dave had the most devious grin and he made you want to be in on what ever it was he was grinning about. Jessy chose Dave to be his spirit guide to the "special services" universe. Dave always had a fresh joint behind one ear that probably explained all the grinning.

Special services was not what Jessy expected and he was astounded by the scope of their responsibilities. They started each day at the movie theatre and made sure that everything was clean and ship shape for the afternoon matinee. They had to inspect the theatre to be sure the night crew had done a thorough job of cleaning up after the late showing of the movie of the week. The crew also restocked the concession stand and ran a shop vacuum around the lobby. When they were done Dave and Jessy got in a grey Chevy pickup truck and headed off to one of many locations in a very specific order depending on certain variables. For instance, if it had rained the night before the first place they went was the officers tennis courts and they took four foot wide squeegees and dried the courts so that, heaven forbid, some "Top Gun" officer wouldn't get his "Converse tennis shoes" wet, or slip and fall and break his shiny white ass. The enlisted men had to play on wet courts if they wanted to play that bad. To be honest most enlisted men didn't play tennis when the courts were dry.

Note: there may have been black pilots back then but they were a rare breed. Tuskegee Alabama is famous for two things. First they gave syphilis to 400 black men in 1932 and didn't tell them why. 100 of those men died. Second they formed an all black squadron of pilots to protect our bombers in the second world war. The "Red Tail" squadron had an outstanding record while fighting off German aircraft and allowing a large number of American Bombers to safely complete their missions. There were 600 Black helicopter pilots in Viet Nam but not many flew jets. In Viet Nam Jet pilots got all the glory while helicopters ran search and rescue missions and got shot down...like quail at a Texas bird hunting ranch.

The next stop on the route was the bowling alley where they would pick up Dave's friend Terry and drive out to the car wash. The car wash was just a quonset hut with both ends knocked out so you could wash your personal vehicle in the shade. Here they would pull into the shelter and spark up a "doobie" and get their "smiles warmed up." Most of the time the next stop involved a trip off base to the closest "Taco Bell," "Jack in the box," or of course the ever popular "Mickey D's," for a "Big Mac". However the "Bell" had the best deal if you were really hungry. You could get four of anything for a dollar. Four taco's, four burrito's, four bell burgers, four tostado's or any combination. Taco Bell was very popular with sailors, hippies, and street people alike.

After the morning break Jessy and Dave would drop Terry off before anyone noticed he was gone. Not like that was ever going to happen. Next Dave and Jessy would cruse over to the base car shop to hang out with an off duty "Hells Angel" who everyone called "dick finger." Not to his face and not because his first name was Richard, or that his last name was Finger. The true story was that when he was younger he had blown off his right index finger in an unfortunate M80 (giant firecracker) mishap. When the doctors tried to sew the thing back together it wound up looking just like a short stubby hard on. I'm sure it probably was not intentional and they didn't charge him any extra for it. I'm also reasonably certain that his girl friends found his disability something they could live with.

Dick finger worked on the trucks and was a serious biker and a truly amazingly gifted mechanic. Jessy and Dave would tear up their trucks something awful during one of their escapes from the base police. After laying low for the appropriate interval they would sneak their bent and broken vehicle over to the car shop and after taking an extra large portion of cursing out (if you've never been verbally abused by a Hells Angel you have not lived a full life) They would watch in awe as Mr. finger would tear into the truck and have it back up and working like new in no time flat. It was like being back stage at a "NASCAR" event.

After the car shop it was time for lunch at the chow hall. The road trip for fast food was just a mid morning snack, but the chow hall was food heaven. You may think I'm joking but, seriously, the food on base was awesome. The Miramar chow hall had won awards for having the best food in the US military. Even the chipped beef on toast was delicious. At Miramar they didn't refer to this traditional GI meal as "shit on a shingle" like they did every where else.

The only unpleasant part of the chow hall experience was the "apple watch." The Navy paid a sailor to get all dressed up in his white summer uniform, with a yellow lanyard over his shoulder and a night stick to protect our nation's apples. It was the job of the apple watch to make sure no one took two or more pieces of fruit. Really? You could take all you wanted on lobster, or king crab day, but if you put two apples on your tray the apple watch was on you like...grey paint on...well everything. Everyone hated the apple watch because he took his job way to seriously. His favorite line was "If you have a problem, meet me after work at Judo class." As fate would have it, and quite by accident, Jessy managed to do just that.

One particular afternoon Jessy took a friend up on his invitation to try out the Judo school. This person knew Jessy was a wrestler in high school and he reasoned that Jessy might enjoy the experience. He had to put on a short white bath robe (gi) and white short pajama pants. The instructors lined up the whole class and since Jessy was the new guy he had to fight every one in order to find out where he would fit in. They started with the easiest and each opponent got progressively better. Jessy defeated all but one of the students using his wrestling skills plus some totally made up shit. When the last guy stepped up he realized it was the apple watch. Jessy hadn't recognized him out of his white uniform and night stick.

Suddenly the fruit cop started screaming some crazy Japanese stuff and came running across the mat like he wanted to kill somebody. Jessy waited until the very last second and when the apple watch was just close enough Jessy used all that forward momentum and picked him up and slammed him to the floor. The screaming changed from Japanese to loud American cursing and screaming almost instantly and continued for what witnesses considered "Way To Fucking Long." He had suffered a broken collar bone and the class got real ugly after that. They dragged the sobbing "fruit dispenser" off to the infirmary and the black belt instructor stepped onto the mat and tightened the belt on his robe and motioned Jessy to the center of the mat. The teacher was a scary looking older "lifer." (someone who joins the military for ever) This hardened warrior looked like a bald Clint Eastwood. They bowed and circled each other until the teacher made a move where he grabbed Jessy's robe by the collar and rolled backwards in an attempt to throw Jessy out the front door. Jessy didn't know that much about Judo but he had good balance and basic instinct told him to place a foot between the instructors legs and drop on top of him. That part worked to perfection. If they were wrestling Jessy could have pinned the guy but in Judo you have to hold your opponents shoulders down for like three days. Jessy was doing his best to pin the master when the instructor reached up and grabbed the collar on Jessy's robe with both hands and choked him with it. This technique turned Jessy off like a light switch. Just so you know, your brain needs a constant flow of oxygenated blood to work properly, or at all for that matter.

Jessy really had no idea how long he was asleep but when he woke up everyone was standing around like he was a pile of money. Jessy slowly got to his feet and tried to figure out where the hell he was. What ever happened after that is a little fuzzy but he did remember not ever going back to Judo class…ever. Jessy was however somewhat of a folk hero with the guys in the chow hall after that. The apple watch had his arm in a sling for quite some time and was rather timid from that point on. Jessy of course, stocked up on apples like they were gold doubloons at Mardi Gras.

After lunch Dave and Jessy would drive out past the golf course and down a dirt road to the fish pond. The fish pond was a small lake stocked with trout that was a secret to almost every one, like no one was ever there. Perhaps the absence of anglers had something to do with the fact that, on base, there was absolutely nothing you could do with a fish once you caught one. They were on a friggin Navy base for Christ sakes. It's not like a sailor could take a trout back to the barracks and light a fire in the middle of the day room and have a fish fry. This was before the popularity of sushi in America. Consequently the fish pond was deserted most of the time.

Now and then they got to stock the pond with new fish from a hatchery somewhere far away. So far away that a good number of the fish were already dead or dying when they dumped them from the truck mounted container into the lake. Jessy and Dave then tried to jump start as many "floaters" as they could by swishing them through the water by hand and forcing the water into their gills. Despite their best efforts they still wound up in a row boat skimming dead fish out of the pond with a net in one hand and a doobie in the other. This wasn't exactly what Jessy had imagined when he joined the Navy but they were in a boat and this was better than helping to kill people who never did anything to them. Dave and Jessy spent many hours smoking pot, telling stories and successfully staying out of everyone's way. There is an art involved with staying out of the way and Dave and Jessy were artists. Dave was Andy Warhol and Jessy was Van Gogh. They disappeared in the morning like smoke on a breezy day, they covered their tracks, touched all the bases, and knew exactly when it was important to be somewhere.

One of the places they knew they had to be was the warehouse detail. The Commander who ran special services also ran a private impromptu supply operation on base. He was a bit of a crook on some level and Dave and Jessy were his trusted minions. He was well aware that Dave and Jessy had their quirks and secrets and they knew that he knew. It all made for a finely tuned mixture of trust, mistrust, obedience, fear and loathing. While complicated the arrangement ran like a good knock off of a Swiss watch.

A call would come in to the movie theatre at exactly 08.00 hours. (8:00 AM) The call involved some very expensive piano or billiards table or sometimes just a big crate that needed to be loaded onto a certain sized trailer from a ship that had just docked at the ship yard downtown.

Due to some very good fortune Jessy had earned a license that allowed him to drive just about every kind of land vehicle that the Navy owned including dump trucks and tractors. He was the logical choice whenever a driver was needed and Dave was his logical shotgun. They were a team like in the buddy movies and no one ever even thought of them working alone on one of their "Projects." They would drive down to the San Diego Naval docks then out toward a specific the dock and then pull onto the pier along side some big grey ship. All of a sudden, like magic, a crane would drop their cargo into the bed of the truck or trailer. There was no paper work, no questions, no names, just a load of stuff that they then drove over to the marine base at North Island, across the Coronado bridge past the place where Navy seals come from. Once there they would make their way to a warehousing area and hunt down their contact.

The North Island guy was named Chief Manny and he looked like someone from an episode of McCales Navy. He had a large brimmed hat with fish hooks, football tickets and a pack of cigarettes. There were also a couple of live 44 caliber cartridges. His fishing vest had dozens of little pockets that were all full of something but only a few had things that you could see, like the three Cuban cigars in the pocket over his heart. He wore a huge Bowie knife and had a Colt, 1911, 45 caliber semi-automatic military issue pistol in a holster on his belt and I'm guessing a big heavy 44 caliber derringer in one of his boots. He was like a walking sports store. You would not have been surprised if he had unzipped his fly and an inflatable canoe popped out.

Jessy arranged for the chief's workers to unload the piano, or pool table, or pallet of pinocle cards, and then they would reload the truck with some other crazy assed traded cargo. They discovered that their commander was a master of the rules of supply and demand and that huge quantities of anything had inherent value. If you corner the market on some commodity like size 10 bowling shoes, well then, you are the "size 10 bowling shoe godfather." This may sound stupidly mundane but their commander had the market cornered on so much shit that he commanded some real power over anyone who wanted almost anything. They once drove back to the base with a marble statue of a hot naked Greek goddess and two tons of rubber bands. If you had all the rubber bands in the Navy you had real power over anyone who needed a rubber band. Please don't get me started on why any one would ever need ten thousand tubes of "Dr. Johnson's Joy Jelly." Jessy and Dave didn't ask questions, they just carted all this crap back to the base and unloaded what ever the hell it was into the special services own giant warehouse back at the base. Dave bet Jessy that the naked marble statue was going to wind up in the commanders rose garden.

Dave and Jessy hardly ever personally touched any of the stuff they hustled to and fro since there were always plenty of low ranking sailors, who Jessy had some authority over. He could make them do pretty much what ever he wanted them to do. It was kind of like being a slave owner except for the whole whipping thing. Jessy just told them to do it and they did it. Power is a drug and some people got off on bossing people around but Jessy always felt guilty whenever he told someone to do something that he wasn't willing to do himself. This particular trait isn't something you would want to put on a resume. This is just an observation based on personal experience.

Special services was a dumping ground for the human refuse that had screwed up so badly that the only evidence that they had once held any rank at all was the insignia shaped unfaded area on their shirt sleeves.

You would think that the sailors hanging around the loading dock would cringe when Jessy and Dave showed up with tons of rubber bands, or golf balls, or size 10 bowling shoes, but they jumped up the minute the truck pulled into the lot. I'm not sure if they were trying to redeem themselves for the crimes they had committed or perhaps they knew that as soon as they were done unloading the truck Jessy would repay their efforts by sparking up a joint or two and hanging out with them until it was time to go back to the movie theatre. Jessy always believed that keeping the spirits of the young men and women who defend our shores at a "high" level. Some would think the military would do more to improve morale among the troops. For the most part, the troops have always done just fine when left to their own devices, thank you very much.

All the while, Jessy and Dave were doing their part to protect our country from the dreaded "commies." As taxpayers who read this story some may think that your money was just getting flushed down the toilet but I will have you know that this country didn't get "nuked" once and Russia didn't invade us even the least little bit while Jessy was getting paid to defend it. Coincidence? Well...you be the judge.

CHAPTER 13

The Golf Course

When you are in the service you are provided with all the basics. Food, shelter and health care are not a concern as long as you stay on the base. The small pay check you receive every two weeks is enough to cover your expenses. You can pay for cheap bad haircuts, cheap on base movies, Cokes and snacks, laundry expenses and of course cigarettes. Most of the money spent on base went for beer at the enlisted men's club. Jessy didn't drink much beer and he didn't smoke so he was one rich sailor minus the ton of quarters he spent calling home on the pay phones. That was at least until he got that whiff of freedom from outside the fence.

If one chooses to move off base all the rules change and you need to come up with extra money to pay for a vehicle, gas, rent, food, and some entertainment. This usually meant getting some shitty part time job like the one you had in high school. In 1968 part time pay was $2.50 an hour if you were lucky. There were plenty of jobs for those willing to work...for less. If you didn't mind working like a coolie for junk wages you could scrounge up enough to make ends meet. Some guys, of course, took the easy road and sold or transported pot because it was, well...easy, and profitable. The war on drugs provided jobs that required a minimum amount of time and effort. Jessy, on the other hand, was born with a fatal flaw. Jessy grew up with the words, "If you work really, really, hard, you just might succeed in life. But don't get your hopes up." Those words from his step dad were ringing in his ears and were words to live by and no one can fault Jessy's stepdad for screaming them at him every chance he got. As someone who, has since worked more man hours in his life than all the people who built the Empire State Building combined, (perhaps a slight exaggeration) Jessy took those words to heart and started signing up for anything that offered a pay check.

When Jessy was old enough he began working jobs that would make todays young people run away in terror. He started out mowing lawns and shoveling snow. Later Jessy found work in factory's that put perfume and hairspray in spray bottles and cans. This is where he learned to drive a fork lift, he also ran deliveries for a pharmacy. Jessy dug ditches, hauled cinder blocks up ladders and mixed cement for a brick mason. He nailed shingles, all hunched over like a monkey fucking a football, for a roofer. He worked for landscapers, and was a longshoreman on the docks in San Diego. He learned to sweat copper tubing while laboring for plumbers, and even put in some time in a pinball arcade. One of the most interesting jobs however was when Jessy worked as a grounds keeper for the Miramar base golf course.

While in the Navy Jessy was constantly short of money because he loved to party and go on dates with "Copper Tone" girls. He drove around in a car that only cost $65.00. The car was a four door 1956 Buick Road Master and was nearly a block long. This car burned up gas like a jet air liner and was constantly in need of parts and that meant he spent much of his spare time down at the local junk yard. One day a friend told Jessy of an opening that involved making short grass out of only slightly longer grass all day every day. Jessy asked if there was any money involved and when they said, "Sure." Jessy said, "I'm in."

Jessy had always been a huge fan of power tools and the more power the better so when he first got a look at those magnificent lawn mowers with freshly sharpened blades and finely tuned gas engines, well that was all he needed. "Sign me up." Jessy would have to admit that the sound of a powerful gas powered engine gives him a hard on. Is that weird? No, it's not.

The following week Jessy went to work with the weirdest group of guys he had ever known. That is saying something considering he was from New Jersey. The job was on the base but Jessy was the only government employee who was also working as a greens keeper on the golf course and at first there was a certain level of suspicion among the menagerie of social misfits he was working with. Try to imagine a small group of people who couldn't get jobs with a traveling carnival who were also all as different as night and... frozen fish sticks.

"Glen" was a surfer who loved to get high and was a free spirit. Glen was also a woman magnet who was balling many "Cougars" in the San Diego area at the time. Jessy met a few of these women and was totally impressed. They were beautiful, smart, some had rich and powerful boyfriends but they all loved being boned by Glen. Glen was like a god to the rest of the crew and he made everything he did look way to easy. Glen and Jessy became good friends and he showed Jessy the ropes of their weird work place environment.

"Robbie" was a creepy, little, actual ex-carnival ride operator, who had gotten fired for letting one to many kids fall out of the "Tilt - a - Whirl" ride. I'm no expert but you would think it only takes one. Like so many carnies Robbie was an ex-con who had more tattoos than the Easter Bunny has jelly beans. Robbie had swastikas tattooed on all ten of his fingers and wasn't much fun to be around. A comparison might be, Charles Manson wasn't much fun at parties, that is of course unless, you were the kind of person who wanted to go out and murder people after the party.

"Tommy" was the old pro and knew everything about the grass cutting business. He was kind of like the Bill Murray character in this little version of "Caddie Shack". Tommy taught Jessy how to mow in perfectly straight lines and in a different direction every other day so that the grass didn't "lay down." Tommy was a master greens keeper and Jessy was in awe of his talents. They aerated the greens and spread sand to fill the holes and those greens responded like pool tables to the stupid little white balls that mostly white guys insisted on hitting at them. The greens were perfect, why couldn't people dressed in clown outfits just leave them the fuck alone?

Golf rant: I think that golf was invented to allow white guys to dress like black guys on the weekends but they never pulled it off. I'll admit that Tiger woods managed to add a high level of class to the golf dress code but when Jessy was working as a greens keeper in the late 60's the outfits were to say the least...colorful. Plaid is not a color, just so you know.

Jessy learned how to move the hole. They have this tool that cuts a neat perfect hole to a precise depth. They would pick the perfect spot for the new hole and cut it out then move the plastic cup insert just far enough below the lip. The last part was to replace the cut out back into the old hole and make sure it came to the perfect level so that a golf ball passing over it didn't wobble or bounce. It was a science and Tommy was the scientist that kept it all running. If a good grounds keeper wants to make a particular hole nearly impossible to sink a putt, there are a few tricks that are invisible to the eye, but absolutely deadly to a perfectly lined up putt, and it makes the best golfer look totally stupid. Don't tell anyone this because some people take the "sport" of golf seriously.

Then there was "Bernie" who was a human golf ball magnet. Whenever they heard a golfer yell "FORE" everyone suddenly looked to see where Bernie was and ran in the opposite direction because he was invariably going to be ground zero. Jessy was told this by the other guys but assumed it was just bullshit until one day he was standing next to Bernie when out of nowhere a golf ball smacks Bernie right on top of his head. He staggered a bit and then shook it off and shrugged as if this happened every day. Bernie must have really pissed off the ghost of Bobby Jones because his ability to attract those stupid little white balls was truly uncanny. The day Jessy saw him get beaned there weren't any golfers around anywhere. After making sure that Bernie was all right, Jessy looked in every direction and they were all alone out there. It was then that Jessy realized that there were powers at work here that were just plain spooky and from that day on made it a point not to get within ten feet of poor Bernie unless they were indoors and not near any windows.

The actual leader of the group was "Jack." Jack was a freakishly small red headed Irishman who looked like he had just jumped off a box of "Lucky Charms." The little leprechaun over compensated for his stature by being as loud and annoying as was humanly possible. Some bosses teach by example and are protective of their subordinates. Jack wasn't one of those. As assholes go Jack was in a class all by himself. Jack reveled in explaining the most simple, mundane, tasks over and over to people who already knew how to do whatever it was much better than he did, but he did it purely to hear himself talk in his thick Irish accent while his workers sat squirming, and wanting to stomp him out, like a little green cigarette.

Jack was afraid of most of the crew, especially Robbie, so he took out his vertically challenged wrath on Bernie who was the most sincerely sweet innocent and helpless worker on the team. Poor Bernie would almost break into tears after some of Jack's pointless tirades. One such reaming lasted for twenty minutes and revolved around the capital crime of forgetting to check the gas level in a mower that had just been serviced and sharpened in the shop. As a rule the guys didn't need to touch gas cans as that was the job of the mechanic who maintained the mowers. It wasn't Bernie's job to check the gas in his mower but that didn't protect him from the ass chewing he received from Jack, who managed to waste ten times the man hours it took to fill up all of our damn mowers. Jack was yelling and screaming as if Bernie was responsible for the sinking of the Titanic. As they sat and watched Jack take Bernie apart, piece by piece, Jessy made himself a promise to screw this nasty, cruel, little prick, in some deviously appropriate yet imaginative fashion.

Jessy was inspired by the story of a previous employee who hated Jack much the same as everyone and when he had finally had enough of the constant flow of Jacks Irish bullshit, he came up with the perfect plan. Jack's birthday was approaching and he decided to retire from his course maintenance duties on that very day. His plan required rising at two o'clock in the morning, and after gaining access to the tool shed with a crow bar and borrowing a "Cushman" cart he visited all eighteen greens and removed the flag and cup from the first seventeen. He then used the hole cutter to plant all eighteen flags evenly around the edge of the eighteenth green. Indeed, it looked a little like a birthday cake when every one arrived the next morning. Naturally Jack had a meltdown and went off on everyone in sight, everyone that is except the actual party planner himself. He was long gone and we guessed he was off somewhere drinking some Irish whisky, and doing his own rendition of the "River dance." He was never seen again. Jessy loved the story of the "eighteenth hole" and aspired to do something equally as gratifying. The gauntlet had been laid down so Jessy picked it up and kept it in his pocket.

One morning as the crew was just about to go do their duties of giving haircuts to billions of blades of grass, Jack marched in and demanded to know if any one of the crew had any plumbing experience. Jessy had worked with his stepdad and uncle one summer installing heating and cooling systems. He knew how to cut copper tubing and sweat joints. He had worked with plastic tubing as well. Jessy was good with tools and figured he could do whatever Jack wanted and perhaps get some sort of raise. God knows $2.30 an hour wasn't very good money even by 1968 standards.

Jessy raised his hand and took a half step forward. Jack dismissed the rest of the crew and told Jessy "get in the pickup, we need to talk." The deal went like this. They had gotten a shit load of cash from the Navy to replace the old sprinkler system and Jack was going to do the job as cost effectively as was humanly possible. He would keep whatever was left over for himself. This explained why he wasn't going with a union plumber. He was hiring a crew of Mexican ditch diggers who he had helped sneak across the border from Tijuana. Ten Spanish speaking, sturdy looking guys who were being paid much less than the rest of the crew. That was simply ludicrous.

Jessy assigned half of his crew to dig up the old sprinkler heads and the other half was filling in the holes and putting the grass patches back in place. Jessy's job was to cut out the old sprinkler heads, replace the plastic fittings and install the new "Rain Bird" sprinklers. Jack was going to give him a dollar for every installed head. Jessy did the math and after an unsuccessful attempt to get a buck fifty each he agreed to the deal. Alas business negotiations was new to Jessy and he didn't know enough to get the deal on paper.

The following day Jessy put together a Cushman cart with all the tools and equipment he needed. Next he identified his translator among the crew of laborers. Jose was from TJ (Tijuana) and spoke decent English. Jose was once the guy who stood outside the strip bar and talked horny marines into spending their money on cheap drinks and very young women. Jose could communicate everything to all of the workers except for the little Mayan guy. Jessy named the Mayan "digger" because after handing him a shovel and pointing at the ground he went to work like a badger. Dirt flew out of the hole so fast they were afraid he was going to strike oil.

Jessy became very good at replacing the sprinklers and with the crew working at full throttle they were doing about seventy heads a day. Jessy would be making good money, "On paper." He worked full time starting at six in the morning and still had time to get out to the line and work his four to twelve shift for the Navy. You can pull off shit like that when you are nineteen, and more or less bullet proof. After the first two weeks he had earned close to seven hundred dollars and for the first time in a long time was looking forward to getting a paycheck. That Friday morning Jack, once again, let the crew go on ahead and asked Jessy to stay behind. He thought that perhaps Jack was so impressed with his performance that he was in for a bonus. Jessy was young and hadn't learned that the definition of the word bonus came from the Latin, "Bone Us."

Note: When your boss offers you a bonus it means he will insert a few extra dollars into your next pay check and cancel your medical benefits the week after.

Jack was acting strangely as he shuffled the papers around on his desk and he finally broke the silence. He said he had to leave in a few minutes so he could get downtown in time to appear on the local San Diego, TV morning show. Evidently Jack was some sort of hometown personality who dressed up in a green blazer and plaid vest and pleased the audience by telling marginally amusing golf course stories. Jack spiced up his tales by laying on his charming Irish Brogue like it was peanut butter.

Jessy began to get an uneasy feeling in the pit of his stomach and he knew the other shoe was about to drop. Jack looked up at Jessy and told him with a fake sincere look that, "the board" had decided that the dollar for each sprinkler head was more than they could afford but they had agreed to give him a nickel an hour raise instead. Jessy stood perfectly still, using all of his self control to keep from grabbing a shovel and smashing the lying little dwarf square in his red cheeked face. Jessy knew perfectly well that if "the board" had made some sort of decision Jack was behind it. He ran the place and he was the controlling factor in anything that went on at the golf course, outside of the front office.

Jessy didn't say a word as he turned slowly and walked out the door and pondered his next move. Jessy was a firm believer in well conceived retribution, as opposed to physical violence. While secretly craving to go the medieval route and pound jack into Irish pudding, he started up the cart and began the short drive to where the crew was working that day. He turned and looked back toward the yard and saw Jack begin his long climb into the cab of his giant pickup truck. Jessy stopped and watched Jack adjust the cushion that allowed him to see over the dash board. He started up the big Dodge and drove out toward the freeway. Jessy was seething mad when suddenly he realized Jack was going to be in town, all damned day. There was a big golf tournament starting the next day at the base golf course and Jack was going to be hanging out with some local celebrities promoting the tournament at the Coronado hotel after his big Television appearance. Jessy smiled and headed over to the ninth hole where his guys were patiently waiting for their orders.

Jessy informed his Mexican foreman, Jose, that they would be doing something a little different that day and that instead of five guys digging up heads and five filling in the holes, he wanted all ten men to dig up as many heads as they could by three o'clock. Jose looked at Jessy like he was a little loco but he obeyed the orders perfectly. Jessy dropped off the cart and walked out to the parking lot, started up his big Buick and headed for the beach. He spent the rest of the day trying to forget that he was going to need a new job. The day was perfect and there was a film crew doing some kind of suntan lotion commercial with more than a few beautiful young girls in bikini's. His mind was soon on something much more pleasing than some tiny Irish "Umpa Lumpa" with whisky breath.

Just a note to clarify. Jessy himself was of Irish decent and I'm not trying to degrade an entire race of heavy drinkers because of one tiny jerk off, who incidentally was to short to ride the rides at Disney Land but sometimes you just need to take a stand.

When Jessy returned to the base after an exceptionally pleasing day of fun in the sun he noticed that there was a sizable portion of the golf course with fairly large piles of dirt evenly dispersed in a pattern strangely similar to the layout of the sprinkler system. You could see the smile on Jessy's face from outer space. He never went back to pick up his last pay check to avoid the wrath of the "mad Munchkin." The stories of what happened when Jack returned that afternoon was the stuff of legend.

Jack had spent the afternoon drinking and glad handing with the San Diego elite and was quite drunk and happy when he drove up in his pickup that afternoon. At first he didn't notice the landscape. As he carefully climbed down from the big truck he looked like a rock climber descending a cliff. Jack really needed to consider getting himself a smaller rig. Finally he made it down safely and after making a few adjustments old Jack turned around to inspect his beautiful course just to be sure everything was perfect for the tournament. It is said that Jack stood absolutely still for the next few minutes while his eyes darted feverishly, going from one pile of dirt to the next. Then he started to sputter and shake, suddenly he was yelling and screaming like a madman. He grabbed a shovel and ran like a monkey over to the closest pile of dirt and started to fill in the hole. He was still wearing his TV suit and was soon covered in dirt and grass stains. Good thing it was mostly green. He was still trying to scream at no one in particular but was gradually loosing his voice until finally only sad little sounds like a kidnap victim in the trunk of a Cadillac were coming from the hole in his pissed off face.

Purely out of misplaced pity the rest of the workers picked up shovels and started filling in the two hundred or so holes. By morning the grounds crew had managed to get the place looking halfway respectable for the big event on Saturday, but Jack, took his hatred for Jessy to his grave. He wasn't a forgiving soul and probably never came to see the humor in the situation and the fact that being a huge perpetual douche bag has certain consequences. That and the part where he deserved everything he got…Karma is a wonderful tool…as long as it's aimed in someone else's direction.

Jessy found another job as a warehouse worker down on the docks at the port of San Diego. He drove a fork lift and repackaged and shipped Mexican products for an Indonesian family, but he longed for the soft green rolling hills of the golf course. It was a private paradise to him and he missed the smell of the freshly mowed grass even though he was the one mowing it. Jessy would have to admit that to this day he still isn't crazy about the sport of golf and the poorly dressed "athletes" who play it. OK, that's a lie. Since those days when he was ducking golf balls, Jessy has hit a few long amazing drives and sunk a couple of impossible puts, which is all it takes to lock you in forever. You really can't explain how chasing that stupid little white ball all over acres of well groomed hills and dales is so addicting but it is a very real addiction. However Jessy will always cringe whenever some cock sucking sack of shit takes a huge divot out of that gorgeous green work of art. That includes Tiger Woods and Lefty. When Jessy is at the "tee" he always uses "one." even on the short holes because he was once the guy who had to replace all those little pieces of grass after some silly turd in plaid pants and white patten leather shoes made Swiss cheeze out of his perfect garden.

Golf note: Say what you will about Tiger Woods but that guy did show the sport of golf how to dress. I mean I've seen pictures of Elin and like every other guy in the solar system and at least half the women, say to themselves "Tiger, dude? What were you thinking man?" In spite of his inability to control the brain in his pants...those are some really outstanding pants.

CHAPTER 14

Training Day

Dave and Jessy really had a stressful job…sort of…and they had to give themselves some quality down time whenever possible. This occurred on a regular basis and usually involved finding a quiet spot to smoke some pot and stay out of sight until the redness in their eyes cleared up. They had plenty of choices on base because of the sheer immensity of the airstrip. Miramar was, after all, a pilot training facility and the bigger the base the better. When large, very expensive, flaming balls of metal come falling from the sky it is only prudent to have an extremely large fenced off parcel of range land for them to crash into. It was hard not to feel sorry for the young men and perhaps women who piloted their aircraft to a fiery date with eternity. The irony of the fact that these people were training to drop napalm canisters on poor people in their own country wasn't lost on them either.

Fact was, most pilots managed to eject safely and lived to crash another day. With a few notable exceptions the only people who paid for their errors were taxpayers. Jessy tried to separate himself from the realities of the situation the best way he knew how. Most of the guys in his crew were there because of drugs and the madness surrounding the war had brought them all together for similar yet varied reasons. The dynamics of the pro, and anti war movements were reaching a crescendo and no one knew what would happen next, so they dealt with it each in their own way. Jessy was heroically creative in dealing with the trials he encountered along his chosen path and he faced these things head on.

One seemingly uneventful morning Jessy and Dave were in the process of training a new member of their tightly woven group of misfits. There was a very cool aspect to being in charge of an (ABB) "Already Been Busted" work force. These people had a lot in common with each other, and... they also had little to lose and very little in common with their superiors. When Jessy took the time to properly indoctrinate these people into the group the result could be quite stunning.

The "fresh meat" on the menu that day was a young kid who had been busted for going awol. (absent without leave) He had tried to escape back to Tennessee to be with his girl friend but only got as far as the Greyhound bus terminal downtown. The cops found him asleep waiting for the ticket counter to open. It was 3:00 in the morning and when he couldn't present his leave papers they turned him over to the MP's. (military Police) The Navy gave him a court martial and busted him down to a pay grade that wasn't even legal in India. Fortunately what was bad for him was good for Jessy. His crushed spirit was pitiful to behold but Jessy was there for him and everyone had their own baggage so it wouldn't take long to bring him over into the "special services fold." There was only the initiation portion of the indoctrination process remaining and the new guy could "legally" become a member of the coolest outfit in the whole damn US military. The new guy's name was John, "John Lennon." Jessy and Dave decided that was just plain wrong. They renamed him "Ringo."

The initiation generally revolved around a hair raising ride in the 1952 ford pickup truck at a stupidly high rate of speed and the more initiations they performed the better they got at making them seem like actual near death experiences. Jessy and Dave persuaded Ringo to ride between them on the bench seat of the pickup, based on the fact that Ringo had no power and wasn't qualified to "call shotgun." They certainly didn't want him trying to jump out the door in the middle of the desert at 70 or 80 miles an hour. In 1952 seat belts were severely optional.

There were several long dirt roads that traversed the base from end to end so they drove down the longest, scariest one of all. There was a huge cloud of dust closely following them down that road. "Who knew dust could travel at that speed?" The curves were coming at them so fast and they hit the bumps so hard that it was sort of like being on all the hairiest rides at Disneyland at once. Poor Ringo had nothing to hang onto and his head bounced off the roof of the cab of the truck several times with so much force that his eyes were starting to spin. Jessy slowed down to a safe respectable speed somewhere around sixty so they could take a deep breath and get on with the initiation. They found their way down to the fish pond and parked in the shade at the far end of the lake. By this time Ringo was nearly in shock. There was only one road into the fish pond and from where they were situated they could see anyone headed in their direction from about a half mile away.

Dave had already sparked up a joint by the time Jessy shut down the engine and he passed it to Ringo who didn't hesitate to take a big long deep hit. Almost immediately he began coughing like he had swallowed a hair ball. Ringo, as it turned out had never smoked anything before, ever...not even a Newport. In no time he was smiling and telling the "A" team stories that had them crying with laughter... at first.

Ringo, as it turns out, had worked for a funeral home back in Tennessee and it was his job to repossess the suit of the deceased during the hearse ride from the funeral parlor to the grave yard. Some people didn't have the money to buy a new suit for a dead relative so the discount funeral came with a rental. Also if the deceased showed up dead wearing a really nice suit the result was that he was destined to spend the rest of forever wearing nothing but a flattened out subdued smile. Ringo was already in the back of the hearse when they loaded the casket and he had the drapes pulled. There was enough privacy to strip the body of its clothing...as well as any rings and any other valuables he might find along the way. Just so you know, some people slip money into the pockets of dead friends and relatives when they give their last respects. This is probably a result of guilt for not spending more time with the horizontal loved one when he or she was, well, more...vertical. What ever the case all this was Ringo's now. Jessy and Dave were engrossed in the story that Ringo laid out before them.

The rental suits had a slit down the back to facilitate the speedy removal process. They were stunned and amazed at this revelation but somehow they couldn't stop laughing. Jessy and Dave were waiting with eyes widen open in breathless anticipation as Ringo told them the story of this really fat old gentleman who he had to wrestle the clothes off of, in the summer heat. The body started farting as the gases found their way out while poor Ringo fought to retrieve the suit before the hearse arrived at the cemetery. I'm guessing that not as much care is taken in the discount funeral to sew things up and replace all the body fluids with formaldehyde. The fat body was naked by the time Ringo was finished. Most dead people don't wear underwear, and our poor goofy friend didn't even have time to pull the gold teeth from the corpse's mouth with his pliers...WAIT, WHAT? HUH? Jessy and Dave both went silent and looked at each other like they had just witnessed Pam Anderson making love to Larry King. Eeeyeeww. It was then that they decided Ringo should never ever be given a position of authority in their organization.

The timing of the gross punch line was strategic. As they sat in silence, slowly trying to absorb the twisted revelation, they heard the sound of a badly tuned six cylinder engine in the distance. Jessy looked up toward the road and saw a beat to shit, grey, Chevy, pickup truck with two "turtle heads" (military police in very small, unflattering, grey, plastic, helmets) bearing down on them in as big a hurry as they could manage. Jessy started the big V8, revved it up and popped the clutch causing the tires to spin at first. Rocks and dirt flew as he worked the clutch to let the tires grab the hard dirt road. The truck popped a little wheely and they took off. It was similar to being fired out of a cannon. (this is a guess as I my self have never been fired from a cannon nor am I in line to be the next to do so) Jessy told his faithful, if slightly petrified crew to hold on tight as this was going to be a very bumpy ride.

They were charging headlong at the grey truck at full speed. Jessy could already see that the driver of the other vehicle was beginning to question his core beliefs of just how important it was to break up a three person pot party and was this mission really worth dying for. His grey truck wobbled from side to side and he was about ready to drive it into the lake. Jessy waited until they were perhaps seventy feet from his bumper and certain death before hanging a hard hairy left turn into the slope. He geared down and spun the rear wheels just enough to get them pointed up the hill. This move also kept them from rolling over. They turned over quite a bit of dirt and rock at first and the truck shuddered as it began to climb up the hillside. The new off road tires were launching a great deal of crushed rock in the direction of the grey shore patrol truck. Remarkably they started to gain momentum and soon were heading up the hillside at an ever increasing rate of speed.

Note: Dick finger must have souped the shit out of the drive train and that suspension. The engine seemed to get stronger as they headed for the crest of the hill.

When they topped out the truck went air born as in they just kept going up for a while after the wheels left the boundaries of the earth. For a few seconds the three of them were staring at nothing but blue sky. The nose of the truck rolled forward and came down extremely hard on a road at the edge of the hill top that Jessy didn't even know was there. They crossed the road and spun out into the desert. Clouds of dust and smoke were everywhere but they were safe for a brief time at least. The engine was purring like a sleeping tiger and the rear tires were smoking a bit but were still intact. The front tires were still mostly attached to the truck but it was going to take a serious front end alignment. Jessy got things straightened out and headed for more familiar territory.

There were a series of winding dirt roads that meandered and intersected all over the west end of the base and Jessy just needed to head east parallel to the runway with the afternoon sun at their back and they would be able to find their way back to the movie theater in no time.

Jessy and Dave were damn proud of their escape from the turtle heads but they let Ringo believe that shit like this happened every day. Dave had a huge shit eating grin on his face and Jessy was trying to act cool so he turned toward Ringo and gave him a knowing wink. There are times that are just so special and this was, by Pam, one of those times. The windows were rolled down and the wind was in their hair. "White room" by "Cream" was playing on the AM radio and Jessy turned it all the way up. Ringo was still in a state of shock, his eyes were rolling around in his head like a dolls eye and he was moving his lips but no words were coming out. He most likely could have used some sort of medication but this was not the time and Jessy wasn't driving an ambulance.

They started winding their way back to a real road when they spotted the car wash up ahead. Jessy smiled at Dave and yelled over the music "Now that was something special!" Dave began to crack up. Just as they were approaching the quancet hut Jessy noticed a grey Chevy pickup, come blasting out of the East end of the building and it was clearly going to get to road first, and cut them off. Jessy cranked on the steering wheel and began to circle back to avoid the impending roadblock when he saw that a second truck had just emerged from the same building from the West end and was getting into position to block his retreat.

Jessy also noticed one other thing at that precise moment. The harder he pressed down on the gas pedal the larger the cloud of powdery sand behind the truck grew. He made a snap decision that their only chance was that growing dust cloud and he accelerated to a speed that started churning out dust like a volcano. Jessy kept on the steering wheel hard left and felt the tires slip smoothy like those Nascar drivers do after winning a race. The pursuing trucks just disappeared as did every thing else. The truck was completely enveloped in the light brown dust cloud as they spun doughnuts for what seemed like a ridiculously long amount of time. They had to roll the windows up just to breathe and it was then that Jessy noticed the unmistakable aroma of someone's soiled pants. It wasn't him and judging from the giant Cheshire cat grin on Dave's face, it damn sure wasn't him. The only logical choice was Ringo who was trying to climb over Dave so he could jump out the window.

This was more fun than Jessy had had in a long time but all good things must end. Jessy straightened out the wheel and crossed his fingers. There was a very good chance, after all, that they would slam head on into a truck full of really pissed off sailors with "Billy clubs" at any moment. Somehow, magically, they emerged from the giant dust bubble without ever seeing either of the base police vehicles. They quickly rolled down the windows and slowed to a crawl and could hear the groaning "six bangers" (underpowered six cylinder grey piece of shit pickup trucks) tearing away at the desert. Suddenly they heard a loud extended series of crashing noises and metallic thuds emanating from the dust storm followed by the unmistakable sound of angry overweight white sailors, wearing tiny grey helmets, swearing at each other at the top of their lungs. Jessy and his riders took off like a class full of eighth graders on the last day of school.

When they got back to the theater Jessy made Ringo clean himself up, and then made him detail the truck, really well, inside and out. Then he made Ringo clean himself up again. Ringo also had to promise not tell a soul about their little adventure or Jessy and Dave would swear he was the one driving. The next day they drove the old trusty pickup over to the shop where they received an awful reaming from Dick Finger. No wait…Sorry, that sounds terribly wrong. What I meant was, he called Jessy and Dave every name in the big book of words no one wants to be called.… ever. Apparently they had blown out all four shocks and broken one of the leaf springs. Dick really wanted to know what the hell had happened to his prized machine but Jessy told him that it was better that he didn't know anything, just in case the CID guys came to call.

Dick smiled knowingly because there were already rumors flying around the base about some crazy civilians who had snuck onto the base and somehow evaded capture after an amazing chase and getaway. As it was, none of the shore cops who had tried to set them up that day had gotten a good look at their license plates and even though their truck was the only tan 1952 ford pickup in the whole goddamn Navy, no one ever figured out who the hell they were. It's possible the whole thing was so embarrassing to the shore patrol that they just decided to try to make believe it never happened. Mr. Finger had that old truck back up and running like a Ferrari in no time. He made a hell of a noise but he loved working on that truck. Dick knew Jessy and Dave knew his love for his job and how much they appreciated his abilities. Secretly Dick was creaming in his jeans every time they pulled off one of their spectacular escapades without getting caught. He was a Hells Angel after all and like it or not he was an important part of the operation. He once told Jessy "If you guys ever get caught it better be because you ran out of gas"

There was more going on here than they knew, and Jessy was sure there was a reason that they seemed invincible at times. It was like either the authorities were, dumber than a bag of ball peen hammers, or they didn't get hauled off to the brig due to some higher purpose. Jessy and Dave knew something was up and Jessy was reasonably certain it had something to do with his pending investigation. The FBI/NCIS was involved and all sorts of crazy shit can happen that just don't make any sense when the "Men in grey" are involved.

CHAPTER 15

The Case

One evening Jessy decided to visit the legal aid office in down town San Diego. Jessy had decided that the legal counsel assigned to him by the Navy might not have his best interests on their agenda so getting a second opinion just seemed to make sense. Jessy had been handed a news letter after donating a couple of bucks to the "Black Panthers" downtown one day. There were numbers to free clinics, places to get free food, and the local legal aid office. There were also the locations of several events that were taking place around the city. San Diego had a very well established underground network at the time and there was always something cool going down that didn't appear in the local paper. Free concerts were very popular at the time and they were even better when you didn't tell the cops you were having one.

That evening Jessy found his way to an old red brick, three story office building with a steel stair way in the back. It was chilly and raining and Jessy was wondering if he had picked the wrong time and place to be looking for free legal assistance. The office was on the third floor and the lights were on. There was also a street light and a couple of porch lights in the alley that made the stairway visible. There was a zero moon that night.

When Jessy made his way up to the office the door was partly open and he could hear a young woman crying. Jessy could just see into the office through the filthy windows and realized he would need to wait for the girl to finish up because the back stairway was the waiting area. Jessy waited patiently for his turn as he pondered the fact that alleys in San Diego and the alleys he had grown up with in New Jersey were pretty much the same. The young girl finally left, still sobbing as she descended the black painted steel stairway. Jessy was summoned into the tiny office and took the only empty chair while the lawyer finished filling out some paperwork from the previous client. Jessy looked around the office and was reminded of a small pawn shop.

There were a couple of paintings on the walls next to a law degree next to a stuffed and tanned baby alligator next to a very old baseball glove and a signed picture of Micky Mantle. Jessy perked up as he was huge fan of the Yankees and Micky Mantle was his all time favorite player. There was some kind of alter with beads and incense and a couple of lit candles.

The legal aid Lawyer was named Quincy Beaumont. He told Jessy he had grown up in Brooklyn but his momma and daddy were originally from New Orleans. He explained that the alter was some kind of Voo Doo thing his mom made him put in his office for good luck. Jessy just said "OK". Jessy had learned a little about Voo Doo in boot camp but didn't need to know more on this particular evening. Quincy was a "Mr. do good" kind of person who was trying hard to heal the wounds of a troubled nation. He obviously wasn't making a ton of money at his chosen profession and his clothes reminded Jessy of a door to door vacuum cleaner salesperson.

They made small talk as Quincy moved some papers around and emptied the ashtray.

Note: Back in the day everyone had an ashtray on their desk or kitchen counter or coffee table. Even if they didn't smoke because so many people did at the time.

Quincy Beaumont smiled and finally asked Jessy how he could be of help. Jessy paused, took a deep breath and slowly explained the whole Viet Nam war resistor/FBI/NCIS, drug charge, while serving in the Navy, thing and sat back and waited for Quincy to work his magic. After a very long awkward pause of his own and several beads of sweat Quincy looked Jessy in the eye and said calmly, "You are totally fucked and there is not one thing I can do to un-fuck you. This is way out of my league." Quincy explained that most of his clients were young teenaged mothers trying to get some money out of their child's father. Some were teenagers who got caught with a joint in their pocket when they were stopped and frisked by cops trying to meet a quota. Jessy's case was in a league of his own. Quincy wasn't going to risk a giant career ending fight with the United States government. His sad, broke, clients needed him to not do crazy shit.

Jessy was suddenly scared and dejected while at the same time he understood Quincy's reluctance. Lawyers don't become lawyers so they can get their law office shut down by an angry government for defending a lost cause. The FBI/NCIS can be very intimidating to some people, Being a "Jersey Boy," Jessy never took cops all that seriously, even when the cops in question were wearing dark grey suits, bad haircuts, and dark mirror sunglasses. Jessy realized this lawyer was indeed out of his league and he respected his wish for him to move along. Jessy felt like a dangerous poison that had the power to hurt the people who got to close to him. This is not a positive emotion to have and since that time Jessy has tried to develop his twisted sense of humor to fend off the loneliness gene in his personality that makes him do crazy ass shit sometimes.

Note: Our "For Profit Prisons" are full of innocent people who couldn't afford a good lawyer. Country clubs are full of actual crooks who can bend laws, lie, steal tons of money and their law teams handle the paper work. This makes total sense to people who attended law school except perhaps for people like Quincy Beaumont.

Note: Note: Our country was built "of, by, and for" wealthy white men. They wrote the laws that made it legal for people to be kidnapped and shipped from their own country to this new country to work for free for wealthy white men who got filthy rich from all that free labor. The ancestors of those white men wrote more laws that assured that the wealthiest people could pay little or no taxes on their assets. Those laws had complicated details that made it almost impossible to put those wealthy people in prison no matter how serious their crimes as long as they had a "Dream team" of expensive lawyers.

CHAPTER 16

The Visitor

One beautiful Saturday morning something so strange and bizarre happened that Jessy started to finally grasp the weight and scope of what he had done to himself. Up to this point he had this imaginary image of him being in control of his own destiny and by using a little trickery and guile he could prevail and emerge relatively unharmed by this latest tangle with the United States government.

Jessy and his roommates had just returned from a trip to Tijuana where they had danced holes in the floor at the "Blue Note" bar all Friday night and well into the morning. They danced so good that night Jessy was sure they would be on Mexican television the next day. Before leaving "TJ" they slammed an enjoyable yet affordable breakfast and plenty of strong coffee and headed home to San Diego in the big Buick. Once they got back to town they dropped off a long haired, hippy friend they had smuggled into Mexico the night before. He was white so they brought him back into the United States in the back seat. The American border guards mainly concerned themselves with keeping large amounts of drugs and the brown people who pick our fruits and vegetables from coming to America. One unfortunate border agent tried to speak broken Spanish to Sunny thinking she was from Mexico. Sunny went off on the poor guy with a profanity laced tirade that would make a rap artist blush. She pointed out that her people had been living in California centuries before Columbus got the ball rolling on the whole plundering, raping, murdering and enslaving the occupants of the new world thing. She dropped so many "F" bombs on the poor agent that he had tears in his eyes and would probably need therapy and possibly some of those drugs they took from under the seats of other peoples cars.

It was about eleven o'clock Saturday morning when they arrived home and Sunny and Mario opted to take a shower together so Jessy hit the living room couch and closed his eyes for a long awaited siesta. He was fast asleep in about forty-seconds and was about a half hour into a dream about being on a date with Joey Heatherton (beautiful movie star of the day) on the beach at La Jolla doing absolutely amazing barely legal things to each other when suddenly the front screen door burst open with a crash. Jessy was asleep but was always ready for unexpected visitors and this was totally unexpected. At first he didn't move a muscle, but opened one eye just the slightest bit. He heard the back door to their first floor apartment slam. As Jessy slowly looked up there was a large balding man in a bad suit standing almost on top of him. As Jessy peeked up at him, his first question was, "Who do I know with bullets on his belt?" This gentleman had two 38 caliber speed loaders on his left hip and what appeared to be a shoulder holster up under his cheap grey sport coat. There was also a gold badge and a giant radio clipped to his belt. The radio made his coat bulge out as if he had just shop lifted a toaster. The holster was empty and as the detective turned Jessy saw the short barreled 38 caliber revolver in his right hand. The cop awkwardly pivoted around while sizing up the situation.

This is where Jessy also started to evaluate the situation. They clearly had a cop in their living room and incriminating evidence was lying around everywhere. There was a four foot tall water pipe on the coffee table and the huge bowl was almost full with at least an ounce of partly smoked Mexican weed. There were the only three copies of "Horse Shit" magazine ever printed at the time next to the pipe and a very large Mexican plaster Buddha with a pile of flash powder in his lap, in the corner. The flash powder came from a military battle flare that had somehow found its way to their home and the associated parachute was hung from the ceiling. No one knows how it got there.

They would light a conical shaped piece of incense during a party and set it, very carefully on top of the pile of flash powder and the effect was really quite astounding when the giant ball of white fire erupted spontaneously in the middle of a "Moody Blues" song. Just when everyone was about to nod off, FOOM, the place looked like the surface of the Sun for a second or two and of course the only ones wearing sunglasses were Jessy and his roommates, oh, and of course Smacks. Smacks was also the only one of their guests who wouldn't react with screams and panic. Smacks simply smiled as he enjoyed the fear and chaos all around him. He was either totally wasted or the coolest person on the face of the earth.... or quite possibly both.

The detective slowly took a look around and just as slowly backed out of the room and onto the front porch. He then whipped out his monster radio and called his station. Jessy naturally assumed he was calling for backup on the scale of the Waco incident. (No, Waco hadn't happened yet, please try to stay focused) Jessy considered making a break for the back door but he knew that police detectives, like ice dancers, snakes and Siamese twins usually travel in pairs. There was possibly someone waiting in the alley out back, with his weapon drawn. Jessy waited for the sound of sirens and helicopters while he alerted Mario, and Erik that the cops were on the way. Sunny was already good and gone. He figured that it was her that he had heard leaving the very second the detective first entered the apartment. As it turned out Sunny had lent her Pontiac to a friend who went by the name of "Son of Moon Dog." I'm making the assumption that his parents didn't name him "Son of Moon Dog" but this was California in the late sixties so naming kids while stoned was a popular sport. Besides being a severely flaked out street person, Son of Moon Dog was also fond of snorting heroine and should never have even been allowed to borrow a skate board, no less a giant purple Bonniville convertible. Sunny certainly had a few seriously bent out of shape friends but Son of Moon Dog was in a category all his own. Jessy later discovered that Sonny's friend had driven the giant car down the alley near the apartment and totally ruined it. The alley I mean, the car didn't look to bad but the alley was trashed. Son of Moon Dog must have run into six or seven back walls and a telephone pole but the giant chrome plated General Motors steel bumper had done exactly what it was designed for. The pole stopped the car, but it paid a terrible price and was broken off and leaning at an angle somewhat less than ninety degrees. The heroine induced driver became a missing person at that very instant in time.

By the time the dust had cleared everyone in the immediate area had called the police. The accident helped explain the sudden visit from one San Diego's finest but it didn't begin to answer the question they all had from that day on. Why the hell didn't they come back? Jessy and his roommates were all waiting in breathless anticipation for a full scale siege. California police departments live for shit like this. Drugs, crashed cars, native Americans, Navy guys with long hair who were probably AWOL. The cops must have been close to a giant gang orgasm at the very thought of getting to beat a band of twisted malcontents and war resistors to death with night sticks. However something had gone terribly wrong somewhere along the way and they were pulled off the raid at the very last second. The four room mates were all looking out the windows waiting for one of those "urban assault vehicles" that were rumored to be part of the arsenal that the boys in blue had at their disposal. The point is...No one ever came back.

They all came to realize that whatever was going on was immensely scary, and definitely had something to do with the Chevy Nova parked down the block. Indeed, the FBI, and or NCIS trumps local law enforcement every single time, in spite of what you see in the "Die Hard" movies. Finally Jessy decided to just go with it. They had just been given a "get out of jail free card" and something like that didn't come along often and should not be wasted or treated lightly. Eric was freaking out but Sunny and Mario were really starting to get in to the whole thing.

Jessy suggested they throw a party and see who shows up. Jessy reasoned that if the feds were watching their every move, then one or more of them could be in attendance. At least they might be able to figure out who their friends were. Even though they were all very tired and perhaps still a little high, the decision was made to push the envelope and they started to plan a truly epic event that would either get them all busted or at the very least, drive the guy in the piece of shit Nova and his superiors fucking crazy.

Note: I chose to bad mouth some truly bad choices in American automobile history in this book. The Ford Pinto, the Chevy Nova, along with some very average low powered pickup trucks among others but make no mistake, I love American steel and muscle cars in a way I can't describe. It seems like the best cars ever made in this country were built in the late 1950's all the way thru the 1960's and early 70's. The early Corvettes and Thunderbirds, and Mustangs were legend. The GTO, the Olds 442, the Dodge Challenger and Charger, not to mention the Barracuda and Cobra. The list goes on and on before you come to any cars from somewhere else. I want to see Detroit come roaring back with the baddest fastest yet seriously fuel efficient cars ever built. Wouldn't that be cool? I'm now researching electric SUV's and pickups with solar panels on the roof. I'll get back to you.

    As far as finding people to attend the party, that was not going to be a problem. As a group, Jessy and his roommates knew a shit load of people and those people knew a larger and way more diverse group of people. Barbara was Eric's girl friend at the time and she worked for Ron, a sort of famous artist at his greeting card factory that employed mostly beautiful women. One of these amazing young women was scheduled to be a "Playboy" playmate of the month for Mr. Hefner's Magazine. She was beautiful and smart. Jessy really liked her and they got along great but he was way too intimidated by her to let her know it. Ron and his female employees were on the list. Jessy was inviting a few of his friends he knew from the beach and some of the guys from the base including their old friend Smacks.

    The food was being supplied by the girls. (Sorry this was before a phrase like that was considered sexist by most people)

Note: Airline stewardesses were all female back then. (My stupid computer just informed me that the word "stewardesses" is a sexist gender specific term. My computer can be a real asshole sometimes)

Jessy's female roommates cooked up a mixture of Mexican, German, Italian, and Sunny stew. You never knew what Sunny was going to put in that stew of hers but it was always good and it always got you high. There would be plenty of tortilla chips, popcorn with parmesan cheese, pretzels and other salty snacks. Because this was southern California a giant bowl of guacamole would be centered on the table. The bananas were in the freezer, dipped in chocolate. "Frozen Chocolate Bananas" were considered a fancy hippy treat back then.

Jessy was chosen to be in charge of "special effects" mostly because of his emerging talent as an artist...of sorts. Oh yeah, and because he had more jobs than a Jamaican and always had some (not a lot but some) extra money to go shopping. The very first thing he bought was a four foot long "black light." They had recently purchased velvet paintings during one of their many trips to Mexico and Jessy was dying to see them in living ultraviolet light. There was this particular piece with a beautiful nude black girl with a big afro that lit up quite well indeed. Next, Jessy visited the flea market and found an old but usable tubular vacuum cleaner, and an old pot belly stove and a big round fish bowl, like in the cartoons. On the way home he stopped at a Woolworth's and picked up some jars of glow in the dark paint and a big bag of ping pong balls. "Jessy didn't go shopping for stuff, but rather he just let stuff go shopping for him."

When Jessy got back to the apartment everyone else was gone so he went to work painting the balls with flowers and peace signs and some stuff he just made up. Then he hung the vacuum out the window in the hedges and plugged the hose into the exhaust end, and ran it through the window and into the stove via the stove pipe hole in back. Next he filled the fish bowl with the brightly colored ping pong balls and taped a round piece of card board to the top of the bowl and cut a hole just large enough for the air hose. Then he taped the hose in place and flipped the bowl upside down, and gently set the bowl over the hole on top of the stove. When Jessy was done It looked a little like someone was cooking little round Easter eggs in a space helmet. If Martha Stewart had seen the creation she would have given him a big gold ribbon. It was dark out by the time he finished the project so he set up the black light on the coffee table and lit up the vacuum cleaner. The balls began spinning around the bowl and the light made them glow. It was almost perfect except for the part where you could still hear the vacuum running in the bushes outside the mostly closed window. A rolled up towel helped but not completely so Jessy went over to the stereo and spun up some "Canned Heat flavored vinyl" cranked it up and lit a joint and now It was perfect. Clearly the missing key to his invention was "volume enhanced rock and roll"

Note: To my readers, if this invention winds up on "The shark Tank" Jessy will hunt you down and break your eyeballs. Not really, remember Jessy was a peace loving hippy.

The party began as most parties do, where the people who you were kind of hoping had lost their invitation are always the ones who show up an hour early. In this case that meant Cousin Brucie. (the real cousin Brucie was a famous New York, radio, DJ) This cousin Brucie was their local neighborhood sneak thief and he didn't have an invitation. No one knew how he knew them. He just started turning up. Jessy thought Sunny knew him. Sunny and Mario thought Jessy knew him and Eric didn't give a shit who knew him, he just wanted him to go away. No one trusted this new friend and he was constantly trying to sell or give them stuff that he had recently ripped off. Once he tried to sell Jessy his own skin diver watch after he had broken into his car. Jessy asked cousin Brucie to please stop coming around and he agreed. Then he apologized profusely and gave them a box of stuff to show them how sorry he was. In the box was a dice tumbler like the kind they use in Las Vegas, a radio alarm clock, a giant brandy snifter, an "unopened" box of a dozen relatively unused golf balls, and Jessy's skin diver watch. A week later there he was at the party. No one had invited him but there he was. No one had any idea how he knew we were even having a party. As Jessy looked back, it was possible that their unwelcome stranger was some form of deep cover government informant. However, that would be paranoid, right? The plan was to enjoy the party but keep a close eye on Brucie and if you had any valuables...put them in your pocket.

The next guests to show up were Ron, the artist, and five of his girls. everyone was curious as to the relationships Ron enjoyed with these women. Jessy suspected that he was giving horizontal dance lessons to at least two of them. No one could really figure it out because Ron was not a hunk. Ron was dark, swarthy, (way too much hair where it didn't belong) short, and he reminded you of the Gypsy con man who sells you stuff on the street that doesn't work the day after you buy it. Ron was business smart and wealthy and seemed to have some kind of power over his women. Ron was sort of like Charlie Manson with a new Cadillac and a much better wardrobe. Ron and Jessy never got along all that well. Jessy was a peace freak and Ron said he was an ex-marine who still thought we were going to win the Viet Nam war. Ron was not your typical warrior. When he told Jessy he was a marine Jessy had to bite his tongue. If he was indeed a marine he looked like the guy who cleaned up after the 4th of July parade. Jessy really didn't really care since anyone who brought five gorgeous young girls to the party was an asset.

Smacks showed up with two young girls of his own. The problem was that these girls looked really young. Like "high school freshman" young. Like "isn't there a law against that?" young. Like "we are all going to die in prison" young. Hey, Jessy had a get out of jail free card, right? Jessy kept thinking how in the hell did a "Jimmy Hendrix" looking black man not get pulled over driving a Purple "Monte Carlo" smoking a giant blunt, with two fifteen year old girls, lap dancing him, as he drove down Adams Avenue at ten miles an hour. Smacks was "styling" in his black skintight leather pants and "Beatle boots." His huge "Afro" was wrapped in a tied died scarf. He had a gold peace sign necklace the size of a dessert plate and of course he was sporting his ever present super dark "Foster Grant" shades. Everyone also assumed that Smacks was also sporting eye balls but no one could swear to it because no one had ever seen them.

The college girls from upstairs came to see what the "hippies" were up to. They were from somewhere in the Midwest, Kansas maybe, and they thought Jessy and his friends were cool. The girls were always hanging around asking questions about marijuana and their life style choices and sometimes Sonny would put them on a little and tell them they could come in and see our apartment but they would have to get naked first. They were a little surprised when they showed up at the party and everyone had on clothes.

Jessy was the DJ and he gradually turned up the volume on the turntable and played all the favorite "LP's"(long playing 33 and a 1/3 rpm. records). "Santana, The Who, Buffalo Springfield, Jefferson Airplane, Poco, Sly and the family stone, Ike and Tina, Iron Butterfly, Janice Joplin, Beautiful Day, Richie Havens and Cream." The music of the late sixties was influenced by so many things it was simply perfect. The war, the civil rights movement, the poets in the Village, the hippies in Haight Ashbury, the youth of America finding their place in history, and of course the blossoming drug movement. Everything came together in a wonderful crescendo of voice, strings, horns, and a drum beat you could dance, or march... or make love to.

The dancers hit the floor and Smacks led the way. Say what you will about drug abusers but some of them can rock. No one knew what he was using to enhance his personality that night but Smacks wore out the two teeny bobbers he came with and was free styling with every girl at the party all night long. If we had been in Alabama, or Mississippi, there would have been a cross burning on the front lawn by the end of the party.

At this point many of you reading this are thinking, "What the fuck is a record?" For those people all I can say is blow me. This was the best tech we had, the sound was just so good and you could separate the tracks on a good sound system and just listen to the drummer if you wanted to. There were eight tracks that combined to make music heaven. This is back in the day when all the bands had actual musicians playing real music on real musical instruments and not just some piece of shit electronic synthesizer, doinking out random sounds like a wind chime in a hurricane.

Jessy turned on the ping pong ball machine about half way through the party. Several people sat around his invention, shared a joint, and said, "WOW" and far out.... way too often. Jessy went outside to get some fresh air and the whole street was awash with music. The neighbors had their windows open and many of them were at those windows waiting to see what was going to happen next. Their interest perked up a little when the young, female, mostly naked, flower child showed up. There was a good amount of marijuana smoke coming from the front door, which was open most of the evening and Jessy saw at least one bat fly right into the telephone pole near the apartment as it circled the street light in search of flying insects. He was smiling when he hit the ground, but then bats are always smiling, Bats are born that way.

Amazingly nothing really went south. Jessy was expecting someone to call the "boys in blue" but the cops never came. He was sure someone would take exception to something and a huge fight would break out but no one lost control and not one drop of blood was spilled in anger all night long. One young girl got sick on wine and parmesan cheese popcorn but she was fine. By that I mean she was fine, even while she was getting sick she looked really damned good. How many people can say that?

Toward the end of the evening they set off the Buddha flash powder trick with a crazy amount of flash powder that nearly set everyone on fire. It sure as hell woke their asses up. The plaster buddha cracked down the middle and fell in half but once the screaming subsided they found that everyone had survived with most of their body hair and clothing intact. Jessy was making sure cousin Brucie didn't steal anything although our huge supply of grass did seem to dwindle at an unprecedented rate. Considering the giant water pipe was going all night long that really wasn't all that surprising.

The detective sat in his shitty little car down the street all night, and if there was a government "plant" at the party they never figured out who it was. Everyone had an awesome time and if one of them was a spy they sure as hell didn't pass the drug test when they got back to the "bat cave." Jessy likes to think that they turned someone away from the dark side that night. There is this picture in his mind of a somewhat "less than gruntled" guy in a rumpled dark suit with one shirt tail hanging out, walking slowly into his supervisor's office, throwing his gun, his badge, his other gun, his Captain America ID card and of course his super dark sunglasses, onto the desk. After saluting to the Nixon picture on the wall with his middle finger he pulls a doobie from behind one ear, sparks it up, spins on one heel, and walks off into the California sunset. Nice. Oh except for the part where eleven other guys in dark suits and sunglasses tackle the him in the parking lot, beat the piss out of him and drag him off and "lock him in a room and throw away the room."

Note: I just love that line, I borrowed it from a movie I saw about some kid who hacks into a government computer and almost starts World War III, I don't want to be accused of plagiarism.)

The following morning there were still several guests sleeping on the floor and the couch. Jessy was up early and the first thing he had to do was to cover up a young naked girl who probably came with Ron but didn't leave with him. There is a problem with showing up with too many dates. You should always be prepared to take some sort of inventory before your departure. Jessy was not complaining by any means. Waking up to find a lovely young woman fast asleep on your carpet, missing all of her clothing is right up there with hot coffee, bacon, eggs, toast and mango jam.

Everyone was welcome to spend the night after one of their parties and sometimes someone would hang out for a few days if they were in between deployments and had no where else to go. This did not include the base of course. Their little apartment was crowded at times but still better than life in the barracks, which was closer to a really noisy prison than anything else. The background music on base was roaring jet engines running at 80 percent all night long.

From time to time they would discover some complete stranger, all crashed out on the floor and would try as they might to solve the mystery of the "uninvited tourist." Jessy came home from work one morning and there was some young guy sporting a spiked Mohawk, zoned out on the sofa. Jessy poked him rather hard with a baseball bat to wake him up. Jessy didn't know him but if he woke up angry...he had a baseball bat. The guy didn't wake up but when he slowly rolled over there was a dark colored sock glued to his nose. Jessy didn't really condone glue sniffing but he wasn't going to throw him out on the street or call the cops with a black tube sock hanging off his face. If there was some film in the instamatic camera he would have stripped him naked and put him out in the yard propped up against one of the palm trees and done a portfolio for the guy's new career as a model in the men's hosiery section of High Times Magazine.

All things considered Jessy felt the party was a huge success and people were still talking about it for months afterwards. Several folks who no one knew had attended the affair, if they were there to party or just observe no one knew. If People magazine had been around back then there would have been a spread devoted to their little shindig. Sure there were some people who had fallen asleep around the house but the important thing is that they all eventually woke up. With the number of parties that occurred in the little apartment, they never once had to take anyone to the hospital or the free clinic to be revived or pumped or sewed back together, or have bullets removed from...ever. That's what the dumpster down the alley was for. No, no...I'm kidding.... really. No body knows how that guy got into the dumpster. Some people think he was living in there and somehow slept through the part where the big green truck came along and carted his poor dumb ass away. Jessy and his roommates didn't serve alcohol at their parties, and that explains the lack of bodies and chalk outlines following their get togethers. People would sometimes bring a bottle of wine but once it got passed around no one really got very much and one way or another, everyone got home safely. No Harm No Foul, right? More importantly they never got raided by a hundred pissed off law enforcement engineers from the SDPD. Whatever Jessy's status was with the FBI, it all seemed to be going in the right direction... and that was good. The part where FBI agents came to the doors of Jessy's parents and friends and coaches and teachers... that was bad.

CHAPTER 17

The Horse Ranch

Writers note: When most people think of the United States Navy there are usually very large, grey, steel, floaty things involved. The very last thing you picture is a sailor riding a horse over a desert range in Southern California but this book never claimed to be anything close to the normal every day "Popeye the sailor man" story. If this comes as a disappointment to any of you, well you can go out and buy yourself a comic book. Just kidding, I need you all to hang in there and finish this book and then run out and tell all your friends to buy it and read it so I can retire and move to Costa Rica.

The whole horse ranch thing was a plot to screw Jessy over in the worst way imaginable. Someone on base knew all about Jessy's "situation" and was distressed that due to the pending nature of his drug case, and the ongoing, FBI investigation, there was virtually nothing being done to Jessy as far as incarceration and or torture were concerned. A certain unknown person with a reasonable level power came up with a plan to pile the shit up so high around Jessy that it would take a lifetime to dig his way out. The grand plan revolved around the fact that there were miles of desert east of the base that the Navy owned and used as a secondary landing zone for pilots who couldn't make it all the way back to the main base runway.

Occasionally the Navy base at Miramar would be startled by the sound of a loud explosion coming from the direction of the low hills across the highway. Sailors would run outside to see a plume of smoke and flames raising from a blackened hole in the ground surrounded by large and small pieces of very expensive taxpayer funded aircraft and hopefully a live pilot landing somewhere after a brief parachute ride to earth. One of our young pilots came in way to low on a dark evening and clipped a hill top and in his moment of disoriented panic he pulled the ejection seat handle. Normally he would have been launched clear of the plane and provided his chute opened he would have had a thrilling story to tell his buddies at the officers club. In this case however he failed to notice that the initial impact had inverted his aircraft and he was up side down when he ejected and the rocket seat buried him in the sand so that only his boots were visible when the rescue team arrived. Ironically the plane itself was still in one slightly beat up piece and the pilot might have survived if he had attempted to belly land it in the desert sand.

The vast stretch of undeveloped land was begging to be used for something besides being a handy crash site and that's when some chief petty officer from a tiny spot on the map of Texas, came up with the idea to build a horse ranch out there. It would be relatively cheap because they had some portable buildings and plenty of free labor, and of course Jessy. The plan was perfect as far as they were concerned. The officers would have a convenient place to dump their kids while they spent some quality time in the strip clubs that were scattered all over downtown San Diego. There would be a constant source of quality fertilizer for the golf course and the best part was that Jessy would be spending his days shoveling horse shit from dusk till dawn and back to dusk again.

Alas, some of the best laid plans sometimes contain one fatal flaw that turns the whole "plan thing" on it's axis and the desired results are twisted into something entirely unexpected. The fly in this particular ointment was Jessy's military Navy drivers license. Along his long strange and winding road, Jessy had taken the time to get certified on every piece of wheeled machinery that the Navy owned. His license had been stamped so many times that he was certified to drive just about everything short of a tank. When Jessy was transferred to the still to be built horse ranch, the first thing he did was to use his vehicle passport to sign out some needed equipment from the motor pool.

Jessy was quite fortunate in that he had friends in moderately high places. These friends pulled on some strings that granted him access to a very well rounded stash of government vehicles. He checked out three pickup trucks, two standard grey Chevy pickups, and the choice little souped up 1952 ford that came with a mechanic named "Dick Finger." Next he acquired a two and a half ton dump truck and a cool Ford tractor equipped with a PTO, (power take off) that connected to a detachable post hole digger and a back hoe. The tractor also came with a drag rake that made short work of cleaning up after a herd of horses that only knew how eat and shit, all day long. There was only one draw back and that was he would now be forced to learn how to operate a dump truck and a tractor. Jessy was certified, but not trained on all of these vehicles so there was much to learn in a short amount of time. The tractor took a little practice and some paint for the stuff he crashed into but mostly he was ready to rock in a scary short amount of time.

Jessy and motorized machinery had always enjoyed a great working relationship. The good news was that now he was able to complete his appointed rounds at the ranch in an hour or two and not endless days as his unknown superiors had planned.

They soon built a corral using railroad ties for fence posts and thick nylon straps that were once used to capture runaway aircraft on the flight line. The post hole digger came in real handy for planting the railroad ties, and his crew nailed three rows of straps to the ties to form the corral. The "base" welding shop built a wide swing gate and their own base special service commander's office (Jessy's friends in the commanders office) came up with saddles, harnesses and a whole "tack shed" full of other horse related leather items that reminded Jessy of some of the stuff you see hanging up on the back wall of a full service strip club in Texas. It wasn't long before their little ranch began to take shape. Soon the only things missing were the long legged creatures with those gigantic faces, and hooves that could kick you into an alternate universe if you weren't careful.

Their chief had the horse issue covered. The Navy had given him five hundred dollars per horse and the chief knew some guys in Mexico who had "caballos" for fifty bucks each. For an extra five bucks you could even get a "pink slip." That's Four hundred forty-five dollars profit per animal. There was an issue with the actual transaction that involved a freeway underpass, some illegal border crossing and the dark of night. On one trip the Texas horse trader bought this poor, beat up, Picasso looking horse that was missing a right front knee cap. Jessy wasn't a vet but he guessed it was going to take much more than five hundred bucks to repair all the damage. Jessy asked the chief what the hell he was thinking and he just said. "Cost of doing business in the dark, under a bridge son." Jessy mentioned "It must have been real god damn dark under that fucking bridge." The chief knew he would get his fifty bucks back because people and dogs still ate horse meat and you can't build furniture without glue. Life can be cruel sometimes, and if you happen to be an animal of any kind sometimes it can get real cruel in a real damn hurry.

When all was said and done Jessy and his ranch hands had over fifty head of horses to feed and care for, oh yeah, and one little pissed off pony named "Sarge." Ponies were bred to haul mine carts out of holes in the ground that were way to small for normal sized horses. Ponies were just as strong as normal sized horses, only mini size. Sarge was a little prick of a pony who drove all the other "real" horses nuts. Sarge would break out of his stall on a regular basis and run circles around the big corral causing a horse riot until Jessy chased him down and roped him. You couldn't chase the little stallion pony from "horse back" because the horse you were riding would be going crazy the whole time. You didn't even think about chasing Sarge while riding a mare because Sarge would try to fuck her, whether you were on her or not. Sarge had a huge dick for such a small animal and he was in a constant state of "horn." Sometimes they would let Sarge try to have his way with one of the mares just because it was so much fun to watch. These horses were twice as tall as Sarge and he would try to mount them from behind with his big dick sticking straight up but at least a foot short of the horse pussy he was craving. Sarge often got kicked for his efforts but he never stopped trying. You have to honor and respect that level of dedication.

The chief purchased a goat one day and everyone wondered, "a goat? What the hell are you thinking chief?" Not being ranchers themselves they couldn't make the connection. It turns out that a goat is like a Zen Buddhist monk to a herd of horses. If they didn't have that stupid little goat the gang of Mr. Ed wannabes would have been trying to kill each other. The goat worked like marijuana and the vast majority of four legged corral dwellers became totally mellow and subdued,... most of the time, except when the damn pony got loose.

There however was one holdout that nearly kept Jessy from attending his next birthday party, and the rest of them for that matter. This particular specimen was huge and white with little black speckles that made him look dirty even after they had hosed him down. His eyes were like snakes eyes and were yellow with little black slits. He looked like pure evil and he more than lived up to that first impression. The ranch hands eventually tried to hang a sign around his neck that said DANGER and that became his name. "Danger" didn't put up with the sign for long and no one had the guts to put the sign back on after he ripped it off with his teeth and stomped the ever loving shit out of it.

One strangely cloudy day Sarge broke out...again and it was Jessy's "turn in the barrel" to chase him down. Jessy walked over to the fence post where they kept the coiled throwing rope and took the rope coil in his left hand and the throwing loop in his right hand and after uncoiling a few feet Jessy climbed through the nylon straps, took a deep breath and began the pony hunt. For those of you who have never hunted ponies, you have to start slowly with stealth and cunning. Of course stepping into a fenced area packed full of large animals, with a rope is as about as inconspicuous as a cop with the lights on his "crown vic" flashing and the siren blaring in Watts on a Saturday night. Jessy began his pursuit by trying to triangulate the corral and he attempted to get the pony to move toward a corner and then slowly move in until he was close enough to launch his rope at Sarge's face. This practice almost, always ended with Jessy running around like a lunatic, chasing a crazy short horse with a hard on until he was totally out of breath and patience. Hey, give Jessy a break. He was from New Jersey, not New Mexico.

Phase two of the hunt had begun and Jessy was running his ass off waving the rope at the stupid pony when out of the corner of his eye he happened to notice something as he approached one of the horse feeders in the middle of the corral. The feeders were wooden and slatted and stood about seven feet tall. You could see through the part of the feeder that wasn't full of hay. At first Jessy saw a tail flick at the far end of the feeder. Upon further inspection he happened to catch a glimpse of a yellow eye gleaming at him through the slats. The stare was cold and threatening and sent a chill down his spine. Jessy was running directly toward the far corner of the feeder at full speed and couldn't stop in time. Instinctively he dropped as if he was sliding into third base. At the same time both of Danger's steel coated rear hooves flew past his face at a thousand miles an hour. Jessy sprang back just as Danger spun around and rose up on his hind legs and tried to finish him off with his front feet. Jessy was just fast enough to avoid certain death or at least having all his bones crushed to powder by a ton of raging equine monster with a Hitler complex. Jessy bolted for the fence and dove through the straps with Danger hot on his heels. Danger pulled up at the fence and just looked at Jessy as if to say, "I'll get you next time asshole."

There was another very dangerous yet beautiful contestant in the "worlds most badass horse contest." There was this magnificent Indian palomino named "Moncho." Moncho looked very similar to the palomino "little Joe Cartwright" rode around the Ponderosa on the show "Bonanza." Moncho however was bigger and stronger and had huge hind quarters and thigh muscles. He looked like he could jump over the tack shed without benefit of a running start. There was only one person on the ranch who could go near Mancho and her name was Natasha. Natasha was like a female version of Mancho. She was tall, beautiful and extremely dangerous. All the men on the ranch knew not to screw around with either one of them. All of us that is except corporal Merf. Merf was assigned to the small marine station at the North end of the corral. The marines patrolled the base perimeter on horse back and most had all seen action in Viet Nam. Merf was a tall, slender, country boy and only a little bit smarter than a coat rack but not nearly as useful. One afternoon horny corporal Merf decided to put the feelings of his constantly erect, yet still inordinately small penis ahead of his better judgment and asked Natasha out on a date. No one knows exactly what happened that night, but speculation had Merf saying and or doing something really stupid that resulted in Natasha going all medieval on him. When he got out of the VA trauma unit his arm was in a sling, his left eye was swollen shut, and he had a mild concussion. Wisely Merf claimed to have fallen down a flight of stairs. Natasha was back at work the next day as if nothing had happened. She looked tip top and fine as always.

The Cowboy

They were running a riding stable and most of the riders were young teens who got a couple of hours of guided quality time aboard a slightly over used but basically well treated Navy issue horses. Every now and then however they would get a special request from a much more experienced equestrian and Jessy and Natasha did all they could to accommodate these "special needs riders." By far the most memorable customer at the ranch was the "Texas Cowboy." Being from New Jersey Jessy thought of cowboys as the guys that hang out in Times Square wearing big hats and leather jackets who make a living selling blow jobs to tourists in the subway restrooms. Out west it seems they have relatively actual "cowboys" who apparently know absolutely everything you always wanted to know about all the magical things boys can do with or to cows. Without cowboys there would be no Big Mac's.

This particular cowboy was an unnecessarily loud Texas douche bag who, like far to many Texans, thought that the more noise you make while expressing your self, the more people will want to listen to what ever it is they have to say. Of course they are mistaken but no one bothers to tell them. We could all hear him coming way before he showed up. First, this noisy, smelly, diesel, entirely too large, black pickup truck came racing down the road stirring up all of the horses. The truck skidded to a stop causing a really big brown cloud of dust and smoke that pissed everyone off. Next, after descending from the giant truck like he had just conquered Europe, the super boisterous cow person was bragging and yelling orders at a crew of people he didn't even know. He was acting like he had the lease to the ranch. The cowboy was wearing a Green leather cowboy hat with a big silver badge that he loudly told everyone he had won at "the rodeo" in some Texas town with a name like "Cow Pie" or "Turd City" or

"Cowturdyville." He also had a belt buckle the size of a goddamned frying pan, also supposedly won at the rodeo in some god forsaken Texas burg whose only claim to fame was its best in the west Dairy Queen. Jessy thought to himself "Do they have a worlds biggest asshole contest at these Texas rodeo's?"

The "Cowboy" said he didn't want to ride no sorry beat to shit stable pony. He wanted the toughest, meanest, badass horse on the ranch. Jessy squeezed out a little smile as he realized that this country nut bag had no idea where he was and who he was screwing with. At first Jessy was considering putting him on "Danger" but there were two serious issues involved with that option. The most important drawback was that by attempting to put a human being on Danger the result could be quite similar to the crime of murder. Jessy was already in a reasonable amount of trouble with the government and a homicide would make his case a lot harder to defend. Second, and this was the show stopper, no one had ever successfully put a saddle on "Danger." Not that a few brave souls hadn't tried and those who did had paid the price. Suddenly the lights came on and Jessy arrived at the perfect solution. He looked over at Natasha and gently nodded his head toward Mancho. At first she frowned at Jessy like he was bug nuts crazy but after a few low rent comments from Tex about her "big old Texas size titties" Natasha nodded back at Jessy and he detected a dark evil smile that he had never seen on her stunning face before. Jessy politely asked Natasha if she would be so kind as to saddle up Mancho. She gave him a brief salute to the brim of her black cowgirl hat as she turned and walked off toward the tack shed with a sly grin as she whistled the theme song from "The Good the bad and the ugly." Go see the movie...... (Get high first)

A few minutes passed and Natasha brought Mancho out, all saddled up and ready to go.... sort of. "Bronco Billy" was impressed and he exclaimed loudly enough to be heard on Mars "Wooeee, that there is what I'm talking about boys and girls now stand back, watch, and learn." He did his best "John Wayne" walk as he sauntered over to the amazing animal and grabbed the saddle horn and effortlessly rose into the saddle. The great horse stood motionless, his steely blue eyes straight ahead, like a beautiful statue. At this point everyone and by everyone I mean the whole damn ranch including the horses was holding their collective breath in anticipation of what was certain to be a memorable event in horse history. Have you ever been to a carnival were a daredevil gets into a box with a large amount of dynamite and everyone is on the edge of their seat waiting for the explosion, and possible death or dismemberment of the misguided soul in the box? This was their carnival and they quietly awaited the explosion.

The noisy Texan gathered the reins in his left hand and took off his big green leather "Texas douche bag hat" and he used it to whip Moncho's muscled hindquarters. The horse didn't move an inch and the cow person looked a little perplexed as he made this silly clicking sound with his tongue and cheek. He had wanted to wear his spurs which looked like big sharp fancy spiky earrings for his feet but Jessy made him take them off. If he was going to ride this horse, he certainly wasn't going to be wearing sharp metal things on his brightly colored high heeled cowboy shoes. He tried kicking Moncho's ribs with the heels of those shiny painted boots but nothing happened so he kicked harder and the horses ears began to ever so slowly lay back on the sides of his head. Jessy looked at Natasha and she looked back at him and both had goose bumps as they realized that all holy hell was about to break loose.

What happened next burned into Jessy's memory like his first kiss. Just a helpful note to anyone who has ever wondered what to do when their horse doesn't start. Jessy obviously didn't know the answer to this horse conundrum but that day, he learned the one thing...you do NOT EVER want to do EVER is hit the horse you are sitting on In the side of his giant horse face with your big green leather douche bag hat. No one had told Tex this, so when he did it the result was spectacular. Moncho turned his giant head and in an instant grabbed the hat in his teeth and ripped it out of the cowboy's hand and dropped it on the ground. The magnificent animal began to stomp the stupid hat violently with his front hooves while his helpless rider did all he could to hang on to the giant beast writhing between his legs. When Moncho was absolutely positive that the hat was good and fucking dead he reared up on his immense hind legs and did a complete turn before dropping back down where he crouched down like a cat charging his muscles and took off so fast everyone did a "Scooby Doo" double take. Vwoooof?

There was nothing but a cloud of dust and the corpse of the dead douche bag hat lying on the ground. The ranch hands were jolted back to reality by the cries of a desperate "man" hanging on to the powerful neck of an animal who was approaching the speed of light. The road east of the ranch was long straight and flat so they all got to watch the whole damn show. To this day Jessy has never seen anything quite like it. A grown up rodeo star screaming at the top of his lungs like a little child who had just had a lollypop slapped out of his or her mouth, and she (he) was growing smaller and smaller by the second.

There was a dry river bed about a quarter mile out. The road took an abrupt hard left at that point. When they got there Moncho didn't turn left, he simply planted his sturdy hooves dropped his head and stopped. Mancho didn't slow to a stop or skid to a stop he just fucking stopped. He was so strong that this maneuver would have blown out the legs of a lesser creature but not Moncho. The physics of the abrupt halt launched the farm boy like a ground to air missile. The screaming cowboy flew half way across the rocky dry river bed where gravity made damn sure he returned to planet earth.

From their vantage point all Jessy and Natasha could see was a tiny human shaped object flying spread eagled into the unknown. His faint screams faded as he went out of sight. Jessy instantly jumped into the ford pickup with Natasha right next to him, riding shotgun. She was worried that Moncho had hurt himself, and Jessy was worried that he had just helped kill someone. Perhaps a someone, that the world would be better off without, but still being party to the death of a rodeo star would be a scar on Jessy's antiwar credentials.

He certainly didn't need accessory to murder charges on his paper work. In a very short time, (Jessy was driving the 52 ford pickup) they arrived at the edge of the abyss in time to hear a special brand of Texas cursing. They couldn't see the source of the profanity but every other word was "sheeeit." (not really a word but you have to consider the source)

When they inspected the arroyo they found one damaged but still loud and annoying rodeo clown. Jessy had demoted him from bronco buster right about the time he started screaming like a scared little school girl. No offense to rodeo clowns by the way. Those guys are super brave, or just plain crazy. In retrospect lets just rank rodeo boy down to third grader in a funny hat and leave it at that, except for the hat...That hat was deader than Billy the kid. Natasha found Moncho in good spirits and in excellent health, all things considered. Some might think he was smiling, if that is even a thing. The same could not be said for their new friend from the flat dry ego enhanced second largest state in the union. Tex had a broken arm and was so beat up Jessy really didn't want to let him bleed all over the seats in his truck so they split open a bale of hay into flakes for him to lay on in the bed of the pickup. Jessy drove slow, mostly to keep the yelling and screaming to a minimum and got the broken cowboy over to the base sick bay where they dropped him off after a brief explanation of a terrible accidental fall down a hill side while he was taking a leak. Tex didn't want the truth to get out and neither did Jessy and Natasha. This was the last time they saw the Texas cowboy, and that was good, like for so many reasons good.

Jessy was beginning to get a feel for this whole horse ranch thing and he even jumped aboard one of the less lethal animals from time to time and learned some cool horse stuff along the way. Did you know that there is a correct side of a horse to climb up on one...on? It's the left side for those of you who didn't know. If you grew up in the country, your daddy taught you all this horse stuff at a really early age, however the only stuff Jessy's step dad taught him about horses was how to guess which one was going to win the third race at

Monmouth. Thinking back, he didn't even teach him that or Warren wouldn't have come home from the track all broke...every damn time. If Warren was winning he sure as hell wasn't bringing that money home and giving any to Jessy.

At the horse ranch Jessy learned how to persuade a charging herd of stampeding horses to turn suddenly at the last second into the corral by standing firmly in their path and waving his arms in a convincing manner. Jessy was (told) how to do this circus trick (not shown) by Natasha who seemed just as amazed as Jessy that it worked. Jessy wanted to think she would have felt terrible if he had been trampled into a bloody pile of sailor paste. Jessy liked and respected Natasha but she could be a little scary sometimes.

The ranch was the perfect duty station for a person like Jessy. He liked animals, even the homicidal ones, especially them actually. He enjoyed the pace of the job and was becoming rather fond of the cute girls who their dirty old chief kept hiring to help run the place. These young women, were competent ranch hands, and they all knew what they were doing. That's more than could be said for the Navy washouts they kept sending to the ranch. Most of the girls had been recruited from ranches and 4H clubs in the area. No one knew where Natasha got her skills but she was head and shoulders above the rest...Literally Natasha was tall and strong and very competent. Evidently the chief was an advocate of the women's rights movement because, not some, but all the civilian ranch help he hired were attractive, young girls. There was the element of distraction to deal with at times. That fact helped hone Jessy's concentration skills to a razors edge.

One afternoon Jessy had spent the morning gathering several hundred pounds of fresh grade "A" horse shit into a neat pile using the rake on the back of the tractor. He was in the process of loading the fragrant quality fertilizer into the bed of the dump truck with the front end loader/tractor. Jessy had just plowed into the steaming pile with the scoop and was raising the load to the proper height when a shiny red pickup pulled up and parked next to the corral. At this point a simply gorgeous, young cowgirl jumped out of the cab. She was wearing the tightest pair of perfectly faded Levi's Jessy had ever seen. Her white long sleeved shirt was tied at the waist and she had a cute cowgirl hat tilted back on her long wavy light brown cowgirl hair. Of course while Jessy was making these observations his right hand was still on the lever that was raising the scoop. As luck would have it, he waved his left hand and caught the cowgirls eye and she smiled and waved back. Just then the load of range dumplings came to a very sudden stop as the hydraulic arms of the tractors scoop couldn't go any higher. The bad news was that almost the entire payload emptied out on Jessy's stupidly smiling face. In about a second he was sitting under a giant pile of ripe road apples and spitting out partially digested hay and dirt.

Laughter is a wonderful gift from god or gods or Mario as the case may be, however when the laughter is loud, continuous, and directed in your general direction, it can be more painful than wonderful. There was literally no place to hide and the crowd of people who were gathering at the corral fence seemed to grow to the proportions of a New York City, street scene. Jessy bowed his head, as the mind in that head, slowly, but surely, began to see the humor in his predicament. Jessy smiled weakly and began shyly laughing along with every one else. He realized it would be a long time before he lived this one down. It would also be a long time before he smelled right to his human friends. The horses didn't seem to notice. If the mishap had occurred today it would have been the lead story on "You Tube" for a week. "Now you know why ranch hands wear those big old hats,".

Once every six weeks or so one crew member had to pull "night duty" and would spend the week putting the herd down for the evening. They got the days off but had to come into work while everyone else was leaving. They slept in the bunk house and got up early each morning for a week to feed the horses their breakfast. This was a chore "horse breakfast" is very much the same hay as horse lunch and horse dinner but it had better be on the table at the same time each morning or the crazy long faced bastards would find a way to break out of their makeshift corral in search of greener pastures.

Whenever the horses escaped the ranch hands would have to round them up with their pick up trucks, because...well...all the damn horses had escaped. Jessy and Natasha would drive all over miles of California desert chasing down a herd of very large, very dumb, very swift, animals with a bad case of "I don't want to live in a corral anymore." Jessy would jump out of the truck once they had herded up all the escapees into one large group.

Then he would swing the gate to the corral wide open and position himself between the gate and the bunk house and Natasha in the other truck would drive the herd directly at Jessy and he would attempt the whole " stand in front of the stampede, waiving the arms thing." Jessy was starting to lose confidence in this procedure because the last time he had tried it he saw this look in Danger's eyes as he came way to close to him on his way through the gate. It was like Danger was telling him "Hey fuck head, next time I'm not turning at the last second, I'm going to run your silly stupid ass over and turn you into a bloody pile of dead, government issue, finely ground, sailor meat."

Most of the horses on the ranch were dumb, docile and mostly easily manipulated, however one or two of our four legged friends were cunning and deadly and "Danger" was certainly in the second category. Jessy was constantly on guard whenever Danger and he were on the same side of the fence and the deadly animal always seemed keenly aware of Jessy's every move as well. They developed a relationship based on fear, respect, and hate. Jessy's fear and respect, and "Danger's" hate. Danger made Jessy understand that he wasn't born to be confined in a corral, and they were really kindred spirits in that respect. Some animals and people for that matter are perfectly content surrounded by boundaries and rules but Danger and Jessy were not woven from that thin fabric. Jessy respected Danger and even liked him in a strange way but he was a big wild animal and not to be taken lightly. Some such relationships just are what they are. Jessy wasn't going to change Danger and Danger wasn't going to change Jessy and this was the wonderful deadly glue that kept their bond intact.

CHAPTER 18

The Night Shift

One particularly beautiful moon lit evening as he was getting ready to turn in for the evening Jessy heard a blood chilling high pitched screaming sound coming from out side the bunk house. He was all alone, except for "Major," the super nasty smelling, beat to shit, boxer dog. Jessy knew the sound wasn't coming from him because Major couldn't make a sound. Major was like most of the other animals that the crazy chief brought back to the ranch. Major was a defective dog, he couldn't bark. Major was a watch dog...that couldn't bark. Either Major had been born without vocal cords or he had eaten one to many of his own rotten ass turds and had gotten some kind of horrible throat infection. Whatever had caused the sad creature to become bark-less, the result was the same. He was useless when it came to warning anyone of danger.

Jessy left Major in the bunk house because dogs tend to overreact and he didn't want to put him in a situation where he could be killed and eaten. Slowly Jessy ventured out into the moonlight and tried to focus in on the origin of the screeching noises that had grown much louder once he moved outdoors. There was a giant stack of hay bales piled up into a wall eight bales high, four bales wide and about twenty bales in length. They had pulled several bales from the stack to provide ventilation leaving void spaces variously spaced along the sides of the pile. As Jessy approached the hay depot the ear splitting screeches seemed to be coming from one of those holes. Just as he was about to peek into the dark space where the noise was coming from this giant "Rodan" looking monster of a bat flew at Jessy's face. He leapt backwards and the huge bat narrowly avoided him as he flip flopped his way up into the night sky, silhouetting himself against the full moon before he disappeared like an invisible horror story that will live in your mind forever.

After the live nature exhibition Jessy returned to the bunk house and made a fateful but fortunate decision. It was getting cold so he decided to let "Major" stay in the bunk house for the night. Normally Major slept on a pile of straw just outside the bunk house where he could silently defend the bunk house from any intruders Major was like a Ninja guard dog, but just this once because of the cold night air Jessy was granting Major temporary amnesty. He was hoping that his horrible smell wouldn't keep him awake all night. Jessy had no idea that this simple choice would prove to be a life and death decision.

Inside the bunk house there was a giant, ancient, World War Two era oil heater that had a reservoir of fuel oil and Jessy wrongly decided it would be a great idea to light that sucker up. After twenty minutes or so he finally managed to get the beast of a heater lit and adjusted. Slowly but surely the old wooden building began to get all warm and toasty. Jessy was really tired by now so he climbed into his bunk and soon was dreaming of Catholic school girls in plaid skirts riding surf boards. This dream wasn't nearly as weird and twisted as it sounds because the school girls were all wearing plaid berets.

Exactly what happened next Jessy could only speculate, his best guess was that a strong gust of wind had sucked the flue in the heater's chimney closed causing the old oil burner to start belching out smoke. Not a little smoke like when some guys play poker all night puffing on "cigars and Lucky Strikes." We're talking about thick greasy black as coal oxygen free smoke, like when a pile of tires catch on fire in a closet. Within minutes Jessy was in mortal danger and was completely unaware of his impending demise. Luckily Major was on the case and jumped into action. When the building began filling with noxious fumes he initially tried waking Jessy by licking his face with the same god awful tongue he used to wash his dog nuts and nasty ass hole. Jessy only stirred long enough to slap him away and went back to sleep. Major was desperate and he opted to use the most potent weapon in his arsenal. He turned around and backed his rotten ass as close to Jessy's face as he could and let loose with the most atrocious dog fart of all time. The sound alone was enough to wake up dead people but the smell was something that could peel the paint off of a battleship. Jessy woke up instantly and thought he must be inside a giant fried goat turd. "OH MY GOD what in holy hell is that?" He began choking and was blinded by the smoke and the darkness.

When he had gone to sleep the moon was coming in through the blankets that they used for curtains, but now he couldn't see a thing. Jessy lost his bearings as he tried to feel his way toward the door but kept crashing into walls when the old nasty dog came to the rescue again by clawing loudly at the front door. Jessy worked his way in the direction of the sound while trying not to breath. Jessy was aware of the danger now and realized how much trouble they were in. He was dizzy and close to passing out when he found Major, the door, and the door nob all at the same time. Jessy blasted the door open, grabbed the dog, and staggered out into the bright moonlight. He fell to his knees and started choking up thick black gooey crap and kept on gagging for several minutes. It was like puking but this stuff was coming from his lungs not his stomach. Finally Jessy was able to stand up and take a big deep breath of fresh clean air and try to figure out what the hell had just happened. He looked back at the building and the filthy black cloud was still pouring out of the door as if the gates of hell were in the basement.

Jessy's lungs were burning as he pieced the story together in his head including the "stuck flue and the flue suck" theory and realized that the only reason he was standing outside the building and not fast asleep, forever, inside it, was that nasty, smelly, silent, boxer dog who at the moment was happily bathing his rotten ass hole with his sloppy foot long tongue. Again Jessy dropped to his knees but this time it was to grab Major around the neck and hug him. The dog licked his face and Jessy didn't even cringe or throw up. Looking back that was really so gross. Jessy had tears in his eyes but that was because Major had farted again and Jessy almost lost consciousness. From that day forward Jessy became Major's benefactor. He defended him whenever someone tried to give him any shit. Jessy also made sure Major got regular rations of beef, even though he had to trade a few pairs of size ten bowling shoes and other items to the guys working over at the chow hall. What the hell, his commander would never miss them and there wasn't a hard copy of the inventory. That poor smelly old dog was not a heroic figure in the traditional sense but he was and always will be a hero to Jessy.

RANT ALERT! I'm an animal lover and always have been. Some of my fondest memory's revolved around the dogs and cats...and squirrels in my life. I'll never understand the goofy morons who think we need to put an end to scientific experiments involving embryonic stem cells, but these very same misguided, uninformed, missing links, (this statement by no means is meant as a slur against actual missing links) think it's fine to do truly terrible things to beagle dogs that are bread only to get injected with bugs that all the other bugs are terrified of. Then when all their hair falls out they get injected with stuff that will either cure them or kill them or make them grow flippers. If they die somebody puts them in a red plastic bio hazard bag and they throw what was once a cute little brown and white puppy in the bio hazard dumpster. I'm sorry but there is just something very wrong with this picture. "Dogs are people too. They put "Michael Vick" in prison and his dogs at least had a chance to fight for their life. The poor dogs in medical labs don't have a chance. I suppose the fact that they don't use human minorities to test scary stuff on was a step in the right dIrection. Hey Alabama! You did stop experimenting on African Americans in Tuskegee, right?

For those of you who think a tiny cell on a petri dish is more viable than a cute little puppy. Why don't you simply adopt the cells and raise them as your own? Perhaps you can convince the pet food company to come out with "Purina stem cell chow." Good luck with that by the way. I can see you now taking your petri dish for a walk in the park with the tiny red plastic dish in a stroller as normal people point at you and chuckle. Then you could sign your cell up for soccer, or God forbid football. How would you even know if your cell had a "hammy?' Maybe you could take George Bush or Herschel Walker or Donald Trump with you when you take your super smart stem cell to get him enrolled at Dartmouth or MIT. Although I'm willing to bet that your stem cell would probably be smarter than all those other three guys combined.

It's all about priorities and actual humanity. When people are starving in Newark, or drowning in New Orleans, or raising a family in the back of a Dodge station wagon just about anywhere, and the tiny brained folks are more concerned about a stem cell or god forbid a fetus then they are about caring for the less fortunate among us? Come on people, you have got to stop living your lives based on the absurd talking points you hear on "Fox fake News" and right wing talk radio. You were born with common sense and misplaced it somewhere. Go back in your head and look for it now and don't go outside until you find it. Oh, and please don't send me any more stupid E-mails about President Obama being a communist, born in Africa, Muslim terrorist, Nazi, with an expired library book on his record. Really please I'm serious. You dick heads are driving me fucking crazy.

CHAPTER 19

This is the end my friend

    Jessy's Navy days were nearly numbered. His enlistment was due to expire in a few months but there were several loose ends that still had not been determined. Jessy was still on legal hold, pending prosecution for possession of an amount of illegal...something or other. The seed he was accused of transporting was sort of chubby as seeds go. No one had contacted him since the giant drug bust in the parking lot and the useless subsequent assignment of free legal counsel. Jessy was curious but for the last year he was trying to forget that this legal matter was hanging over him like a big black go directly to jail cloud. Jessy imagined that he could be shipped off to Portsmouth Naval prison for a very long time. One of his fellow sailors at Miramar had written a document explaining his feelings concerning the war and the military in particular. He turned his manuscript in to his superiors and was never heard from again.

    Besides the legal issues Jessy had to deal with, there was also the issue of finding a suitable replacement to take over for him. Jessy was either going to be discharged or chained up and hauled off to room some where that doesn't have a doorknob on the inside. This was a heady decision because his job in the Navy didn't exist. The Navy has patches that defines your job description. You Iron it on your denim work shirt or sew it on your dress uniform. There was no such patch to describe a Navy sailor who works on a horse ranch. They have a patch (Jessy's old patch) for people who work on aircraft, a propeller with wings. They have a patch for people who dispose of explosive stuff. A mine with crossed torpedoes. Try as he might Jessy could snatch no such patch with a horse of any sort. (sorry Dr. Seuss) that was pitiful.

At the ranch Jessy's second in command was an Italian kid named Vinnie Badetto but everyone knew him as Bandit. He was a city kid from New York but he caught on to the ranch routine in no time. The initiation Jessy put him through didn't seem to bother him a bit. He was smiling the whole time as Jessy drove him all over the base at break neck speed. Jessy and Dave nearly rolled the truck trying to get him to break a sweat but he was like a kid on the Magic Mountain ride at Six Flags. Alas, Bandit was soon to be discharged for the crime of setting up a nice little gambling operation on base. He would have been the perfect choice to run the ranch when Jessy was gone. The place ran like a Swiss watch and Bandit knew all the tricks to keep their little piece of horse infested heaven Tip Top.

Another candidate to run the ranch operations was almost too scary to take seriously but was very cool and quite funny, for an alcohol abuser. This persons name was Pat and he was usually wearing a cast or bandage or using a crutch, from a recent accident. Pat was always in the wrong place at the wrong time. Jessy met Pat when he showed up for duty on his first day at the ranch. He had been busted for selling small amounts of pot around the base. He was wearing a short sleeve denim work shirt with the tell tale unfaded area on the shoulder where his rank patch had once lived. He also had a large bandage covering the top of his head and another under his chin. Everyone was curious about the gauze so they asked Pat to explain his injuries. It seems Pat was at a party, got drunk, and walked thru a glass patio door. Twenty-two stitches and a series of little haircuts on his head and he was ready to rock. Hard to look at perhaps, but ready.

A week later Pat showed up for work with an abbreviated version of his original bandages plus a cast on his left arm. Jessy asked Pat to tell all in attendance how he had broken his arm. Pat explained how he was at a party at the same home where he had injured himself a week earlier. This time he got drunk and performed a perfect jack knife from the diving board of the swimming pool but didn't notice that the pool had been drained so that kids who lived there could shred the pool with their skate boards. Jessy told Pat he might want to consider smoking pot. Pot smokers might think about doing dangerously stupid stuff but usually never get around to actually doing it.

The third week Pat had lost the bandages on his head, he still had a cast on his arm and was walking with a limp. Jessy said. "Hey man, what the hell did you do to yourself this time, for Christ sakes?" Pat sheepishly told him that he had gotten drunk, yet again, and he was riding his 650 Triumph motorcycle back from another party at the same home that had been so cruel to him in the past. Half way to the base he blasted through a stop sign and got run over buy a sports car. When I say he got run over I don't mean that in a figurative way. There was a cop parked close to the intersection who saw the whole event. The patrol officer jumped out of his cruiser and ran over to Pat expecting to find a crushed and bloody corpse.

The automobile had rolled directly over Pat's chest. By the time he got to the scene Pat was getting to his feet and dusting himself off. The officer was stunned and asked profusely if Pat was all right. Pat assured him that he was fine so the cop wrote him his ticket for the whole stop sign thing and then got back in his "Crown Vic" and drove away to give out some more tickets and if he was lucky hit somebody with a stick. California cops were trained to collect revenue first and deal with lawsuits later. All things considered Pat would have made a fine choice to take the reins, (so to speak) of the horse ranch. Jessy however had to choose someone with a better chance of living long enough to actually do the job.

One person near the top of Jessy's short list was a very intelligent Irish guy with all the qualities he was looking for. Jessy and Shawn were friends and Jessy knew Shawn was smart enough to deal with the chief as well as the personalities that would challenge his sprit on a daily basis. Shawn could be trusted. Trust was a rare commodity but absolutely a necessary component to their ranch machine running smoothly. They all had a lot to loose and were dependent on one another. What happened at the ranch stayed on the ranch. Unfortunately for Shawn there were things going on in his life that were far beyond his control. Shawn was from Los Angeles and his father had been chosen for jury duty. Not a big deal normally but the trial that his father was sitting through involved a strange little crazy person named Charles Manson and his misguided mob of murdering minions. The story was unfolding all around southern California and Shawn's dad was stuck right in the middle. This story isn't about the Manson trial but the Manson trial is a part of the story.

Shawn started showing up late for duty or not at all. The ranch didn't operate the same way as the rest of the base and Jessy had no problem covering up for someone who needed a personal day or two or six. The chief would ask "Have you seen the red headed Mic?" and Jessy would respond "Shawn drove out to La Mesa to get a load of Omolene for the herd" Omolene is a Purina product made from oats and molasses and horses can't get enough of the stuff. The horses couldn't live on hay alone and they used the Omolene to supplement their diets. There was plenty stored up but now Jessy would have to hide it someplace until Shawn showed up.

Jessy was worried about Shawn and when he finally came to work the next day he was drunk and hungover. Jessy took him aside and Shawn told him, very slowly, that things were not going well a home. The family was falling apart as the Manson trial dragged on. The jurors eventually would be sequestered for 255 days. The longest trial in history up to that point.

Note: Jurors get $15.00 per day in LA today. Whatever they were getting in 1970 wasn't enough and employers are supposed to hold your job open for you but they don't have to pay you in your absence. If you are ever chosen for jury simply tell them. "I don't believe in law and order" … I'm not certain how this will turn out.

Shawn was finally discharged for personal reasons due to his family issues caused by a blood thirsty lunatic with a swastika tattoo between his eyes. Jessy's search for a replacement continued. When a new guy showed up one day to fill in for Shawn Jessy looked him up and down and said, "Screw it, you will have to do." The stunned and bewildered look on the new guy's face told Jessy that he had left something out of his welcome aboard speech. "Too late now" Jessy thought, he had work to do and his last days in the worlds most dangerous navy were at hand. Jessy grabbed the new kid and led him over to the old stake truck they used for mending fences, looked him sternly in the eyes and just said. "Get in." The new guy did as he was told. Jessy out ranked him and he was already in tons of trouble or he wouldn't have been assigned to this outfit. Jessy had no Idea why he got sent to the ranch and frankly he didn't give a shit.

Jessy was going to get the fresh meat up to speed or die trying so he fired up the truck, ground it into gear and sped off just slightly ahead of a giant cloud of dust. The truck was an old deuce and a half (two and a half ton) from one of our past wars. It was like the truck you see in all the war movies with a bunch of American soldiers riding in the back. Some had a canvas cover some were open, this one was stripped down to the flat bed with stake fences placed into railing slots on the sides. As they picked up speed the new kid looked a little scared and he yelled over the roar of the engine. "Where are we going?" Jessy yelled back "It doesn't matter. This ride is all about the trip not about the destination." Now the kid really looked scared. This was his initiation and the sooner he got it over with the better. The truck was running well but still took a while to get up to scary speed. Jessy yelled over to the kid riding shotgun "Hey, what's your name kid?" Jessy was like twenty-one years old and he's calling somebody kid. The new guy looked at Jessy fearfully and yelled back "My name's Frank." Jessy thought that somehow Frank just might be the perfect name for someone who was going to take over for him at the ranch. You know, like in Jesse and Frank James. Billy would have been an awesome name as well. Jessy glanced over at Frank as he was about to piss in his pants and decided this wasn't the time to ask him if he wanted to change his name.

They were up to speed. Jessy had no idea what that speed was because he had used the speedometer cable to tie the muffler to the frame of the truck on a recent trip to the base. He didn't need his muffler flying loose and taking out a ranking officer when there was possibly pot in the glove compartment. Ranking officers were a dime a bushel but freedom had no price...at the time. This was before the O. J. Simpson trial.

Frank was just starting to enjoy the ride down a stretch of dirt road when he saw the 90 degree left turn up ahead. Jessy had pulled this maneuver with other new guys in the past and it never failed to provide the desired results. Sometimes it got a little smelly depending mostly on what the individual had had for dinner the night before. Instead of slowing down for the curve Jessy sped up. You could see the hard left turn from a half mile away. Straight ahead the earth seemed to disappear. Frank was screaming "stop you crazy bastard we're going to die" That was Jessy's cue. He reached up to the top of the steering wheel with both hands and squinted his eyes almost shut and hit the gas as far as it would go. Frank was screaming so loud you could hear him all the way back in where ever it was he came from. Jessy didn't turn at all and simply drove over the cliff. It wasn't much of a cliff really, just a five foot drop that wasn't visible from the road. They went airborne for a few seconds that to Frank seemed like an eternity. They came down hard but more or less unharmed and Jessy was already pondering how he would explain the damage to the truck to Dick finger. The front shocks were toast but the leaf springs were still intact. About then was when Jessy heard the banging on the roof of the truck." What the hell is that?" Jessy wondered.

Suddenly Jessy remembered why he was driving the flatbed that day. They were preparing to go out and repair some sections of broken barbed wire fence when Frank showed up. Jessy had already loaded up a roll of barbed wire, some tools, and a bag of U shaped fence nails, and the two guys in the back of the truck. Jessy had completely spaced them out. If he had looked in the rear view mirror, even once, He would have noticed their legs directly behind him out the back window. Jack and Danny, a couple of misfits who worked as laborers sometimes were standing on the flatbed, hanging on by their finger nails.

Jessy slowed down, stopped in the middle of the dirt road and jumped out to survey the damage to the truck and his passengers. Jesse was fine, apart from the mental stress he had just endured. Danny was bleeding from a cut on his chin. His face came down on the roof of the truck when they went over the cliff. Jack did have a number of small puncture wounds he suffered when he fell backwards onto the roll of barbed wire and he was going to recover but was badly in need of a new work shirt. The truck shocks were bleeding red fluid from the ruptured seals but the six tires were still attached to the axles. All things considered they were looking good. By they we mean Jessy. Everything and everyone else was going to need a little work. The side rail fences of the truck were out on the range somewhere as were the tools. The barbed wire was safe thanks to Jack who used his body to save it from certain death. The Barbed wire saved Jack as well by clinging to the deck of the truck with it's hundreds of tiny claws. That last line makes more sense if you have ever had to deal with barbed wire on a personal level. The flat bed was mostly...well flat...and empty. Looking back Jessy could see how things could have gone badly but Frank had gotten a well rounded tour of the east side of the base and it's likely he understood the people running things at the ranch...weren't to be taken lightly.

Note: A day without blood is like a day without sunshine. If you work with sharp tools or telephone poles or horses or barbed wire and you come home from work and you aren't bleeding from somewhere...you just aren't trying.

Jessy drove over to the base one morning, unannounced. They didn't have a phone at the ranch and no one had a cell phone back then. I know, right?

Rant Alert: What the hell did we do before cell phones? We didn't communicate with one another constantly and we got a whole hell of a lot of work done and we didn't crash into the guy stopped at the light just as we were about to hit send. Today they say the American worker is the most productive worker on the planet. "They" might be exaggerating a bit but imagine how productive we were when we weren't sitting in front of a computer all day playing electronic games and checking up on our Facebook and Twitter accounts. And don't get me started on porn hub. At least the people who eat lunch in their work trucks and take showers when they get home are still getting shit done, like every god damn day done.

Jessy went directly to the legal office and asked to speak to his lawyer. They were expecting him? Wait? What? Jessy's case was sitting open on the lawyers desk. Shit like that happened to Jessy all the time during his last two years in the service. No one knows why. Well, somebody knew but it certainly wasn't Jessy. His new lawyer was sitting behind his temporary desk. (Apparently Jessy had six other lawyers since his first) but no one had told Jessy. The new Lawyer guy had a proud grin on his not very smart looking face. He informed Jessy that all charges had been dropped due to a lack of evidence. They never had that much to start with. One little burnt up seed wasn't something anyone would want to spend the rest of their life in prison over. Perhaps keeping a loose lid on his feelings about the Viet Nam war these last two years was more important to them. This fact was something Jessy has always believed. They knew what they were going to do with him for quite some time but waited until his last days in the Navy to tell him. Whatever had happened, in a few days, Jessy would be allowed to pack up all his shit and go on his way.

Jessy thanked his new lawyer...for what...he had no idea. About then he calmly walked out of his lawyer's office. There was a strange sense of relief as Jessy felt the warm California sun on his face. Jessy had put the possibility of prison away in a closet in the very back of his mind. For two years he made believe that the government wasn't going to drop the hammer on him, but he knew, all to well, that at any moment the worst could descend on him like a swarm of hungry, rabid, sewer rats. Now he could finally let it all go. Somewhere inside, Jessy secretly wanted to rip all his clothes off and dance around the parking lot until his feet got sore, but discretion took hold and, shook him a couple of times and reminded him that if he did his whole freedom dance thing he might need another bad, government issue, lawyer. Thanks discretion you have served us well.

CHAPTER 20

Much Closer to The End My Friend

So far this book hasn't mentioned the part where Jessy went home, got married to his high school sweetheart and had a son during his last year in the service. His wife was a good woman and a great mother. Nichole had nothing at all to do with what was happening to Jessy on base and that was how it had to be. They lived off base in a small but beautiful apartment in a quiet neighborhood in San Diego. Their small apartment complex looked like a Spanish hacienda with fresh white stucco walls and a vivid red tile roof. There was a long wide stairway up from the street and it was painted dark red in contrast to the bright white stucco. Vines with red bougainvillea flowers hung from the top of the stairway and there was a court yard at the top. In the courtyard you walked on a red painted concrete sidewalk, past some goofy little banana palms with tiny bananas on them. The courtyard had a coy pond and a small Japanese foot bridge in case you wanted to cut across to one of the apartments on the other side. There were ten units situated around the courtyard and Jessy and Nichole lived in the first one on the right at the top of the stairs. It was a little slice of paradise and they loved it there. The best part was that they were only paying a little over three hundred a month rent including utilities. They got along great with the landlord and his wife and they became best friends.

Jessy and Nichole got to know some of the neighbors and one couple in particular made them feel right at home. John and Michele lived in the big apartment directly across the foot bridge from them and they were invited over to their place on a regular basis. John always had a quantity of quality marijuana and he; Michelle and Jessy would get high and talk and laugh until late at night. Nichole wasn't a pot smoker but she enjoyed watching them get stoned and listening to the crazy shit John and Jessy came up with together. John wanted to start a magazine that would be a Mexican version of Playboy and he wanted Jessy to do the artwork. Jessy was glad that he didn't want him to write the captions for the cartoons because he never understood the humor in Mexican jokes after they were translated into English. Humor is hard in any language but to try translating "Jokes" is Einstein hard.

One weekend John and Michelle threw a party at their apartment and even went out and got a real tiger skin rug for their living room floor. The rug was huge and you had to be careful not to trip over the immense tiger head. Jessy wasn't a fan of the dead tiger he had to walk on but the party itself, was off the hook. The second and third things Jessy and Nichole noticed when they entered the apartment (first being the tiger rug) were two identical beautiful young women in mini skirts and high heel boots. As it turned out, they were Playboy playmates, the "Collinson" twins. They were the first paired set in Playboy history to that point. Jessy and Nichole were in awe as they checked out the people who showed up at the party.

The men were dressed in elegant suits. The women were wearing the most expensive designer clothes they had ever seen, in person. Jessy had never been to a runway fashion show but the clothes worn by some of the women at the party would certainly rival anything found on Rodeo Drive. The women them selves gave you the impression that at least some if not most of the men hadn't brought their wives. At first Jessy and Nichole were embarrassed to be in the same room with these people but everyone was very respectful and friendly. Jessy surmised that some of these people were politicians and the only thing worse, lawyers. Jessy took John aside at one point and asked him who all his friends were. He started to list them off as the San Diego elite. Lawyers, artists, business owners, politicians, and of course, playmates. The Mayor showed up for a while but Do Not quote Jessy on that last remark...but he looked just like the Mayor.

John was involved in some kind of business with several of the men at the party but he was not very specific and Jessy didn't ask. This was not a business meeting, this was a party and John spent most of the evening entertaining his prominent guests and Michelle spent quite a while talking to Nichole and Jessy. Michelle was just as intimidated by Johns friends as they were. The party was a little boring compared to what Jessy was used to but the food was amazing and there was an excellent wine selection. Not one of the wines came in a gallon bottle with a finger hole on the neck or a box. Someone was lighting up joints in the kitchen and that made the food taste even better. Jessy and Nichole didn't stay all night long but the party was still going strong when they said their good-byes. They took the short walk over the bridge and past the banana trees back to their apartment and both of them had a new found appreciation for their friends across the courtyard.

About a week or two after the party Jessy was returning from work at the ranch. He had parked his Olds convertible in the lot next to the apartment. He didn't lock the car or bother to put the top up. No one was going to steal it and there was zero chance of rain at this time of year in San Diego. Jessy grabbed his lunch box and thermos and started climbing the red steps when his neighbor Michelle came blasting out of her apartment leaving the door wide open. She was carrying a pile of clothes and a woven bag stuffed with personal belongings. Michelle ran past Jessy on the stairs screaming "turn on the NEWS!" She disappeared around the corner on her way to the parking lot. Jessy heard the Jaguar fire up, the screech of burning rubber and then just the sound of the finely tuned 12 cylinder driving machine as it sped away. That was the last time they ever saw or heard from their friend Michelle.

Jessy hurried up to the front door and rushed into the living room like a crazy man and turned on the second hand television. There were only six stations on the antenna and at this time of day only two of them would be broadcasting the national evening news. The used TV slowly lit up to the CBS news with Walter Cronkite. Walter was just announcing breaking news from San Diego, California. At first Nichole was startled and a little pissed at Jessy for not taking time to say hello. But now she was glued to the image on the screen, as was Jessy. There had been a big drug bust up the coast and suddenly they were looking at a photo of their friend and neighbor, John. They said his name and address. His address was the same as their address. They showed video of a big Hertz rental van parked by a dock with huge piles of cellophane wrapped kilos of what one had to assume was high quality Marijuana.

John and a group of very high profile residents of San Diego had been busted after a long investigation with eight thousand pounds of marijuana. The pot had been shipped up from Mexico on a Yacht.

Note: Most of the drugs that make it across our southern border get here on trucks, boats, or thru tunnels under the border. Not in the backpacks of people trying to swim or walk across. Some of the drugs that Americans purchase do get here that way but it is likely that the cartels use that as a way to take the DEA's eyes off the actual pathways that are supplying our nations insatiable appetite for drugs.

Note, Note: President Nixon started the war on drugs but President Reagan put that program on crack, literally. The CIA under Reagan flew tons of coke into the US, specifically Los Angeles and delivered it to the drug dealers who converted the coke into crack and sold it to young black and brown kids and created the drug epidemic and the huge central American drug cartels that we see today. (Google Iran Contra affair)

This was the biggest bust in the history of Nixon's drug war at the time. Jessy and Nichole turned toward each other and said in unison "HOLY SHIT" before turning back to the TV. Both of them realized that some of those people they had met at the party were part of this story and at least one of them owned a yacht. Jessy didn't think that the Playboy playmate twins had anything to do with the conspiracy but John sure as hell did. They guessed that John may have been the idea man and had brought the rest of the group and their resources together at the party. Many of the people they had met at the party were investors in the enterprise and they expected, but never got, a return on their investment. You have to wonder if insurance covers this sort of thing.

The story really hit home to Jessy, especially the part about the long investigation. Someone was at the party who didn't belong there…besides Jessy and Nichole. That same someone knew Jessy was there also. Jessy was nearly about to be discharged from the Navy. He was finally being cleared from all his legal difficulties and was about to embark on the next chapter of his young life. Now, something new and unexpected could put an end to that chapter if he wasn't careful. Nichole really had no real understanding of what Jessy had been going through up to this point and that he was still under some kind of investigation by people in grey suits. Jessy will always regret that Nichole had to share this strange time with him. She didn't deserve it but she dealt with it while giving birth and raising their son in the government funded mad house that government had created.

They were preparing for Jessy's discharge and getting all of their ducks and chickens in a row. Jessy had been looking around town for a job in case they decided to stay in California. He tried the airlines first, thinking that being a veteran with jet engine experience would get him a job. They told him at the recruitment office that jet school was a ticket to a good job in civilian life. They lied. You need an A&P (airframe and power plant) license to work on aircraft in the United States. In Russia all you needed was a pair of pliers and a roll of duct tape. Jessy would need to attend classes, and get a certification before he could even apply for a job with the airlines even though he had worked on military aircraft and served as a plane captain in the navy. Jessy couldn't wait that long for work. He needed a job within a week or two of his discharge from the service. You don't save up much money on military pay, especially when you are married with children.

Jessy resigned himself to the fact that they were homeward bound. He loved California and would have sold oranges on street corners if it was just him. Jessy and Nichole's families were back in New Jersey and they could provide support for them until they got back on their feet. They had a baby son to think about and didn't want to end up with no money, no job, and no home that far away from their roots.

Note: When you see a family pushing a shopping cart filled with all there be longings, it's just people who made some bad choices.

With a few days to go on his enlistment Jessy rented a Hertz rental truck and they started to pack up their stuff and load it into big cardboard boxes. One thing that worried Jessy was the fact that his ex-neighbor, John, had used a truck similar to the one they were loading in his attempt to smuggle huge amounts of pot into the country. At first Jessy thought that his fears were just left over paranoia from the crazy FBI/NCIS investigation he had just gone through but when he got home from work on his next to last day he pulled into their parking lot and there were two men wearing black warmup jackets poking around the Hertz van. Jessy approached them after parking the convertible in the shade. It was hot and he wondered why these two guys were wearing jackets. He understood the dark Foster Grant sunglasses. It was very bright late in the afternoon, but he suspected these guys wore theirs all night long. As he walked toward the men they hurried to their "dark grey" sedan and drove off.

Note: When I say their that car was dark grey what I mean is the car was regular grey but what was going on inside that car made it seem much darker.

Jessy told his wife about the agents in the parking lot when he entered their apartment and she said she thought she had seen some people wandering around the courtyard that afternoon. Jessy heard the old saying "It's not paranoia when they are really out to get you." ringing in his head.

CHAPTER 21

The End of Days

Jessy still had some chores to do before leaving the base for good. On his last day he arose early and headed off toward the Naval air station at Miramar. He thought this was going to be like the last day in high school, visiting friends, signing yearbooks but Jessy was in for a few surprises. On his way through Murphy Canyon, he saw smoke up ahead and what appeared to be a car on fire by the side of the road. Normally Jessy would have pulled over and given the stranded motorist a helping hand. As he got closer to the car that had a growing case of flames leaping from beneath the hood Jessy realized the car in question was his old 1956 Buick Roadmaster from days gone by. Not only was he able to recognize his ex-car but also the guy he had sold it to. When Jessy and Nichole got married they thought it only fair to upgrade their ride. They used $500.00 of their wedding money, or more accurately most of their wedding money, to buy the 1960 Oldsmobile convertible.

Jessy needed to get rid of his old Buick due to parking issues. There was a first class petty officer from the base who needed a reasonably priced vehicle so Jessy sold him the Buick for $5.00. Nichole was really pissed but Jessy calmly explained that he had only paid $65.00 for that giant piece of shit over two years ago. She was still pissed. The buyer was a big man. Not football player big but more like too much time at the lunch counter big. Jessy didn't know his real name but his full nick name was "Meat and Potatoes," he went by "Meat."

Meat was all happy when Jessy sold him the car. He thought he was getting over on him and he loved making good deals and ripping people off whenever possible and then bragging about it later for way too long. He went freaking nuts with glee when Jessy quoted him the price. That was then but now he looked like he wanted to kill someone as he franticly threw handfuls of sand at the car while the flames grew and grew. Jessy slid down in his seat and sped up a little as he passed the horrible scene that was getting much worse every second. Jessy was looking in the rear view mirror from a short ways up the highway when the car blew up. It was a fireball explosion that threw Meat back a few feet but he didn't look badly injured. Meat didn't have a lot going on in the eyebrow department for a while after the explosion but Jessy didn't feel guilty. After all, Meat was the one driving around in a five dollar car for the last year.

When Jessy got to the base he headed over to the dispersement office to get his military status changed so that he could pick up his last pay check that included separation money that was going to pay for the rental van they'd be driving to New Jersey. Jessy was in and out in no time. These military paper pushers could be really efficient when they wanted to be. It was Friday and they needed the office completely devoid of work at the end of the work week so they could enjoy happy hour.

Jessy had his check folded safely in his shirt pocket as he strolled down the sidewalk toward the sort of new car. He was just starting to enjoy his feelings of freedom when he suddenly noticed a wave lieutenant headed in his direction. She was very attractive and her uniform was perfect in every respect. The dress shoes were black patent leather and the creases in her pleated skirt were straight and sharp. She wore a cunt cap tilted just slightly to one side. (I apologize but that's what it was called) Jessy noticed she was glaring at him as they passed each other. He could hear her spin on her heel as she barked at him to stop right where he was. He stopped about ten feet away and turned slowly in her direction, smiled and asked if he could help her in some way. She stared and exclaimed "You didn't salute me sailor" Jessy considered her statement for a brief moment and answered "No, I did not" Then she yelled at him "You didn't salute me because I'm a woman" Again Jessy paused in thought and responded "That is not true, I have nothing but respect for women, my mother is a woman, I didn't salute you because you are an officer." She was visibly shaken and her eyes started to blink. She took a quick step in his direction. Jessy took an even quicker, and much longer step backwards. Again she strutted toward him and again Jessy jumped back away from her. He was wearing sneakers, she was wearing two inch heeled patent leather shoes. She didn't have a snow cone's chance in hell of catching him and she knew it. The lieutenant was way to uptight to start screaming and there weren't any people within range to hear her if she did. Jessy was holding all the cards so he simply turned and walked away. Jessy had stuff to do.

Note: Authority has a place but in Jessy's world, at that time and in that place the need for supervision was a small concern. If you want someone's respect...earn it. Don't tell a person to give you respect or you will have them locked up in chains. That's not respect, that is fear, and people should try very hard not to let fear run their lives. Shit happens, and when it does you have to deal with it, but don't waste your life being afraid of things that you can't control. If the base had been suddenly attacked by the Viet Cong, or Nazis, or little green men Jessy would have reacted in an appropriate manner and if someone with a higher rank started giving him orders he would have obeyed those orders.

The next thing on Jessy's agenda was a trip to the sick bay for his exam. They need to find out if you are too physically and or mentally screwed up to be released back into society. There is also the need to establish if you are eligible for benefits based upon a service related disability. Jessy explained it thusly. If a service man or woman entered the military with X number of limbs and only had Y number of limbs when he or she was discharged they would be eligible to Z amount of dollars forever or until death which ever came first. Z was a number dependent on the difference between X and Y. The size of the compensation, Z, changes regularly and is adjusted for inflation. In high school "they" told Jessy he really sucked at algebra... obviously... "They" were mistaken.

Jessy drove over to the sick bay and walked into the sterile waiting area. The person behind the counter was neatly dressed in his perfectly ironed and starched summer white uniform. It had been a long time since he'd seen that look on a sailor. On the flight line the sailors always wore the standard bell bottom Seafarer jeans a denim shirt and a blue ball cap. Jessy personally wore an army, khaki jacket on his night shift. Working on the ranch the only piece of clothing that resembled anything Navy issue were bell bottoms. They wore tee shirts and hats. Most of the hats were baseball caps but there were a few white "Dixie cups" (the round folding sailor hat that could be fashioned into any number of interesting shapes) Most guys shaped their sailor hats into a square and then rolled down the top edges. The girls at the ranch wore cowboy hats and they wore them well.

The seaman at the front counter sent Jessy to the audio department for an ear exam. When you work on the line on an airbase the first thing they want to know is, did you go deaf while working around jet engines all day for four years. Jessy went into the sound proof booth and listened for the faint sounds emanating from a pair of head phones. Some of the sounds he was listening for sounded like the constant ringing he had in his head all the time. Many years later he found out that the noise in his head is called "tinnitus" When they asked Jessy if he could hear the high pitched sound he said yes. There were other sounds that had been completely erased from his hearing spectrum. Many years later Jessy would apply for, and get, a disability for hearing loss and would receive a compensation check from the VA. What's 40 years times $120.00 a month? That's what he lost by not getting a service connected disability after his ear exam that day. It's $57,600.00 by the way. There was also the issue of saying "huh or say again" for all those years. Both of Jessy's wives thought he was just an inattentive douche bag.

After the hearing exam Jessy returned to the waiting room and waited to see a doctor for his physical exam. The magazines in the waiting room were "Sports Afield" and "Hot Rod" and that was cool. Jessy loved cars and had a subscription to Hot Rod when he was in high school. There was a wait but it wasn't terrible and he had the time to learn how to replace and adjust a four barrel carburetor. Finally Jessy was called in to see his doctor. He walked into the office and sat in the chair next to the desk. A cold stern looking man in a white coat came into the room but Jessy didn't know if this person was a doctor or not. The Navy has people who are designated as "corpsman" that function as doctors but are not what the rest of the world would consider doctors. You didn't need a degree to be a corpsman. Jessy once saw two corpsmen flip a coin to see who would get to give the totally hot woman in the waiting room her pelvic exam. It is quite possible that the young goddess didn't need a pelvic exam but she got one that day.

As it turned out Jessy's doctor did have a degree and had the rank of commander as well. The commander, doctor, took one look at Jessy and told him he wouldn't examine him until he got a proper hair cut. Jessy blinked and smiled because he instantly thought, incorrectly, that his doctor was just screwing with him. Jessy explained that this was his last day in the Navy and all he wanted was a signature on his paperwork. The commander doctor re-explained to Jessy that he would not examine him unless he got a haircut. He was a commander, doctor, super gigantic asshole, who saw what was going on around him and that his generation was headed to the garbage dump of history. The politics of continuous everlasting war were being confronted by huge numbers of young people that weren't going to take it anymore. This didn't mean that commander doctor was going to take it lying down. He made it his mission in life to make sure that those young warriors of change would pay for their futile misguided attempt to move the country in the direction of peace. Long hair was a symbol of that movement and it had to be crushed or at least shortened to within an inch of its life.

Right about now Jessy came to realize that this day was going to be a long one. He grabbed up his paperwork and headed on over to the base barber shop. Jessy had never seen the inside of the barber shop on base. Generally he got haircuts off base done by a very cute hairdresser in Claremont, the town across the airfield from the base. He had just gotten his hair neatly trimmed the day before his discharge and thought he was looking pretty damn good. He realized that his hair was a we bit long but he would be a civilian in a matter of hours and didn't want to step out into the real world looking like the top of a fucking flagpole.

Jessy asked around for directions to the base hair removal center and found it after a couple of tries. When he entered the unattractive concrete block building everyone inside went silent. People were looking at Jessy and his hair like he was Bigfoot. This was very bad and Jessy started to flash back to the redneck barbershop scene in Tennessee where he was surrounded by the cast of Deliverance. Jessy was torn between running out the door or staying for the second worst haircut of his life. Some of you are thinking "So what's the big deal, suck it up and get the damn hair cut. " Having hair was a big deal to some people in the service, or at least it was until buzz cuts came back into style. Jessy had an Italian barber back in New Jersey who did razor cuts that were worthy of Frankie Valli (reference to the lead singer of the Four Seasons) what ever was going to happen next could destroy Jessy's soul.

(Note: To the guy driving the car in front of me with a head about the size of a sixty watt light bulb. You were ill advised when someone told you that you would look cool with all your hair cut off. Perhaps the, "Just got out of prison" look is cool for someone with a normal size head, but when I pull up behind a car being driven by a doorknob...it freaks me all the way out.)

The barbers in the shop hurried through their other customers like they were Lucy and Ethel in the chocolate factory. They all wanted to get a shot at Jessy's poor head. The winner hustled his last victim out of the shop and motioned Jessy to step up. When his turn arrived

Jessy slowly walked to the chair and kept telling himself "It will grow back...someday it will all grow back." Jessy's hair was really quite long compared to everyone else and the barber really let him have it. Jessy asked barber guy to just give him a trim but he thought he said. "Make me look like a prisoner of war." and he did just that. When he was finished he spun the chair around so Jessy could see himself in the mirror. His hair looked as if it had been attacked by a pack of wolverines on meth. He also noticed the sly grin on the barbers face. Jessy was depressed when he walked out of the "little shop of hair horrors." He didn't want to go home on his last day in the Navy looking like he had lost the war all by himself. Jessy returned to the doctor's office and after listening to commander doctor ream him out for twenty minutes for what he had no idea, the commander doctor finally signed the form. He didn't examine Jessy but he did sign the form. Jessy put on his blue ball cap and walked out.

Jessy finally took his paperwork back to the movie theatre where the commander who was still his superior officer worked. When he walked into the commander's office Jessy's CEO had a strange look on his face. "Don't I know you from somewhere?" he asked. Jessy answered that yes indeed he did because he had been in special services for two years and the commander had been his boss for both of those years. The commander shook his head and said, "I knew you looked familiar." Jessy explained that he worked at the horse ranch and that this was his last day in the Navy and that he could do Jessy a huge favor by signing his release papers. Jessy's commander looked puzzled and asked "This horse ranch? Is that mine?" Jessy told him that he was sure the ranch was a part of special services and that he was the commander in of that, so yeah. Then the commander asked "Where is this horse ranch?" Jessy told him that he had worked there for well over a year...for him, and that it was probably best that he didn't know where it was. After a moment of deliberation the commander agreed. People in management are typically experts at covering their own backsides. Being in charge of something and not knowing it could pose a problem to someone in a position of authority, career wise, however when people in charge of stuff but are too dumb to know it...well that can actually be an asset. The arrangement had worked well for Jessy and it would be a shame if the commander tried to get involved at this point.

The commander realized there was a real possibility that something rather huge had slipped between the cracks, and by cracks that would be his ears. The space occupied by his standard size, government, issue, brain had missed something quite large. That something was a horse ranch that he knew not one little thing about. He had signed paychecks, he had signed purchase orders for everything at the ranch, that wasn't stolen. This included the horses, tons of hay and a truck load of horse shoes but like a typical administrator he never read any of the stuff in his in-basket. He was much to busy dealing in pool tables, bowling shoes and rubber bands to keep track of tiny details, like the ranch, even if this tiny detail was as big as half of the airbase. There is a very good chance that Jessy's commander never signed any of his own paperwork but had one of his subordinates do it for him.

Note: You have to love management. When you realize that the people in charge of you don't know who you are and yet without all of that college educated guidance you still manage to do a superior job and build a fully operational horse ranch with only the help of a few convicted felons and several very good looking female ranch hands, it is very gratifying. To be fair Jessy couldn't have done his job without those lovely young cowgirls. The young women knew how to work around the animals and they loved every minute, and so did Jessy. The women at the ranch taught Jessy a valuable lesson that he kept close ever since. When you choose a course for your life, don't let the money you'll make be your only guiding light. You need to find a path that makes you happy, something that makes you feel fulfilled and valuable. The paycheck is an important bonus but sometimes the less money you have to live on the happier you are. This dynamic, if taken to extremes, makes living impossible. Minimum wage laws are a way to make the divide between the obscenely wealthy and the devastatingly poor less of an issue. Universal healthcare also releases the pressure on families who have to choose between paying hospital bills or paying rent or buying food.

After some friendly negotiations Jessy managed to get his commander to sign his discharge papers. Jessy had one more stop before taking his last drive home. He headed out the front gate and crossed the freeway overpass that lead to the entrance to the horse ranch where his fellow cowboys and cowgirls were waiting to throw him a going away party. Unlike his commander the ranch hands knew who he was but also were aware that this would be the last time that most of them would ever see him again. The Hertz rental van was packed up. Jessy had collected the damage deposit from his landlord. He, his wife and baby son would be New Jersey bound the next morning.

When Jessy arrived at the bunk house the place was full of friendly faces. A while back he had learned to get the unfriendly faces transferred simply by stating that they were scaring the horses. Everyone was cool with this and there were plenty of shitty jobs on base that needed low rent workers to do them. There was always a place to send people who would otherwise mess up the well tuned machine that was the ranch. Someone needed to paint and polish all the cannon balls and other military yard sale junk that decorated every open space and all the buildings. Brass cannon shells make lovely ashtrays when polished with a liberal amount of Brasso.

The girls were all dressed in their finest country outfits that made the rest the navy ranch hands look like rag dolls. Those cowgirls were looking extra good and one in particular...Jessy had to admit, made him take a second look. Debbie was the same young woman who had caused him to dump a giant load of warm wet horse shit on his distracted head one day. It was his own fault but he blamed her just the same. Debbie seemed to be in charge of the party and handed Jessy a beer when he entered the bunk house. She was extra friendly towards Jessy and they sat together on a bunk while the other ranch hands reminisced and told stories of their own experiences with Jessy while he was running the ranch. Jessy was flattered by the attention he received from Debbie that afternoon and noticed looks of longing from several of the guys at the party. Debbie was the fantasy of most of the male workers at the ranch and Natasha was acting a little weird also. Jessy wanted to think Natasha was jealous of Debbie but he had a feeling she was jealous of him. Natasha was tall, beautiful, mysterious, and no one was sure just where her sexual desires led her. Jessy was simply fascinated with the many layers of beguiling woman that was Natasha. If Natasha had a necklace with her name on it that name would be "Danger," just like the killer horse out in the corral. Natasha was the woman you would bring along to rob a bank not the woman you would sit in front of the TV or go shopping with.

Most of the stories told that day revolved around wild drug enhanced thrill rides in the ranch vehicles and everyone was laughing at Jessy's expense. He had to remind some of them that they were laughing now but at the time they were crying like babies and shitting in their bell bottom jeans. At this point Jessy wants to make one thing clear to the friends and relatives of those young men and woman who worked with him at the ranch. Not one of them died or was seriously injured. Did they have a story to tell? Yes they did. The cowboy who spent some time in the ER was the only serious casualty but that was his own damn fault and no one felt the least bit guilty for his misfortune. Near death experiences are good for you. Take it from Kelly Clarkson, "What doesn't kill you makes you stronger."

The party went on all afternoon and they drank the beer stored in the horse feeder. The feeder was a long aluminum half can that was once used to transport helicopter rotor blades. Originally our chief thought that the metal boxes used to ship the soldiers bodies back from Viet Nam would make great feeders to replace the wooden ones. The transport caskets were only used once and there were thousands of them to be had for the asking. The problem with the wooden feeders was that the horses chewed them up faster than the ranch hands could build them. The problem with the caskets was that the horses wouldn't go near them. Horses are weird animals and they have scary instincts. Jessy's crew steam cleaned those metal boxes but the damn horses could still smell death and refused to eat the hay they put in them.

The ranch hands had cleverly covered the ice and beer with hay just in case the chief showed up. Of course when the chief finally did show up he parked his pickup, got out and helped his new girlfriend get down from the passenger seat, and then calmly walked over to the feeder and reached in and pulled three cans of beer out from under the hay. The chief hadn't been born yesterday and like the horses he could smell beer just like they could smell death. The chief was a beer Ninja. He pulled the tabs from two of the cans and dropped them into the cans to prevent the sharp tabs from winding up on the ground where a horse could step on it and tear up the soft underside of its hoof.

Note: The beer cans of old required a can opener that cut a little pie slice into the top of the can but you needed to cut two holes one on each side so air could get in on one side while you sucked the beer out of the other. By the early 1970's their was a pull tab (pop top) that came all the way off. (see Jimmy Buffett and the story of his blown out flip flop).

The ranch hands watched from the window as the chief handed a beer can to his cute, young, girlfriend and headed toward the bunkhouse. Everyone wondered how their old, fat, beat to shit supervisor always managed to surround himself with good looking young girls. Personally Jessy guessed that the chief had plenty of cash stashed away from all his shady business deals and shared some of it freely with gorgeous young women. This was pure speculation on Jessy's part, for all he knew the chief had a dick that would make the horses jealous.

Note: For those of you who may have never seen one, fully aroused horse dicks are as big around as a soda can and nearly two feet long. Pony dicks aren't as long but they are twice as determined.

The chief entered the crowded room and found Jessy and Debbie still sitting on the bunk chatting and enjoying the party. He was well aware that this was Jessy's last day, unlike their commander. The chiefs only concern was that Jessy had picked a replacement so that he wouldn't have to. Jessy chose that moment to announce that he had indeed found a suitable replacement. Frank was all trained up and ready to go. Jessy also decided to say his good bye's and get home and prepare for the trip back to New Jersey. His young wife Nichole would be home, efficiently rounding up all the stuff they would need on their long journey and stashing it in the cab of the van. Their one year old son would be riding in a 1971 version of a car seat propped up on the insulated fiber glass cover of the engine compartment. This arrangement would get you jail time these days but back then you could still transport your whole family around in the bed of a pickup truck.

Jessy started making his way around the bunk house while taking time to say something personal to everyone. He was going to miss this place and these people and he wanted them to know it. Jessy gave Natasha a hug and reminded her to never forget her New Jersey cowboy. She gave Jessy a spooky smile and told him never to forget her either. Jessy assured her he couldn't forget her if he tried. "You better not try" she responded. She didn't include "or I'll hunt you down and kill you" but that part was understood. Jessy told the chief not to buy any more horses with missing body parts. The chief smiled and told him, "Don't get too far off the trail son." This was a cowboy thing and Jessy nodded so the chief knew he was going to do his level best to stay on or damned near the trail. They both knew that the chiefs trail and Jessy's would never intersect. "Not never, not ever, forever, amen."

Jessy walked over to Pat and told him to be careful. Pat was all healed up and his wife had given birth to a baby boy around the same time that Jessy's son was born. He was a proud father and his son was going to need a dad that didn't spend half his life in the emergency room. Jessy wound up his good bye's and headed out to the car where he found Debbie leaning up against the drivers door. As he approached she opened her arms and gave him a big warm hug that lasted way longer than expected and then she gave him a long wet kiss that caught Jessy totally by surprise. He was stunned and like most guys in that kind of situation, confused. Jessy had always liked Debbie, even before he got married but he never guessed she had any feelings for him. Now it was way to late to change anything. Jessy was married with a son a wife and a big truck loaded with all their stuff. For better or not, they were about to head to the East coast. Hey girls it's all about timing and most guys are not real smart when it comes to picking up on hints. This rule is multiplied when the girl is young and beautiful. Oh well, this was not the time for double guessing his life decisions. It was time to move on and try to grow up and find a way to feed and his family.

Jessy gave Debbie one last hug and turned her around, so that he could get at the car door handle. He tenderly put his left hand to Debbie's face and gazed into her beautiful blue eyes then carefully unlatched the door with his right hand opened the door and slid into the car. Jessy softly said goodbye closed the door, started the engine, put it in drive and very slowly drove away. Jessy felt a little sorry for Debbie but he knew she would be over this moment before the sun went down or as soon as he was out of sight and so would Jessy. The big car rolled slowly as he waved goodbye to everyone but accelerated quickly as it pulled away. Jessy's brain was awash in memories as he got up to speed.

Jessy gazed across the desert toward the small hills just east of the base and remembered the time he and Dave had backed up one of those hills in the Ford pickup. They had been careful not to silhouette themselves and parked just below the crest of the hill. The truck was a brownish beige and blended into the hillside perfectly. They were free to light up a joint and gaze over the base as jets came in for landings just to the South. They were telling tales, laughing and enjoying their buzz when both of them stopped instantly as the ground shuddered and shook as a terribly loud thunderous sound grew in their ears. Jessy couldn't see anything but as they looked in all directions at once Jessy happened to spot something in his rear view mirror. There was a giant pipe capped with a large light brown flash deflector advancing over the top of the hill directly behind them. Jessy started the truck, popped the clutch, and stomped on the gas almost all at once. Any other truck on base would have stalled out instantly but their mechanic, "Dick Finger," had that little "52" Ford tuned like a fine violin. The M48A3 Battle tank surged over the top of the hill and nosed down right on the spot where they had been parked only seconds before. Jessy sped down the hill side while trying his best not to hit a rut and flip the truck. At the bottom of the hill he turned back to see which way the tank was going so that they could go in the exact opposite direction. The Marines had thrown a tank party but no one had told Jessy and Dave and they nearly wound up being transformed into under paid tread grease. Those were the days and Jessy was going to miss them. He may have had a tear in his eye as he rolled to the end of the dirt road and prepared to get on the highway and start his new life as an unemployed civilian.

Note: Some say that smoking marijuana inhibits your ability to make correct decisions. In my lifetime I have smoked and consumed a fair amount of this once banned substance and based on my own experience have no personal proof of this analysis. I can't speak for anyone else. I would say that smoking pot definitely leads the smoker to make "interesting" decisions but usually not dangerous ones.

Jessy was looking back one last time when he noticed Frank pulling up along side his car. Frank was smiling and driving the 52 pickup. Jessy rolled down the window, saluted Frank, and told him, "Make me proud dick head" "You know I will chief" he yelled as he gunned the engine and spun the tires. Frank liked to call Jessy chief and Jessy had told him that was cool as long as there wasn't an actual chief around. Frank hung a tight smoking "U" turn on the pavement and sped off in the other direction. Jessy continued on his way, down the freeway on ramp and drove toward his new life. What he missed as the wind blew in through the still rolled down window was Frank trying way to hard to impress him by speeding down the road that paralleled the free way. As Frank tried desperately to catch up, he on his road, Jessy on his freeway, Frank failed to notice the sharp curve in the road ahead. Jessy was cruising south, blasting tunes, with the wind blowing in what was left of his recently abused hair. At that very same moment Frank was rolling sideways down a hillside through a fence and onto the north bound lanes of the freeway.

Jessy didn't hear about the accident until the next day when one of the ranch hands, Bandit, who had stopped by to wish them a safe trip home gave Jessy the news. (Bandit was there that day because he had a bit of a crush on Nichole) Frank was a little banged up but alive and recuperating in sick bay. After hearing that Frank was going to be OK, Jessy's first question was, "How is the truck?" Bandit told them that the old Ford pickup was already in the competent, if somewhat disfigured, hands of Dick Finger who loudly swore he wasn't going to let the savages from the ranch get their hands on that truck ever again.... ever. Jessy just smiled. He knew his beloved machine was in good, penis inspired hands.

This was a defining moment and Jessy realized that the ranch saga was officially over. He had taken on the entire military industrial complex and while he may not have won, he certainly didn't lose, and that simple fact was something that he has carried near the front of his mind ever since. Confidence is something you acquire, something you earn, not something you are born with. Jessy certainly wasn't born confident and self assured but the years in the military had turned him into someone who could be depended upon to complete a task, exceed expectations and do it in record time. This is something that todays employers often overlook when they review prospective employees where one of the applicants has military experience. The military person was taught to think outside the box and improvise when there is a job to be done. Veterans don't depend on a management suit to lead them every step of the way or any steps of the way for that matter. They have been taught to manage themselves and lead when they are called upon. They also become supremely aware that no matter how many assignments they complete in superior fashion their superiors will take all the credit. If they fuck up it's all on them. This dynamic carries over in civilian life and the ability to not go postal in that environment is an asset in all levels of the business world and politics as well.

Many years have passed since Jessy's days in the military but those memories are still bright and clear. His job was to assure that all the planes that he inspected and launched came back in one piece and they all did. Jessy took pride knowing that all of his pilots came back alive, all his drogue chutes opened, and none of our nations horses or ranch hands died on his watch. The one horse that did die did so on someone else's watch. Jessy also felt good knowing that he stepped up and protested and helped end a terrible war that needed to be ended long before it finally was.

Note: The Viet Nam war was like not knowing when to get up and leave the casino when you are loosing. You think to your self "If I leave now all the money I've lost up to now will be wasted." The truth is the money you lost was wasted the minute you walked onto the casino floor. Next time you feel a need to go to a casino just pull up to the front, get out of your car, walk up to the building and throw your money at the door then get back in your car and drive away. Better yet just drive on by. If you feel a need to throw your money away give it to a food pantry. You will feel much better and so will the people you help.

Note: Note: You don't win a war, you hopefully survive a war and then you try to learn from all the wasted lives and treasure how not to blindly get into any more wars. When you are the biggest baddest mother fucker in the valley of death, get the hell out of the valley or those who were there when you showed up, they who control the high ground, will figure out a way to mess you up, no matter how big and bad you are. Viet Nam should have taught us this lesson but our leaders cut that class. Our military budget is larger than the combined military budgets of the ten next most powerful countries and yet 19 bad actors with one way plane tickets and 19 Home Depot box cutters took out the World Trade Center before lunch. This was a lesson, not an excuse to start new wars with people half a world away. We certainly didn't need to attack two nations that didn't have anything to do with destroying an iconic target inside our country. Osama Bin Laden and most of the hijackers were Arabs, none of them were from Afghanistan or Iraq. So why did we invade those countries? The answer to that question is lost deep in the "Bushes."

Note: Note: Note: The price of oil was $3.50 a barrel in the early 1970's. We were paying about $.35 a gallon at the pumps. Nixon doubled it with his fake oil shortage and the oil embargo of OPEC oil. The rest is history. Prior to September, 11 oil was going for $30.00 a barrel, Osama Bin Laden vowed to get Arabian oil prices to over $100.00 a barrel. He got his wish, as of this writing the price of oil is $123.00 a barrel. What does this have to do with the Viet Nam war. There was and still is rumored to be a large amount of oil in the Tonkin gulf and the United states knew it. We used the Ton Kin incident to justify escalating the war under president Johnson. That incident for the most part never happened but that didn't stop us from sending hundreds of thousands of young men and some young women to the jungles and shores of Viet Nam over more than ten years.

This book was written as one man's window into what life in the military might have in store for young men and women who might decide that serving in the armed forces could be the doorway to their future. Just know that doors and windows aren't always what they appear from the outside. you should always look carefully through those windows before walking through the door. Today the internet provides many more ways to obtain information regarding your choices for the future. Also there are people who have been down that path before you. Talk to these people and get a feel from their experience if you think this is the road for you. You might try doing some volunteer work at a nearby Veterans hospital. Just be careful if you talk to veterans who live under a bridge, their opinions may be a little hard to follow but please remember to leave them a tip.

Thank you for reading my book. If you read this far you are a brave and curious person. Feel free to provide me with any feed back through my Email account. My address is chrispeck1@comcast.net. If your comments include hate mail or death threats reach me at blowmedickhead@yousuck.com.

Note: If you feel an urge to kill me because of my views please be kind enough to let me know ahead of time. I have developed arthritis in both feet from climbing telephone poles and ladders for the last fifty years and my escape will be very slow and painful. A good head start would be greatly appreciated. If however you enjoyed my first attempt at writing I'm planning to start a new book about Jessy's adventures as a telephone man in the towns and cities of Northeast, New Jersey. Oddly there will be more guns and near death experiences in the telephone man story than in this war time book. Not so odd if you have ever been to New Jersey or watched an episode of the "Sopranos."

ACKNOWLEDGMENTS:

First and forever foremost thank you to my Mom who was poorer than a church mouse when I was born. Church mice would come by and leave us their leftovers at Christmas. She "chose" to have and raise me the best way she knew how. Some women "choose" to not go through what my mother did and I totally understand that decision. Am I glad she was brave enough to make the choice she did? Of course, but I appreciate more than you can imagine that choice and all of its consequences. My mother was alone until I was in the sixth grade. By then she was taking care of me, my sister and my grandmother and those early years were so very hard for her. When she married my step dad it was her first marriage and all that the statement implies. My father and my sisters father were two different men who knocked up my mother and just simply disappeared. She was in love with both of them and sadly... she trusted them. My mother pointed me in directions that would challenge me for the rest of my life. Thank you Mom.

My stepdad who I've treated rather harshly in this book for his racist views, was a driving force that made me take a closer look at the world around me. He had a big right hand, an Irish wit and he was a story teller. Those things had a positive influence on my formative years. He also pushed me to succeed in whatever I chose to pursue in life. Most of all...in spite of everything...he hung around, Thanks Dad.

The writers who've influenced me are to numerous to mention without starting a new book but I'll try to give some of them their due.

GENE SHEPHERD:

You may think you don't know this person but if you have a television and have ever turned it on during the Christmas holidays you have most likely seen the movie Christmas Story. Mr. Shepherd wrote and narrated this story and his night time radio program was a mainstay in my home as a child. His humor and his story telling molded my young mind and helped keep me somewhat sane during my challenging formative years.

Dr. Hunter S. Thompson:

You took on subjects that others wouldn't and you did it with a totally unique style and your own sly twisted sense of humor. You were fun to read and every time I set one of your books down I was forced to open a new corner of my brain to handle and sort out this totally new eye opening information. At the end of the day your readers always learned something important and it was our job to figure out how to live with these new ideas and lessons. Hunter, you made a difference, thank you sir.

Wanda Sykes (writer comedienne)

Brilliant sense of humor with the black, lesbian, Eskimo, government worker, perspective. I'll get back to you on the Eskimo thing. Your sly smile was a wake up call and a call to action. Humor is a powerful tool and you are a craft person with that tool.

Richard Brautigan

Funny, imaginative, you taught me to look way outside the box for my ideas. Check out "Trout fishing in America."

Ian Fleming

You and James Bond taught me to read and enjoy well told stories. Great attention to details. Authors should always keep their readers on the edge of their imaginations and you achieved this with style and exciting grace.

Henry David Thoreau

Gave me the perspective to slow down and view the world around me. Peaceful yet strong and resourceful he showed me how to create a path to follow. A path with a purpose and a well thought out if not a common direction.

Lenny Bruce

A stand up comedian who showed bravery in taking on an unjust and at times a very cruel world. His strength far outweighed his weaknesses. Overlooked, misunderstood, but a very important influence on our culture.

George Orwell

A visionary who saw what we as a society could do to ourselves without soul and humanity to guide us in the right direction. He taught me that socialism didn't have to be a bad thing (remember social security, schools, and libraries are socialist concepts. "1984" is all around us now. It is subtle but governments run by wealthy benefactors are taking the power away from voters and Mr. Orwell showed us what could and probably will happen next. We are more than halfway there.

Upton Sinclair

Formed some of my early political feelings and gave me a sense of right and wrong when it came to the working people who built this country. If you haven't read "The Jungle" ... read "The Jungle."

Thom Hartman

This guy could help save our world, I've read a couple of his books and they are inspiring and informative, "Screwed" is an example of a book that everyone should read. As well as "Last days of ancient sunlight" You will never feel the same about modern politics or our environment again.

Leon Uris

History and story telling blended perfectly. He was a great model for any writer. I read Battle Cry in the seventh grade followed closely by Mila 18. These books opened my eyes to the side of war that make you think about the personalities and politics of the people who get us into wars that never end as well as the young and old men and women who fight those wars.

Sarah Silverman (writer comedienne)

Ironic social satire, nose bubble funny yet so much truth you want to cry while you are laughing at stuff people shouldn't laugh at...ever. Very easy to fall in love with. Her smile makes you smile while she is saying things that are just so wrong yet honest.

George Carlin (writer, actor, comic, social commentator)

The king of political satire and truth telling. George could put anything into a humorous perspective that would make you laugh, think, and squirm in your seat all at the same time. I miss this man, as we all should. He was trying to tell us how to see the world with all it's good, bad, ugly, and disturbingly funny

Martin Cruz Smith

I read "Gorky Park" and was fascinated with Smith's detail of the Russian culture while not glorifying the government and how much we have in common with our cold war rivals. The Russian people not the politicians. I've read most of Mr. Smiths books over the years and his research has taught me a great deal. He is fun to read and his hero always gets his ass tenderized before solving his case. I think this is a wonderful way to give his main character a humble human side.

Joseph Heller

Helped inspire this book. He pointed to the insanity of war and taught me how to convey that fact with humor. His characters are complex and vividly real. "Catch-22"...Every high school student should be forced by penalty of violence to read this book, I'm kidding but this book is that important. I'm not kidding.

Did I leave anyone off my list? Yes, of course I did. Do I feel guilty? No but I probably should.

www.ingramcontent.com/pod-product-compliance
Lightning Source LLC
LaVergne TN
LVHW010156070526
838199LV00062B/4384